RENEWALS 458-4574
DATE DUE

WITHDRAWN
UTSA LIBRARIES

About Island Press

Since 1984, the nonprofit Island Press has been stimulating, shaping, and communicating the ideas that are essential for solving environmental problems worldwide. With more than 800 titles in print and some 40 new releases each year, we are the nation's leading publisher on environmental issues. We identify innovative thinkers and emerging trends in the environmental field. We work with world-renowned experts and authors to develop cross-disciplinary solutions to environmental challenges.

Island Press designs and implements coordinated book publication campaigns in order to communicate our critical messages in print, in person, and online using the latest technologies, programs, and the media. Our goal: to reach targeted audiences—scientists, policymakers, environmental advocates, the media, and concerned citizens—who can and will take action to protect the plants and animals that enrich our world, the ecosystems we need to survive, the water we drink, and the air we breathe.

Island Press gratefully acknowledges the support of its work by the Agua Fund, Inc., Annenberg Foundation, The Christensen Fund, The Nathan Cummings Foundation, The Geraldine R. Dodge Foundation, Doris Duke Charitable Foundation, The Educational Foundation of America, Betsy and Jesse Fink Foundation, The William and Flora Hewlett Foundation, The Kendeda Fund, The Andrew W. Mellon Foundation, The Curtis and Edith Munson Foundation, Oak Foundation, The Overbrook Foundation, the David and Lucile Packard Foundation, The Summit Fund of Washington, Trust for Architectural Easements, Wallace Global Fund, The Winslow Foundation, and other generous donors.

The opinions expressed in this book are those of the author(s) and do not necessarily reflect the views of our donors.

Environmental Regulations and Housing Costs

Environmental Regulations *and* Housing Costs

Arthur C. Nelson,

John Randolph,

Joseph M. Schilling,

Jonathan Logan,

James M. McElfish Jr.,

and Newport Partners, LLC

Washington   Covelo   London

© 2009, Arthur C. Nelson and John Randolph

All rights reserved under International and Pan-American Copyright Conventions. No part of this book may be reproduced in any form or by any means without permission in writing from the publisher: Island Press, Suite 300, 1718 Connecticut Ave., NW, Washington, DC 20009

ISLAND PRESS is a trademark of the Center for Resource Economics.

Library of Congress Cataloging-in-Publication Data
Environmental regulations and housing costs / by Arthur C. Nelson . . . [et al.].
   p. cm.
   Includes bibliographical references and index.
   ISBN-13: 978-1-59726-559-1 (cloth : alk. paper)
   ISBN-10: 1-59726-559-4 (cloth : alk. paper)
   ISBN-13: 978-1-59726-560-7 (pbk. : alk. paper)
   ISBN-10: 1-59726-560-8 (pbk. : alk. paper)
   1. Housing—Finance—Government policy—United States. 2. Environmental law—United States. I. Nelson, Arthur C.
   HD7293.E63   2008
   333.33'8230973—dc22
                           2008048248

Printed on recycled, acid-free paper

Manufactured in the United States of America
10 9 8 7 6 5 4 3 2 1

KEYWORDS:
Chesapeake Bay Program; Dallas-Fort Worth, Texas; Denver, Colorado; Fairfax County, Virginia; Montgomery County, Maryland; Pima County (Tucson), Arizona; Washington DC metropolitan region; Affordable housing; Land Use Planning; Regulatory Barriers; Housing Policy; Real Estate Development; Habitat Protection; Environmental Regulation; Compliance Costs; Regulatory Process Benefits; Stormwater Management; Brownfield Development; Environmental Impact Statement (EIS); Land Capitalization Theory; Environmental Policy; Wetlands Permitting

CONTENTS

	Preface	ix
	Acknowledgments	xvii
	Introduction *Housing the Next 100 Million Americans*	xix
ONE	The Link Between Environmental Regulation and Housing Costs	1
TWO	Existing Research *A Review of the Literature*	18
THREE	Excessive Costs and a Comparison of Historical Changes in Environmental Regulations and Approval Processes	35
FOUR	Case Study *Washington, DC, Metropolitan Region*	45
FIVE	Key Lessons from the Case Study	107
SIX	A View from the West *Findings from Denver, Tucson, and Dallas*	125

SEVEN	The Benefits of Environmental Regulations and a Summary of Key Findings	165
EIGHT	Assessment, Lessons, and Future Directions	171

Appendix A: Literature Review References — 185

Appendix B: Chesapeake Bay Program — 191

Appendix C: Outline of Environmental Regulations and Review Processes in Fairfax County, Virginia, and Montgomery County, Maryland — 203

Appendix D: Special References for Cost Reduction and Best Development Practices — 208

Notes — 211

References and Selected Bibliography — 217

Index — 253

PREFACE

MYTHS AND REALITIES ABOUT HOUSING COSTS AND THE ENVIRONMENTAL REGULATORY PROCESS

An unchallenged assumption has permeated the planning, environmental, and development communities: required environmental review of development proposals inherently increases permitting times, thus causing delay and increasing housing prices, but there is a dearth of rigorous statistical assessments. Even statistically based studies that associate environmental regulations with higher housing prices cannot distinguish between supply effects (whether regulations or permitting delay reduces supply thus increasing prices) and benefit effects (whether regulations enhance the quality of life in ways the market is willing to pay). Based on a case study of metropolitan Washington, DC and focus groups in Dallas, Denver, and Tucson, this book challenges long-held myths and illuminate the true effects of environmental regulations—specifically the regulatory process—on housing costs.

> **Myth.** *Environmental review of housing developments increases permitting time, creates delays, and therefore adds significantly and excessively to housing costs.*
> **Reality.** It is true that virtually all regulations add *something* to housing costs. Building codes requiring safe wiring, for example, add to housing costs in the short term but provide greater benefits in the long run. Our study found, however, that regulations in general have little impact on housing prices relative to market forces and other policies (fiscal, infrastructure, and so on). And environmental regulations probably have a

smaller influence on housing costs than do such nonenvironmental regulations as zoning, subdivision rules, building codes, impact fees, and the like. In our case study involving the Washington, DC, metropolitan area, the cost of environmental compliance per unit was less than 1 percent of the unit sales price. Contrast this with new U.S. Department of Housing and Urban Development (HUD) research showing that land-use regulations affecting density, lot size, setbacks, and improvement standards add an estimated 4 to 5 percent to housing costs on average.

Further, our Washington metropolitan area case study showed that regulatory requirements can cost as much as $4 million for a very large housing project, mostly for water-related issues such as stormwater, erosion, and sediment control. Other large expenses include site remediation; wetlands delineation, permitting, and mitigation; tree preservation and forest cover; noise abatement; and archeological resource management. Still, environmental regulatory costs averaged about $8,500 per housing unit but totaled only 1 to 5 percent of land and development costs (not including construction). The environmentally related share of costs relative to total improvement costs and to the imputed price of finished lots is at the low end of the cost continuum developed in chapter 3.

The focus group markets covered in chapter 6 confirmed the increasing emphasis on and cost of stormwater, erosion, and sediment control, but indicated that environmentally related costs relative to total improvement costs and to the imputed price of finished lots is also at the low end of the scale.

Other findings about the relative cost of environmental regulations include:

- Environmental impact assessment (EIA) documentation studies, where required, are expensive and raise costs but not significantly.
- Open space set-asides also are costly, but onsite density bonuses are often provided as noted in the Washington, DC, case study and according to information provided by the focus groups.
- Wetlands permit and habitat conservation mitigation requirements are costly. In the Washington metropolitan area case study, the cost of wetlands compliance ranged from $53,000 to $411,000 for each project, but only about 7 percent of environmental costs (or $300 to $2,000 per finished lot)—averaging quite a bit less than 1 percent of the im-

puted finished lot cost in that area. In focus group areas, these costs seem to be lower and in line with the small share of total finished costs observed in the case study.
- Stormwater management was clearly the major compliance cost, although tree provision/preservation costs were significant. Interestingly, stormwater management and street trees were noted separately in the National Association of Home Builders' (NAHB) *Cost Effective Site Planning* (1976a), showing them to be a very small share of overall improvement costs and an even smaller share of finished lot costs.

Myth. *Whether it's large or small, the impact of the environmental regulatory process on housing costs has increased during the past three decades.*
Reality. We found that the impact on housing costs that arise from environmental regulations has not changed much in thirty years—indeed, it may have gone down—despite the fact that the number and rigor of environmental regulations have increased in the latter third of the twentieth century and into the twenty-first century.

Myth. *The permitting time for residential subdivisions has increased significantly since the 1970s.*
Reality. Between 1976 and 2002, the average permitting time for residential subdivisions increased by only two months, from fifteen months to seventeen months (Ben-Joseph 2003). Whether any of this increase is attributable to environmental regulations cannot be determined. This modest increase in permitting time comes despite reasonably well documented expansions of government review at all levels—especially local government—and the apparently expanding abilities of citizens to intervene in permitting processes.

Myth. *Environmental regulations protecting sensitive landscapes and listed species significantly reduce the supply of buildable land.*
Reality. It is unclear whether federal regulations protecting wetlands and listed species, along with state and local regulations protecting sensitive landscapes, reduce buildable land supply appreciably, even in states where federal and state land ownership is extensive. In the Tucson, Arizona, region, focus group developers indicated that habitat protection under federal and state regulations limited land for development. However, Arizona

has only about 15 percent of its land in private ownership, and only Nevada and Utah have a comparably low percentage of privately owned land. The rest is in federal, state, Native American, and other public ownership.

> **Myth.** *Direct increases in housing costs attributable to reviews and mitigation measures have been offset by technology and increased efficiency of experts representing developers.*
>
> **Reality.** As regulations of all kinds and especially environmental regulations have increased during the past thirty years, so has the rigor of development review for environmental effects. That these increased demands on the development process have not increased the share of costs associated with environmental regulation or the length of review is a testament to:

- *Technology* that makes professionals more efficient and the installation of environmental improvements less costly in real dollars over time
- *Efficiency* of technical analysis conducted principally by experts representing developers

We found it remarkable that environmental costs as a percentage of total residential subdivision costs are about the same as they were in the mid-1970s. There are several reasons for this:

1. Developers have more knowledge about development impacts on the environment today than they did in the 1970s. For one thing, simply knowing what questions to ask has been refined. For another, techniques to assess environmental conditions that may trigger mitigating exactions are far more efficient than in the past. This is a function of improved technical skills of experts representing developers.
2. Relative to the 1970s and later periods, experts probably know far better how to address environmental concerns during the due diligence phase of a development process. Land-purchase contracts may now better reflect these costs than in the past. Experts—such as engineering and environmental consultants—may also know better how to address environmental concerns in more cost-effective ways than may have been possible in the past. The result is that developers can nego-

tiate a land-purchase option agreement reflecting this knowledge and design projects that reduce—but do not eliminate—the costs.

3. The role of experts in the review process has likely expanded generally to the benefit of residential subdivision developers—and perhaps to the benefit of the environment and the community. Through interviews, we heard numerous anecdotes about how a developer's engineering or environmental expert would craft solutions to environmentally related issues in ways that reduced development costs while also gaining staff support and often taking the NIMBY (Not in My Back Yard) group's environmentally related objections off the table. These experts and the environmental solutions they designed certainly added costs to projects, but the additional costs are not out of line proportionately with costs seen in the 1970s.

4. Environmental regulations—at least those in mature jurisdictions with professional, experienced staff—add the very kind of process certainty that developers need. Developers interviewed in the study stated that knowing in advance what is required allows them to perform more accurate analyses and better anticipate costs associated with improvements and the approval process. This theme was prevalent in interviews from both the case study and the focus groups.

5. Technology and the expanding environmental consultant profession have likely reduced environmentally related improvement and investigation costs relative to the past. Interviews with the environmental consulting firms engaged for the developments evaluated in the case study highlighted the growth and sophistication of these full-service environmental consultant companies within the greater metropolitan region of Washington, DC. Although it was difficult to quantify the direct cost savings, we believe these factors may explain why the ratio of environmental costs to total project costs has continued to remain about the same for the past twenty-five years.

Myth. *Indirect increases in housing costs potentially attributable to delay have been held in check through enhanced planning skills and procedural diligence at the local level.*

Reality. The expansion of regulations at all levels of government has the potential to increase delays in processing residential developments.

That these increased demands on the development process have not increased the share of costs associated with environmental regulation or the length of review is a testament to:

- *Planning* that manages an increasingly complex permitting process in ways that add little if any additional time to the overall process
- *Diligence* of locally elected officials who balance the need to enhance the environmental quality of life for the citizens who elect them with the need to facilitate housing production

The extra time environmentally related regulations add to the residential subdivision review process could be zero if responding to environmental issues is concurrent with the rest of the development review process—and, in any event, environmental review may be difficult to disentangle as a separable element of delay. Indeed, we find it remarkable that residential subdivision approvals are processed as fast as they are relative to the mid-1970s. There are a couple of primary reasons for this:

1. Environmentally related regulations may be clearer and more objective now than in the past and may have become part of the routine checklist of things to do as part of development preparation and review. In the past, environmental concerns were evident but uninformed as to appropriate measures to mitigate impacts. Many environmental concerns are now addressed through clear and objective standards or through deference to consultants who are experts that are trusted by public agencies and developers. These experts, in turn, seek solutions and build trust among various parties over time. Finally, administrative systems are probably much more efficient today than in the past in processing environmentally related conditions.
2. A common theme emerged in all communities studied—combined regulatory review. That there are more environmental regulations and review processes now than during the 1970s is a given, but they have been layered on the same timeframes for review and public discussion, not extensions of review periods. While this leads to "thicker" applications, it does not seem to have added to the review time appreciably if at all.

Myth. *Even though the impact of environmental regulations on housing costs is relatively small and has not been increasing, there are still ways to reduce that impact.*

Reality. In fact, *how* to reduce the effects of the environmental regulatory process on housing costs is a major part of this book.

ACKNOWLEDGMENTS

The authors gratefully acknowledge the valuable contributions of several people to this study, chief among whom is Edwin A. Stromberg of the U.S. Department of Housing and Urban Development. Invaluable assistance in facilitating review and production of this book came from Heather Boyer of Island Press. Equally invaluable assistance in making the complexities of the research leading to this book accessible to several audiences was provided by Kathleen Litzenberg and David Martin. Additional technical and review assistance was offered by Kristen Hayworth and Sheila Keyes. We also acknowledge Sharon Oxley, former director of the National Center for Housing and the Environment, for her leadership in advancing research into the relationship between environmental regulations and housing prices. Final thanks are due to Brenda Scheer who provided important resources on behalf of the University of Utah that made this book possible.

We are especially indebted to senior staff and employees of a major national large-scale home builder for giving us access to propietary plans, data, and market insights.

This book is based on work sponsored by the U.S. Department of Housing and Urban Development. The views and opinions expressed herein are the responsibility of the authors.

Introduction

HOUSING THE NEXT 100 MILLION AMERICANS

In the coming years, America will add 100 million people at a rate faster than any other country on the planet except India and Pakistan—faster even than China. This translates into a net increase of roughly 40 million homes between 2000 and 2040. This growth will occur largely in areas already challenged by declining supplies of land suitable for efficient development and in areas characterized by shifts in demand favoring different—often higher density—housing in more mixed-use configurations.

The environmental implications of future growth will be significant, and communities across the United States are grappling with how to meet housing growth pressures in ways that are affordable for people while protecting the environment. Now more than ever, environmental regulations—on top of recent market turmoil (e.g., the subprime meltdown, soaring foreclosure rates, and plummeting house values)—may be viewed as increasing the affordability burden.

At the same time, environmental mandates have proliferated and grown more important during the past two decades, but little research has been done to determine what kinds of impacts these regulations have on the cost of housing in communities across the country. Many people have argued that environmental regulations have driven up the cost of housing and serve as a critical barrier to housing affordability, but there is little empirical evidence of this impact.[1]

This book examines environmental regulations, at all levels of government, that are potential barriers to housing affordability, including:

- Environmental impact statement (EIS) process review (federal [F], state [S], local [L])
- Wetlands permitting (F, S, L)
- Endangered species habitat conservation plans and permits (F, S)
- Air quality permits (F, S)
- Floodplain zoning (F, S, L)
- Other natural hazard mitigation (F, S, L)
- Management requirements for stormwater and nonpoint source water pollution (F, S, L)
- Erosion and sediment control (S, L)
- Coastal zone stormwater and sensitive area management (F, S, L)
- Source water protection provisions (F, S, L)
- Agricultural land protection zoning (S, L)
- Open space set-aside requirements (L)
- Urban forestry programs, tree preservation permits, and landscaping requirements (L)
- Impact fees for environmental measures (L)

Because so little is known definitively about the effects of environmental regulations on housing costs, we need to identify promising areas of research, conduct that research, and then pursue corresponding policy implications. Throughout the book we focus on the policy implications related to the implementation of environmental regulatory review in the residential development permitting process, especially processing time and uncertainty.

This book focuses on four U.S. housing markets, one in detail. Although our study provides some of the first empirical data on the costs of assessments, compliance, and delays from environmental regulations, the limited geographic scope makes the study preliminary. As such, the study is not intended to provide definitive, broad-based, representative findings that can be broadly generalized. The results are suggestive, or heuristic, and are intended to set the stage for more targeted research to be pursued in more detailed studies.

This book offers two types of analyses. The first is a case study of metropolitan Washington, DC, the study of which brings certain advantages.

Specifically, two states—Maryland and Virginia—dominate the regional market in roughly equal proportions providing important insights into the extent to which environmental regulations and their effect on housing costs differ. In addition, the states themselves differ in their political economy with one (Maryland) extending home rule to counties while also mandating some of the nation's most rigorous planning requirements, while the other (Virginia) is a "Dillon Rule" state with no substantial state planning mandate and no home rule powers conferred on local governments to do so. Also, where state-mandated planning in Maryland would seem to create similar regulatory approaches among its jurisdictions, the lack of a mandate in Virginia means there can be wide variation in local regulatory approaches. Given these differences in the same metropolitan market, the case study provides one of the better opportunities to compare the effects of environmental regulations on housing costs.

The book's second analysis centers on a set of focus groups assembled in three western metropolitan areas: Dallas, Denver, and Tucson. Although not representative of all regions, the focus groups (comprising builders, developers, and planning officials) assessed the applicability of the case-study findings in their region. This firsthand fieldwork identified important similarities and differences among the regions and between them and the case study.

SUMMARY OF KEY FINDINGS

Despite anecdotal information and intuitive feelings to the contrary, we found that in general the environmental regulatory process does not add significantly to the cost of housing; that it does not significantly increase the amount of time housing developments require to complete; that the costs and time delays attributable to the environmental regulatory process have not increased significantly during the past thirty years or so; and that the benefits homeowners, society, and developers derive from the environmental regulatory process are considerable. Figure I-1 provides a summary of the role of environmental compliance costs in overall project

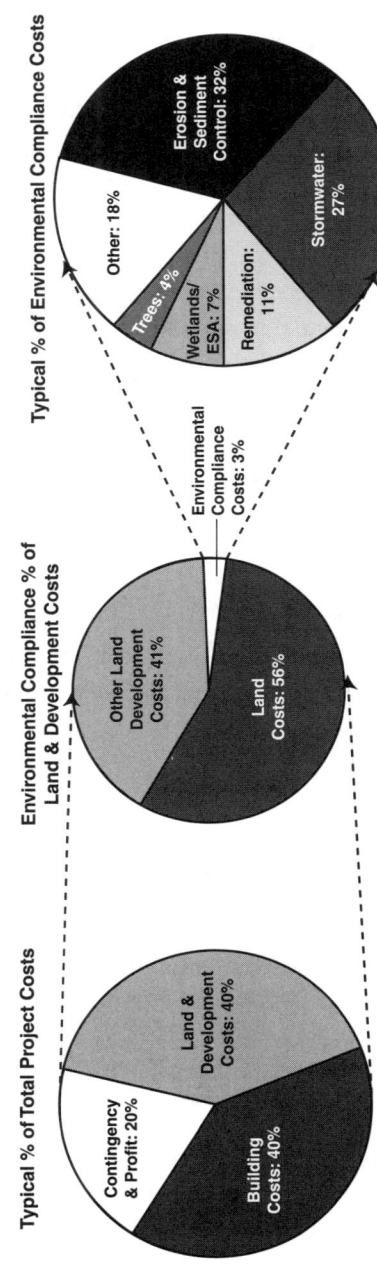

Figure 1.1 Environmental Compliance Costs in Land Development: Metropolitan Washington, DC, Case Study.
Source: Authors' calculations based on pilot study research.

development costs, based on our findings from the Washington metropolitan area case study.

Here are some specific findings from this project:

- Costs of environmental regulatory compliance are about $5,000 to $15,000 (in 2006 dollars) per lot or unit in the Washington metropolitan market. This is comparable to Tucson, but the costs are apparently less in Denver, and considerably less in Dallas.
- Stormwater management, erosion and sediment control, site remediation, tree preservation, wetland mitigation, and habitat preservation are important cost categories. Water issues (stormwater management and wetlands) dominate mitigation costs.
- Developers could do a much better job tracking environmental costs—having more concrete data on environmental costs would greatly assist the home-building industry in understanding where improvements in the process are needed to help reduce expenditures. Indeed, through the course of our research, we were aided immeasurably by a large-scale home builder that began to realize the internal accounting and decision-making benefits of tracking environmentally related costs systematically and was working toward modifying its national accounting protocols accordingly. Project delays for environmental approvals were apparent in the projects and markets studied. However, the twelve- to twenty-four-month approval period revealed in the case-study projects was not atypical compared with historical norms for rezoning decisions, which are increasingly required for major developments. Concurrent permit reviews were important to minimize delays.
- Environmental compliance and expedited approval can be facilitated by the use of knowledgeable and trusted environmental consultants who can develop innovative compliance measures and communicate them to permitting agencies and to the public.
- In certain markets with already limited buildable land (e.g., Tucson), Endangered Species Act habitat conservation may limit land availability and raise land prices. There is no evidence from the study that wetlands permitting and mitigation affect land availability.
- Some state and federal mandates—including FEMA map revisions and U.S. Army Corps of Engineers wetland review—caused delays that

some developers thought were excessive. But other projects showed that concurrent review by different jurisdictions and for different permitting decisions helped shorten overall review times.
- There are opportunities in many markets to reduce uncertainty for developers, to streamline the approval process, and to reduce costs while still protecting environmental resources.

ONE

The Link Between Environmental Regulation and Housing Costs

This chapter reviews the federal concern about the role of environmental regulation as a barrier to the production of housing that is affordable to the largest number of households, summarizes research on the relationship of regulatory barriers to the production of affordable housing, acquaints the reader with the evolution of the residential subdivision process over the past century, and notes the conundrum of ensuring a high-quality environment while also meeting housing affordability needs. The chapter also describes a key consideration from the developers' perspective: how developers decide to proceed with a development proposal. The chapter continues with a review of the research design that guided the study leading to this book. In brief, in addition to extensive literature review, the research relies on a case study and on focus groups to inform its policy analysis.

While often motivated by good intensions, some local, state, and federal government rules and regulations can increase the cost of housing in certain communities. Although this book is not concerned precisely with affordable housing as defined by the U.S. Department of Housing and Urban Development (HUD), we think it is useful to look at HUD's idea of what constitutes a regulatory barrier to affordable housing. These are the requirements that frequently, without intending to do so, prolong the completion and raise the costs of new construction and rehabilitation.

THE FEDERAL CONCERN

The issue of regulatory barriers is not new.[1]

In 1991, the President's Advisory Commission on Regulatory Barriers to Affordable Housing, popularly known as the Kemp Commission, published its report, *"Not in My Backyard": Removing Barriers to Affordable Housing* (1991). Its basic finding—that exclusionary, discriminatory, and unnecessary regulations constitute formidable barriers to affordable housing—is still evident in HUD's update of the report, *Why Not in Our Community* (2005).

The Kemp Commission report stated that, as a result of inefficient implementation, environmental protection regulation processes pose significant barriers to the availability of affordable housing. The report cited the following inefficiencies: (1) conflicting environmental regulations; (2) prolonged review processes; (3) lack of a clear rationale or justification for environmental decisions, and (4) regulations that extend beyond the scope of goals they seek to achieve. These four inefficiencies can result in increased unpredictability, delays, reduced land availability, and increased construction costs. Interestingly, the Kemp Commission report cites very little rigorous research but reports numerous anecdotes as the foundation for its claims and basis for its recommendations. In April 2004, HUD sponsored a Research Conference on Regulatory Barriers to Affordable Housing (the proceedings of which were published in *Cityscape* vol. 8, no. 1), which reaffirmed these environmental barriers as a major issue requiring systematic research (Schill 2005; Listokin and Hattis 2005; Quiqley and Rosenthal 2005; Been 2005; Kiel 2005; May 2005).

The major federal mandates that affect housing development include environmental impact statements, water quality management (especially stormwater management), air quality management, wetlands protection, floodplain management, coastal zone protection, endangered species protection, and site contamination. Many states in turn have added their own requirements, which increase the layers of regulatory review and even conflict with federal efforts.

SETTING THE CONTEXT:
A SURVEY OF RESEARCH ON REGULATORY BARRIERS

Housing developers and affordable housing advocates have raised numerous concerns about the impact of regulation on housing production and especially on producing affordable housing.[2] A 1998 survey by the National Association of Home Builders (NAHB) of its members found that about 10 percent of the cost of building a typical new home is attributable to what respondents describe as unnecessary regulation, regulatory delays, and fees (U.S. House of Representatives, Committee on Small Business 2000). Luger and Temkin (2000) used a more refined research approach to find that development costs associated with their definition of the "direct cost of excessive regulation," including delays plus financing costs affecting residential subdivisions in New Jersey, added $10,000 to $20,000 per new housing unit (in 2000 dollars)—roughly 2 to 4 percent of the sales price of new homes.

To assess trends over time, Eran Ben-Joseph (2003) replicated a survey undertaken in 1976 by Stephen Seidel (1978). In both 1976 and 2002, nearly 75 percent of the development community respondents cited "government-imposed regulations" as one of the three most significant housing problems. One area of particular concern for respondents was the time it takes to process residential subdivision approvals. Ben-Joseph's data indicate that between 1976 and 2002 the national average time to process approvals increased from fifteen to seventeen months, with much of the increase attributable to securing various forms of zoning relief (rezoning, variance, special exceptions, and so on.). One-fifth of the respondents to his 2002 survey noted waiting more than two years for approval. Luger and Temkin add further insights about the sources of delay for residential subdivisions in their surveys of New Jersey and North Carolina planning officials, noting:

"Organized citizen opposition" to subdivisions was cited by the greatest percentages of respondents, respectively followed by contractor or development error, inadequate staffing, and unspecified sources of delay in negotiations. . . . In response to other questioning, from one-third to over one-half of the respondents cited complexity in regulations or regulatory processes as a major factor in delays in regulatory approvals. (2000, 57, 61)

However, the extent to which environmental regulations affected housing costs—if at all—was not noted specifically.

May (2005) notes that solid research about delays is hard to come by with most allegations about delays being more anecdotal than empirical documentation—and the research team learned from local officials that the biggest source of delay is untimely submission of complete information by the developer.

Delays also vary by the complexity of processes. Regarding the high costs of new housing construction in New York City, Salama, Schill, and Stark (1999) note:

Because the Buildings Department is the single most important agency in the development process, its management and operations need to be as efficient as possible. In fact, the New York City permitting process is not—the process is arcane, cumbersome, confusing, complicated and paper-intensive. (108)

Euchner and Frieze (2003) and Field (1997) note that groups that do not want multifamily housing or other forms of affordable housing in or near their neighborhoods often use public hearings and review processes to create roadblocks to those developments. At the other end of the spectrum, however, are examples where affordable housing is given fast-track status (such as in Florida), and in Oregon land-use approvals are required to be given within 120 days of filing a completed application (Nelson and Duncan 1995).

May (2005) further notes that there are numerous anecdotes about how duplication of administrative structures and gaps in regulatory decision-making processes complicate regulatory implementation and often lead to delay. Euchner and Frieze (2003) review the effect's regulatory fragmentation in the Boston area as an example of housing barriers:

> The lack of integration [of regulations] at the state level [then] can lead to confusion among local enforcement authorities such as building inspectors, fire chiefs, and boards of health and increase the number of appeals boards in front of which a builder has to appear. The process is especially complex (and confusing) in the case of environmental and handicap access regulations.
>
> Public officials also regularly defer to "community process" when controversial projects are proposed. Many cities and towns specifically require that projects undergo community scrutiny, even when the projects fit into the existing look and feel of the neighborhood. Community process can be especially problematic in small communities with volunteer governance structures like town meeting and little professional staff in town hall. (7)

Although striking, these are not new insights. Pressman and Wildavsky's 1972 work concludes that decision structures that include multiple decision points between and across levels of government introduce delays as decisions are made and remade. More often, this redundant process introduces multiple opportunities for any given decision maker to veto decisions of others.

As May (2005) laments, however, without specific knowledge of actual situations, it is difficult to evaluate the extent to which regulatory processes actually increase approval periods. Helping close this knowledge gap is a principal purpose of this book.

OVERVIEW OF THE RESIDENTIAL SUBDIVISION PROCESS

America has built or rebuilt more than 2 million homes annually during most of the first decade of the twenty-first century. This does not include residential units converted from existing nonresidential structures such as warehouse loft conversions, recycling of office buildings and schools into residential units, and similar conversions. According to the U.S. Bureau of the Census building permit statistics, more than two-thirds of all new residential units are single-family detached or attached townhouse units on individual lots. The production of these lots almost always requires subdividing land.

The process of subdividing land for residential development has evolved greatly during the past century.[3] Before the mid-1920s, it was common for individual property owners to merely file a plat (typically with the local county recorder or clerk) showing numbered lots and blocks, streets dedicated to the public (not necessarily to any governmental unit, however), and occasionally land dedicated for public uses. The subdivision of land was seen merely as a way to sell lots more efficiently, bypassing the need to engage the cost of a surveyor to document each individual lot and have a title company accept it for title insurance purposes. For local governments, this process made real property taxes easier to assess and collect.

The Standard Planning Enabling Act (SPEA), drafted in 1928 by the U.S. Department of Commerce as a guide for individual states to adapt, saw the regulation of residential subdivisions as a way to plan or guide for community growth—and included giving local governments the authority to approve, deny, or set conditions for proposed residential subdivisions (see Juergensmeyer and Roberts 2007). The SPEA provided local governments with a list of design features—such as street design (length, width, intersections, and curvature), utility placement, lot and block design and dimensions, and open spaces—to consider in reviewing and approving residential subdivisions. Underlying the standard act was the goal of empowering local government to manage its density by setting minimum lot sizes as part of approval conditions. Although the standard act was not adopted uniformly among the states, it *was* adopted in most of the faster-growing ones. This second epoch of subdivision control extended through the Great Depression, the Second World War, and into the first generation of automobile-dependent postwar suburbanization.

In the early half of the twentieth century, subdividers all too often did not install roads or utilities to lots, leaving those costs to the lot buyers or, more frequently, having the buyers put pressure on local government to do so.[4] Local governments came to see residential subdivisions as triggering a need to provide new parks and schools that governments often were unable to meet. In response, many states crafted subdivision statutes that enabled local government to require that subdividers install onsite infrastructure at the subdividers' expense and also to dedicate land for schools, parks, and other purposes or provide funds in lieu of this land that local government could use to acquire the necessary land outside the subdivision. During this period, the environmental and social impacts of new subdivisions were not usually addressed except indirectly as related to infrastructure.

Beginning in the late 1960s and into the 1970s, other issues affecting residential subdivisions began to emerge, many relating to the environmental and social impacts on the community. Water pollution from stormwater runoff, denuding subdivisions of trees during the land-clearing and residential home construction process, altering waterways with adverse downstream impacts, and relying on septic systems instead of sanitary sewers emerged as chief environmental impact concerns. States often amended their subdivision enabling statutes to account for these additional concerns, but in some cases, where states did not pass such statutes, local governments found ways to address the concerns.

During this period the federal government also began to exert its interest in protecting the environment—and, later, habitat. The National Environmental Policy Act, adopted in 1969, declares it national policy to prevent or eliminate damage to the environment and biosphere caused by human activity. It is implemented by the Environmental Protection Agency (EPA).

The process for creating and developing residential subdivisions has changed considerably during the past century. No longer can someone buy and subdivide a tract of land without being subject to planning review or required to install infrastructure. Currently, with the residential subdivision and development process extended, buyers and speculators of raw land will acquire land intending to hold it for several years. Prospective land developers often secure an option to buy the land, and will proceed with purchase only after a due diligence period and then only if entitlements from local governments are secured—a process that can take two to five years. Land developers often face a year of land improvement before selling finished lots to home builders—and if the market softens unexpectedly, the period of time to sell off all of the lots can be months or years longer than projected (table 1.1). For instance, many developers in the early

> **BOX 1.1   Survey of Other Federal Environmental Acts**
>
> In addition to NEPA there are several other federal environmental acts. For instance, the Clean Air Act, adopted in 1967, protects the quality of the nation's air resources and, among other things, facilitate regional air pollution prevention and control programs. It is administered by the EPA.
>
> The charge of the Clean Water Act, adopted in 1972 and also known as the Federal Water Pollution Control Act, is "to restore and maintain the chemical, physical, and biological integrity of the Nation's waters." Among its seven goals is creating a nonpoint source pollution program for the purpose of making the waters of the United States "fishable and swimmable." The CWA contains the nation's most noteworthy wetlands legislation. It is implemented by the EPA.
>
> A companion to the Clean Water Act is the Safe Drinking Water Program, which was adopted in 1974 for the purpose of protecting the quality of the nation's drinking water. It is also administered by the EPA.
>
> The Endangered Species Act (ESA) of 1973 protects endangered and threatened species from extinction. It also provides for the protection of the critical habitats on which these species depend for survival. The U.S. Fish and Wildlife Service (FWS), housed in the U.S. Department of the Interior, is responsible for implementing nonmarine species while the National Marine Fisheries Service (NMFS), a branch of the National Oceanic and Atmospheric Administration (NOAA) housed in the U.S. Department of Commerce, is responsible for administering marine species.

to mid 2000s, invested substantial sums processing "entitlements" (legal authority to develop with little or no additional review) expecting they would build late in this decade. However, by the time the entitlements had been acquired or, worse, as the developers were building homes, the market softened, leaving them with unsold inventory.

The typical residential subdivision process is composed of several steps. Generally speaking, local government makes two important decisions about residential subdivisions: whether to approve the "preliminary" or "tentative" plat including the conditions of approval, and then whether to approve the final plat when those conditions are met. The procedural flow

Table 1.1 Residential Land Conversion Process and Pre-Development Activity

Activity	Land Investor Type				
	Buyer of Raw Land	Land Speculator	Entitlement Securer	Land Developer	Builder/End User
Primary Function	Begins conversion	Holds land waiting for development to arrive	Analyzes markets, conducts due diligence, secures entitlements for development	Subdivides; installs all development improvements	Builds residential dwellings for sale or/and rent
Financing	Institutional; partner equity	Institutional; partner equity	Institutional; partner equity	Construction loans	Construction loans
Typical Buyer	Land speculator	Shorter-term speculators, usually not developer	Land developer	Home builders including internal to firm	Home buyer
Tenure Length	More than 10 years	8–10 years	2–5 years	1 or more years	Typically months

Source: Adapted from Rabinowitz (1988, 26).

chart for each is illustrated in figure 1.1 (for the preliminary/tentative plat) and figure 1.2 (for the final plat). According to a national survey, 92 percent of jurisdictions require preliminary/tentative approval, and 99 percent of jurisdictions require final plat approval (Ben-Joseph 2003).

Combined, the typical residential subdivision approval process entails at least twenty review steps and decisions, any one of which can be delayed for reasons such as backlog of applications, vacation or sick leave of key staff, community opposition, and requests by staff for more information. Additional considerations imposed by state and/or federal agencies invariably extends the review period. If zoning relief—such as variances, special exceptions, and zone changes—is required, the process can be extended as well.

The evolution of subdivision review and improvement standards increased costs of development. While some may view this outcome as a source of increasing housing costs, others will note that such regulations merely have developers (and homebuyers) "internalize" the "externalities" they impose on the community. That is, the costs ("externalities") imposed on the community by a development are mitigated ("internalized") by developers and homebuyers. This creates a conundrum of evaluating the costs and benefits of environmental regulations.

THE CONUNDRUM OF EVALUATING ENVIRONMENTAL REGULATORY COSTS AND BENEFITS

The introduction of regulation may result in higher housing prices by reducing the supply of land or materials or labor to build homes and by increasing the time it takes to build a home (either through delay in the approval process or during the construction itself when environmental issues must be addressed). Of course, regulation might also elevate the quality of life to a level that the market responds favorably. In truth, all these factors are at work simultaneously.

Kiel (2005) reviews the literature to examine the extent to which there is evidence that environmental regulations by themselves have an impact on housing prices, as opposed to exclusionary zoning and other nonenvironmentally related supply restricting efforts. She concludes that

Figure 1.1　Flow Chart for Preliminary Plat Review Process, Approximately 1970s into 1990s. *Source:* Adapted generally from Ducker (1988, 230).

Figure 1.2 Flow Chart for Final Plat Review Process. *Source:* Adapted generally from Ducker (1988, 232).

environmental laws can affect the supply of land but that is not all: such regulations can affect the price of inputs into the house such as on the price of lumber. Regulations can also impact the supply of housing if those regulations extend or exacerbate review procedures or increase the potential for litigation. If effective, however, the regulations might increase the demand for housing if the community environmental quality has been improved relative to competing communities.

Kiel (2005) suggests that academic research and literature have been unable to disentangle the role of specific kinds of regulation on housing prices, or even whether some regulations that appear to raise housing prices do so because benefits of better environmental quality are realized as higher housing values. In short, no definitive work directly links environmental regulations with changes in housing prices or uncovers whether those regulations are merely capitalization of broader benefits. In an unpublished work for the National Center for Housing and the Environment, Sunding (2004b) observes:

> The topic of environmental regulation of housing developments links several academic literatures, in particular those on urban economics and environmental economics. Despite the large number of papers on urban growth processes and on the costs and benefits of environmental protection, it is somewhat surprising that there are so few papers on the impact of environmental regulation on housing development. Given the potential for large wealth transfers and amenity creation, this seems to be a major area of opportunity for economists, policy analysts, and others who study processes of urban growth and development. (2)

We draw the following conclusions:

- Prices go *up* because developable land is scarcer. This can occur if environmental regulations remove land from development potential or if permitting delays are so lengthy as to have the same effect indirectly.
- Prices *stay the same* because environmental compliance costs are capitalized into land costs, meaning that the seller of land to be developed

internalizes costs—this is consistent with conventional theory of land economics.
- Prices go *down* because of lower developable densities on environmentally restricted land. Usually, land allowed to develop at higher densities has more value than land allowed to develop at lower densities. If one result of environmental regulations is to reduce allowable density, land value would be expected to fall.
- Prices go *up* because of demand for the environmental amenities created by restrictions (see also Boyle and Kiel 2001).

Furthermore, three kinds of land costs related to environmental regulation have differing effects on housing development and availability:

1. Land scarcity (affected by regulations associated with wetlands, coastal zone protection, floodplain and hazard protection, and habitat, among others)
2. Site preparation (affected by regulations associated with stormwater controls, erosion and sediment, and assessment for hazardous substances, among others)
3. Operating costs (affected by regulations associated with water and sewer, stormwater management, and solid waste management requirements, among others)

A PERSPECTIVE ON ENVIRONMENTAL COSTS AND THE ROLE OF LAND CAPITALIZATION

Sunding (2004b) provides an important perspective, one that ultimately guides the research reported in this book. Sunding notes that developers are well versed in anticipating potential effects of regulation on development. The general process in which developers engage is as follows:

> In the planning and initiation phase, the development team is assembled, major hurdles are identified, and overall project objectives are assessed. Next, the feasibility of the project is considered through an assessment of market conditions, local and regional governmental ob-

jectives, availability and cost of financing, and potential project sites. Typically, land will be optioned by the end of this phase at the latest. The commitment phase of the development process involves land assembly, preparation and negotiation of environmental documents, assembly of materials needed for other regulatory approvals, preparation of documents needed for financing, and finalizing the design of the project. This phase culminates when the developer obtains the needed financing and regulatory approvals. The developer then moves on to construction and operation of the project. (6)

One important factor developers consider is delay. As Sunding and Zilberman (2002) note, the prospect of delay leads developers to enter into "free look" (low- or no-cost purchase option) agreements with sellers of land, allowing the developers to assess the risks of attaining profitability in light of numerous factors such as clarity of regulations, including those related to the environment, delay, and normal market risks. This is called the "due diligence" process; and it is not a trivial element of the overall development process. The National Association of Home Builders has developed a list of more than a thousand factors that should be considered before acquiring land for development. The factors are organized into the following broad areas:

- Location and neighborhood
- Size and shape
- Accessibility and visibility
- Environmental conditions
- Legal constraints
- Utilities
- Zoning and regulation

Due diligence leads to an informed decision by a developer before proceeding to secure entitlements that ensure development can occur. Under ideal circumstances, the due diligence process allows developers to negotiate the best land purchase price that reflects those factors. In a relatively competitive housing market—which still exists in many metropolitan areas—such knowledge allows developers to discount the purchase price of land to reflect the costs and risks of these factors and ensure normal profit. This is called "backward capitalization" of development costs, where the sale price of raw land is the finished land price less improvement costs, or the "residual" illustrated below.

Finished Lot Price
    minus sales commission and transfer cost
    minus improvement costs including normal profit
    minus risk factor, which is a reduction that hedges unforeseen market conditions or development delay based on developers' knowledge of the local risks,
equals **"Residual," also known as Land Purchase Price**

The improvement cost includes processing entitlements (land-use changes, subdivision approval, development agreements, and related legal decisions), physically improving the land into lots for sale to builders, reasonable delay in securing entitlements and installing the improvements, the cost of financing, and the opportunity cost of the time it takes to complete these tasks. The risk factor helps account for market shifts, unexpected delays, and other unanticipated events.

Usually, developers reduce their risk of land purchase by entering into a land purchase option contract. The option allows developers to engage in due diligence analysis and, if that process indicates positive outcomes, the option then allows a developer a reasonable period of time in which to secure entitlements. Once secured to the satisfaction of the developer, the land is often (but not always) purchased at the agreed-upon price, which is sometimes different from the initially negotiated price—this difference is based on the nature of entitlements secured and the conditions of approval attached to them.

Sometimes the land is purchased in stages after the developer installs the improvements. These are called "lot releases" and the process has two beneficial effects. First, the developer still has not purchased all the land (although once the option conditions are satisfied, the developer will usually make a sizeable down payment), so the landowner essentially carries the financing. Second, the landowner typically is rewarded with slightly higher prices in exchange for agreeing to defer payment. Deferring payment as long as possible is usually more beneficial to the developer than to the landowner because, as our study found, interest on nonrecourse loans to developers with good credit ratings range from about 15 to 20 percent, depending on local market conditions. A nonrecourse loan means that the developer is offering very little or no tangible security, so in default the lender may not receive much if any of the loan repayment. Recourse loans that provide security to the lender can reduce the loan to low double-digit or high single-digit interest rates. This is the avenue taken by many small-production or marginal credit developers. However, the cost of security—such as a bank letter of credit, performance bond, and so forth—adds to the total, so in the end there is little or no difference in the cost of financing between a recourse and nonrecourse loan.

Theoretically, it is possible that all land-development costs, including costs associated with environmental regulation, could be capitalized backward into the land, meaning that the seller of land to developers, not the homebuyer, bears the costs. The extent to which this may happen depends on the elasticity of demand among consumers and the availability of close substitutes and short-term versus long-term perspectives. Theoretically, it is also possible that, in the absence of close substitutes and relatively inelastic demand for housing, landowners may become an informal cartel. Such a cartel may result in landowners refusing to absorb much of the environmental costs by lowering raw land prices. The result may be forward-shifting of the cost to homebuyers and renters.

There is another perspective: What if the environmental regulations generate benefits recognized and capitalized by the market? The book focuses only on regulatory costs, not benefits. As we will demonstrate, we find environmental costs to be negligible in the grand scheme of things. So even a small level of benefit may offset costs. See chapter 7, The Benefits of Environmental Regulations and Summary of Key Findings, for more discussion on this perspective. We conclude that what may matter most is clarity in requirements and certainty in administrative procedures.

TWO

Existing Research
A Review of the Literature

This chapter includes a literature review regarding what is known about three potential cost impacts of environmental regulations: (1) procedural delays; (2) costs added to development to meet environmental conditions; and (3) the removal of land from development supply. Some state and local governments have attempted to remove regulatory barriers by streamlining review processes, clarifying requirements to reduce uncertainty, and encouraging affordable housing through incentives, funding, and regulatory exemptions. Some have developed emerging programs that aim to integrate environment and affordability, such as brownfields redevelopment, compact/mixed-income development, and community revitalization. This chapter also notes that many questions remain unanswered by the literature, including (1) the extent to which environmental regulations actually pose barriers relative to other regulations and market forces; (2) the relative impact of regulatory requirements (standards and measures) versus implementation (review process delays) on housing affordability; and (3) the role of reform and incentives to balance the objectives of housing affordability and environmental protection.

Much of the literature on the effects of environmental regulations advances a tacit assumption that environmental quality is often achieved at the expense of economic development and that costs for environmental quality divert resources and increase costs for development and social well-being. However, there is little research that objectively quantifies those effects, especially the effects on housing affordability.

This literature review is greatly assisted by the U.S. Department of Housing and Urban Development (HUD) Regulatory Barriers Clearinghouse as well as by papers from the April 2004 HUD Conference on Regulatory Barriers and Housing Markets, especially those by Keil and Schill.[1] The literature reviewed here is drawn from survey articles,[2] previous federal government studies,[3] and reports, studies, and plans prepared by states[4] and local governments.[5]

The environmental regulatory framework is made up of tiers, from federal to state to local governments, but there is considerable integration and relationship among the tiers. This multitier regulatory framework is often thought to be prone to duplication problems in the permitting and review process, but there is little empirical evidence to support this theory.

There is considerable variation in environmental regulations across the country. Even federal regulations that aim to provide nationwide uniformity vary considerably depending on location and conditions. However, the greatest variation in regulations occurs among the states and among localities across the country.

The literature identifies land-use and development regulations as barriers to housing affordability, but most references indicate that this impact is "implicit" and often state that there is little empirical data to support this basic assumption. Further, the little evidence that does exist fails to distinguish between the effects of environmental and other regulations. Some studies assert that the overall cost of land and housing is dominated by land and housing markets and not by regulatory barriers. The literature cites several potential barriers created by environmental regulations, including:

- Review process delays
- Project add-on requirements
- Removal of land from development

Some state and local governments have attempted to remove regulatory barriers by streamlining review processes, clarifying requirements to reduce uncertainty, and encouraging affordable housing through incentives, funding, and regulatory exemptions. For example, Oregon's statewide land-use planning program requires local governments to establish clear and objective development standards and to review development applications within 120 days (which is enforced through judicial action). Florida allows developments with affordable housing components to go to the head of the line in permit review, thereby reducing waiting time for public hearings. In addition, there are also emerging programs and approaches, including brownfield redevelopment, compact/mixed-income development, and community revitalization efforts that aim to integrate environment and affordability. Unfortunately, there are too few examples of these efforts.

Many questions remain unanswered by the literature, including:

- The extent to which environmental regulations actually pose barriers relative to other regulations and market forces
- The relative impact of regulatory requirements (standards and measures) versus implementation (review process) on housing affordability
- The role of reform and incentives in balancing the objectives of housing affordability and environmental protection

This literature review covers two main areas:

1. Literature on the types and variability of federal, state, and local environmental regulations that potentially impact housing affordability
2. Literature on the impact of environmental regulations on housing costs

Much of the literature suggests that environmental quality is often achieved at the expense of economic development and that costs for environmental quality divert resources and increase costs for development and social well-being. However, there is little research that objectively quantifies those effects.

On the other hand, there is a large body of literature about the concept of sustainable development, which aims to advance the multiple objectives

Existing Research   21

of economic, social, and environmental well-being. The literature asserts that long-term sustainability of the economy, social equity, and the environment requires that development and public policy balance all three objectives.[6] The following sections present the main environmental regulations cited in the literature as potential barriers to housing affordability, and discuss the principal issues that may affect our findings.

FEDERAL OR FEDERALLY INFLUENCED ENVIRONMENTAL REGULATIONS

The following are federal or federally influenced environmental regulations.[7]

- **National Environmental Policy Act environmental impact statement (NEPA EIS) process review.** These regulations, which are enforced by the EPA, can have process and review impacts on large projects requiring federal approval, funding, or permitting.
- **Wetlands permitting.** These regulations, which are required by the Clean Water Act (CWA) and enforced by the Corps of Engineers and the EPA, can affect the permit process and may require mitigation required by the Corps of Engineers for development that affects jurisdictional wetlands.
- **Endangered species Habitat Conservation Plans (HCP) and permits.** These Endangered Species Act (ESA) regulations are implemented by the Fish and Wildlife Service (FWS) and the National Marine Fisheries Service (NMFS) of the U.S. Department of the Interior. In habitats of ESA-listed species, some development is allowed as long as an HCP is developed and approved. HCP documentation and mitigation can be very costly, but these regulations have affected only a few urbanizing areas (e.g., Southern California; Austin, Texas) to date.
- **Air quality permits.** These regulations are implemented by the EPA through the Clean Air Act (CAA) and by individual states through delegation of enforcement authority in addition to their own standards (if they are more rigorous than EPA standards). EPA permits are required for air pollution discharges in areas of both attainment and nonattain-

ment with federal air quality standards. These requirements generally do not affect housing projects, but large projects in nonattainment areas, such as Atlanta, that have transportation inducing air pollution impacts may require permits. Some states such as California have their own air quality laws implemented by environmental agencies.

- **Floodplain zoning.** These regulations are implemented by the Federal Emergency Management Administration (FEMA) through the National Flood Insurance Program (NFIP). An indirect effect of NFIP is that—to be eligible for national flood insurance—states and local governments must develop and implement floodplain zoning restricting development in flood-prone areas. Restrictions on so-called substantial improvement to existing structures in the floodplain also may block efforts to improve affordable housing in such areas.
- **Urban stormwater management permits.** These regulations are set forth in the Clean Water Act (CWA); the EPA has delegated enforcement authority to the states. The EPA requires that cities with populations greater than 10,000 must obtain water pollution permits through the National Pollutant Discharge Elimination System (NPDES) program for stormwater discharges. Many states, such as California, Florida, and New Jersey, have similar programs.
- **Coastal zone stormwater and sensitive area management.** These regulations are set forth in the Coastal Zone Management Act (CZMA), which is implemented by the National Oceanographic and Atmospheric Administration (NOAA) of the U.S. Department of Interior and by individual states participating in the program. Participating states receive funding from the CZM program for planning and programs to manage the coastal zone. Although some states, such as South Carolina and Georgia, maintain flexible and variable coastal management regulations (provided overall federal requirements are met), other states, such as Florida and North Carolina, have additional, mandatory regulatory requirements. In addition, the CWA amendments of 1987 mandated certain requirements for nonpoint source pollution control in the coastal zone.
- **Source water protection provisions of the Safe Drinking Water Act (SDWA).** These regulations are enforced by the EPA and implemented by states through delegation of authority. SDWA amendments of 1996,

enforced by the EPA, impose source water protection requirements—for both surface and groundwater drinking water sources—on all local governments. These requirements usually are implemented by state health or environmental protection agencies.

STATE ENVIRONMENTAL REGULATIONS

The following are some state environmental regulations.[8]

- **State environmental review requirements.** About half the states have EIS requirements similar to NEPA, but most require reviews for state or public projects only. Some states, such as Washington, California, and New York, require reviews for certain local decisions that may affect large projects.
- **Natural hazard zoning and state building codes.** Most states oversee certain natural hazard mitigation programs at the local level, and these state programs may mandate zoning and development restrictions for floodplains, steep slopes, seismic hazards, karst landscape, wildfire hazards, and so forth.
- **Wetlands restrictions and permits.** Several states, such as Florida, New Jersey, and Washington, have development restrictions or permitting requirements in the vicinity of wetlands that go beyond federal requirements.
- **Stormwater management regulations.** Several states, such as California, Florida, Oregon, and Virginia, have adopted urban stormwater regulations and guidelines to reduce the impacts of development on water flows and quality. These regulations can mean more extensive review requirements and potentially higher costs for developers.
- **Erosion and sediment control regulations.** All states have adopted erosion and sediment control regulations to control erosion and sediment generation from construction sites, including implementation of specific physical measures to keep sediment on the site and review requirements to ensure proper drainage from the site. These regulations may add to the cost of construction.
- **Coastal zone area restrictions and regulations.** All coastal states now participate in the federal CZM program, and many states have their

own development restrictions and permitting that go well beyond the minimum standards of the federal requirements, as noted above.
- **Agricultural land protection zoning.** Most farming states have programs for farmland preservation, but a few, such as Oregon, use a statewide regulatory approach.
- **Groundwater wellhead and watershed protection area restrictions.** Although the federal law does not mandate wellhead protection, some states (e.g., Florida) have developed program elements to encourage local governments to protect important sources of drinking water.
- **Threatened wildlife and natural community protection regulations.** Some states, such as California, have their own endangered species legislation.

LOCAL ENVIRONMENTAL REGULATIONS

The following are some local environmental regulations.[9]

- **Environmental review requirements.** Local governments have a range of review requirements that must be met before subdivision or building permits are issued. Some municipalities require formal environmental impact review, while others require ad hoc approaches.
- **Natural hazard mitigation plan implementation.** These regulations include floodplain zoning, seismic zoning, steep slope zoning, and wildfire mitigation requirements, among others. Local governments are the first line of defense in mitigating damages from natural hazards, and many have developed regulatory programs, such as overlay zoning, building codes and restrictions, and other measures. These programs may reduce land for development and increase costs of housing, but they serve other social needs.
- **Watershed and groundwater recharge source protection restrictions.** Local governments implement state requirements for source water protection, and many municipalities have developed their own additional restrictions.
- **Stormwater management regulations.** Local governments often go beyond minimum state requirements to manage stormwater and runoff

pollution. For example, some municipalities may implement low-impact development standards.
- **Erosion and sediment control regulations.** Local governments implement these state regulations through inspection and enforcement.
- **Open space set-aside requirements.** Local zoning ordinances can mandate open space set-aside requirements that may reduce land for development.
- **Urban forestry programs, tree preservation permits, and landscaping requirements.** These types of programs include regulations for tree protection, planting, and landscaping that may raise the cost of development.
- **Impact fees for environmental measures.** Most local impact fees are imposed for infrastructure or other physical needs or impacts caused by development projects. Some localities impose fees for environmental measures or improvements, such as stormwater management and parks and recreation.

PRINCIPAL ISSUES ARISING FROM A REVIEW OF ENVIRONMENTAL REGULATIONS

Many federal regulations such as air and water quality operate under a state primacy provision that allows and encourages states to take on implementation responsibility if their programs are deemed at least equivalent to the federal standards. Some programs, such as the NFIP's provision for floodplain management and the CZM program, require implementation by state and especially local governments. Most state regulations affecting land use and development are implemented by local governments.

The literature clearly identifies land-use and development regulations as a barrier to housing affordability, but most references indicate this impact as "implicit," and many admit the lack of empirical data that proves much beyond this ambiguous assumption. Some surveys of developers[10] and local government officials[11] indicate that regulations have some effect on housing affordability, but there is little evidence that quantifies the impacts or distinguishes between environmental and other regulations. Some studies assert that overall land and housing markets determine the cost of land and housing regardless of regulatory barriers. In any case, the literature identifies several regulatory barriers to housing affordability.

Problems with Environmental Regulatory Requirements and Processes Identified in the Literature

The literature reveals numerous shortcomings and problems with environmental regulatory requirements and processes. Regulatory review process requirements create delays and, therefore, increase costs, or so the reasoning goes. The review processes and decisions often are inconsistent and unpredictable, especially with wide reviewer discretion.[12] There are often too many reviews, too many departments, and too many layers of government.[13] There is uncertainty about length of time, and outcome of review often impedes projects.[14] Environmental impact assessment (EIA) requirements, where required, are lengthy and expensive.[15] Extensive review processes create opportunities for NIMBY (Not in My Back Yard) opponents to create further delays.[16] Finally, often lengthy delays occur imposing an additional cost on developers.

Much of the literature argues that meeting regulatory requirements increases costs.[17] For instance, EIA documentation studies are expensive and raise costs.[18] Open space set-asides are costly[19] both financially and because they often reduce overall development density. Wetlands permit and habitat conservation mitigation requirements are also costly.[20] Onsite wastewater (septic) standards are becoming increasingly expensive.[21] However, few other documented costs are associated with environmental regulations based on the literature reviewed. Nonetheless, it seems likely that such costs as stormwater management and landscaping/tree protection, among others, are viewed by developers as routine elements of the development process.

The literature also argues that environmental regulations remove land from potential development, thereby increasing the cost of housing affordability directly (onsite) and indirectly (in land markets).[22] Natural hazard and health standards (floodplains, seismic areas, steep slopes, septic systems, water supply source protection, aquifer and watershed protection, and so on) restrict land development, but most agree they are appropriate for the protection of health and safety.[23] Wetlands protection[24] and Endangered Species Act habitat conservation requirements also may reduce the supply of buildable land especially in urbanizing areas.[25] Moreover, farmland protection is sometimes a factor even if not directly related to environmental regulations.

State and local governments have tried to reduce regulatory barriers to housing affordability.[26] Most of these efforts are not directed specifically at environmental regulations, but at all regulatory requirements.[27] Efforts to streamline review processes and reduce duplication include one-stop per-mitting and time limits (i.e., automatic approval if no decision is made after a certain number of days).[28] In addition, some states and municipalities have worked to develop clearer and stronger policy statements and regulations that reduce uncertainty and reviewer discretion.[29] Others provide funding to help affordable housing projects comply with regulations.[30] Some states and local governments offer exemptions from some environmental regulations and review requirements for affordable housing projects.[31] Incentives such as density bonuses and mandates for affordable housing may help,[32] but the literature is not conclusive on the extent to which they encourage the development of affordable housing.

The literature identifies some emerging regulatory and design approaches that can increase affordable housing opportunities while enhancing environmental protection. For example, brownfield redevelopment programs aim to reduce uncertainty and liability and streamline project review, and some programs offer financial incentives for projects that have an affordable housing component. In addition, some smart growth initiatives aim to enhance community revitalization with affordable housing components.[33] Compact development and new urbanism designs often contain mixed-income housing requirements. In addition, green building programs aim to reduce longer-term operation costs through energy efficiency (affordable comfort) and reduced maintenance.[34]

The literature raises numerous caveats and issues. For example, the literature defines the term "environmental regulations" and addresses the important issue of distinguishing environmental regulations from other regulatory requirements, such as zoning, building codes, subdivision regulations, impact fees, urban containment, smart growth policies, and the like. In addition, the literature notes that, relative to market forces and other policies (fiscal, infrastructure, and so on), environmental regulations probably affect high housing costs little.[35] Relative to nonenvironmental regulations (zoning, subdivision regulations, building codes, impact fees, and so on), environmental regulations probably have a smaller influence on housing costs.[36] In the end, however, the literature offers no clear consensus on the effects of environmental regulations on housing affordability.

One issue not addressed in the literature reviewed is whether the public wishes to attain affordable housing at all costs. When assessing regulatory barriers to affordable housing, one must consider the barriers in the context of public objectives other than housing affordability. Any regulatory barrier, especially one that compromises the provision of affordable housing, must have a reasonable connection to public health, safety, and general welfare. For example, floodplain and other natural hazard regulations, wetland protection, endangered species habitat protection, erosion and sediment control, stormwater management, and other requirements will increase the cost of housing directly or indirectly, but they also provide public benefits.

In addition, the literature is unclear about the impacts of regulations per se versus the effects of regulation implementation. For example, barriers and delays often are created by inadequate funding for implementation (e.g., staff for review) rather than by the regulations themselves. In addition, one could argue that there is a learning curve associated with the initial implementation of new regulation. This learning curve requires learning by both the regulator and the regulated, creating delays and barriers that often are overcome with experience.

For the most part, our research reinforces the lessons gained from the literature; that is, uncertainty in what should be done to advance environmental quality persists, is subject to debate, and thus delay. This reality increases unpredictability in the development process leading developers to incorporate a higher-risk factor in their due diligence assessments, which usually leads to the need for higher-priced housing to offset the risk. However, as will be seen in the case study (presented in chapter 4) and demonstrated somewhat less clearly by the focus groups (discussed in chapter 6), the costs of environmental regulations in the twenty-first century are not that different from those of the latter third of the twentieth century—

despite the fact that there are more regulations and thus more requirements. In addition, despite increased regulation, the actual delay associated with environmental review may be negligible considering that approval times have also remained steady during the past three or more decades. We pose some reasons for this in chapter 8. Nonetheless, much can be done to improve certainty, enhance predictability, and make the overall development process more efficient in ways also discussed in chapter 8.

Regulatory Process Barriers to Affordable Housing and Possible Solutions

This section (and others later in this book) is informed significantly by Peter J. May's discussion of barriers to affordable housing.[37] Following May, the section considers two outcomes of regulatory implementation: (1) delays in construction and the rehabilitation of housing; and (2) added cost and procedural burdens that initially discourage housing development.

Among several procedural barriers to environmental regulations identified by May are two that guide this research. One is the barrier of *regulatory approvals* that entail delays because of cumbersome decision-making processes and duplication of regulations. These kinds of delays are of special concern to developers. Another barrier is created by a *patchwork of administrative arrangements* that results from the duplication of administrative structures and gaps in regulatory decision processes.

May suggests several broad administrative approaches to improving regulatory processes. One approach stands out: regulatory and administrative process simplification. This includes steps to reduce duplication and procedural hurdles. In addition, May identified other improvements: (1) conflict reduction and consensus-building approaches that are aimed at achieving agreement about affordable housing goals; (2) smart enforcement practices that reduce deterrents to housing development by fostering a supportive regulatory environment; and (3) facilitative reviews and inspection processes that speed up housing approvals and construction.

Regulatory and Administrative Simplification Efforts

May suggests various approaches to regulatory and administrative simplification, including so-called one-stop permit shops, electronic permitting, and third-party certification.[38]

Electronic Permitting and "One-Stop" Permitting

May notes that although the benefits of these and related approaches have not been systematically analyzed, anecdotal evidence illustrates potential improvements, including the following examples.

- The City of Los Angeles streamlined its regulatory functions, resulting in reduced waiting times by a factor of nearly 10 for permit processing, plan checking, and inspection scheduling.
- Use of integrated permit forms and processes among jurisdictions in the three-county Portland, Oregon, area, resulted in a substantial reduction of delays and confusion caused by the prior fragmentation of services.
- By using an online system for permit processing and inspection requests, Fairfax County, Virginia, achieved $1.5 million in operational savings for these regulatory functions in 2001 and reduced the county's permit processing times to under one hour, from an average of more than four hours.[39]

The National Institute of Building Sciences[40] cites more than 100 jurisdictions as leaders in electronic permitting, while recent planning research provides a broad review of the promise and pitfalls of e-government.[41] The evidence suggests that information technology may help streamline regulatory processes and overcome some of the barriers of fragmented regulatory authorities.

Enforcement Delegation and Third-Party Certification

One novel way to reduce delays in development permitting is to delegate approvals and enforcement to third parties. This approach can accelerate regulatory processes by, for example, having engineers hired by local government to provide inspections and conduct peer review of development applications. May observes that use of third parties can be expanded to the use of qualified private certifiers to review plans, conduct inspections, and perform audits of regulatory compliance.[42] Energy conservation and radon reduction provides important examples of third-party certification of regulatory compliance. In these cases, private certifiers evaluate problems and/or certify compliance. One problem with this approach, however, is the potential of giving poorly trained consultants authority as certifiers.

The viability of third-party certification or plan review depends on a stable source of development permit revenues. Comments from city planning directors indicate that in several fast-growth communities in California, the recent ebb in the housing market translates into fewer building permits and thus less permit revenue. Planning and development services departments are now laying off private consultants and plan reviewers—fewer building permits should translate to less work, right? Unfortunately, several of these jurisdictions relied so heavily on the private planning consultants that their own planning staffs do not have the capacity or expertise to handle the current applications, thereby causing further delays in permit processing of pending development projects.

Administrative Reorganization
According to May, one advantage of administrative reorganization is reducing duplication and clarifying decision-making processes.[43] Of course, reorganization requires that someone decide which functions need to be assigned and to which agency. An obvious approach would be to assign all functions related to environmental regulation to a single agency, much as building permit functions were long ago assigned to a "building" department. This solution may not work, however, when authority for decision making extends across different agencies and departments (e.g., engineering, transportation, planning, water utilities, and environmental services) and different jurisdictions (city, county, state, and federal regulators).

Another approach is to coordinate functions across different agencies and jurisdictions. Information technology, or e-governance, makes it possible to integrate regulatory functions without reorganizing government. Coordination among agencies and jurisdictions may be achieved with the appointment of a central administrator charged with the responsibility for integrating regulatory functions. For example, former San Diego mayor Susan Golding appointed a full-time staff person to become the Czar of Red Tape. This official's job was to coordinate multiple city departments and serve as a liaison with state and federal agencies on the development projects that city leaders considered the most important to the overall economic development of the city. Several cities adopted similar approaches.

The effects of reorganization on the actual production of housing have not been studied. May observes that the literature suggests that reorganization *may* reduce delays, but there is no certainty that reorganization *will* reduce delays.[44]

One of us (Nelson) recounts a personal anecdote of this from when he was a planning consultant in Washington State during the 1980s. The local county created a one-stop environmental review process to implement Washington's environmental policy act, with an administrator facilitating discussions among the dozen or so state and local agencies involved in Washington's environmental policy act. Instead of reducing the permitting period, however, the period actually increased by 50 percent. The problem was that the administrator sought consensus on all environmental issues, including those beyond the legal and professional scope of the individual agency heads. The developer ended up meeting with each agency directly anyway to negotiate issues relevant to the individual agency, and final permitting was received about a year after initial promises of the "one-stop" permitting system. As May notes, rearranging the organizational boxes does not necessarily reduce turf considerations and other bureaucratic hurdles.[45] For a reorganization to achieve improved and streamlined processes, the organizational culture and associated routines need to be transformed as well. This is a principal lesson learned from the Boston example reviewed in chapter 1.

The use of ombudsmen is yet another technique used in the environmental regulatory arena that could alleviate inconsistent interpretations across multiple agencies or jurisdictions.

Conflict Reduction and Consensus Building Strategies

Citizens, acting to preserve their interests and sometimes posing NIMBY opposition to affordable housing, present a different challenge. Burby notes that citizen involvement in planning "tends to be dominated by an 'iron triangle' composed of local business and development interests, local elected and appointed government officials, and neighborhood groups."[46] Interactions among these groups can influence the timeframe for decision making and the conditions of approval.

There are a variety of ways to identify and constructively engage "stakeholders."[47] May concludes that there is no simple taxonomy of approaches.[48] As the dispute resolution profession continues to grow and gain credibility, however, an accepted continuum of strategies and tools is emerging. These conflict resolution approaches may range from formal arbitration and administrative hearings to informal mediation and consensus building. More and more communities request and a few even require (e.g., Baltimore County) developers to convene charrettes with local residents for certain special projects. Engaging residents early in the design phases of a project substantially minimizes the potential for NIMBY opposition. Within the planning profession, the National Charrette Institute's workshops create a standard framework that adds predictability and credibility to the consensus-building process.

Much of the conflict-resolution literature and research relevant to land development has roots in environmental mediation. However, MIT's Consensus-Building Institute study of more than 500 mediations revealed that land development was the primary conflict in most of the cases.[49] Further, based on surveys of the participants and mediators in these conflicts, mediation was an effective way to resolve the dispute in many of these cases. Perhaps the lessons learned from the environmental dispute resolution field will continue to spill over into applications directly related to land development permitting systems. Although conflict-resolution and related negotiation processes have been used to reduce delays and unreasonable approval conditions, there is little solid research into the outcomes of specific applications and situations. Even less research exists about negotiating conflicts involving affordable housing, and this gap points to an opportunity for future research—the adaptation of a menu of conflict-resolution strategies to address regulatory barriers and community opposition to affordable housing.

One pilot land-use program may shed some light on the applicability of dispute resolution to resolve permit problems. From 1988 to 1995 the City of San Diego, with support from the University of San Diego Law School, ran the Center for Municipal Dispute Resolution (CMDR). CMDR trained zoning and building department supervisors to represent the city in nearly 750 mediations that involved violations of the local building and zoning ordinances. Staff from the law school managed CMDR while mediators from the community mediation center were paid a modest fee to mediate each code enforcement case. Written agreements were reached in more than 90 percent of the cases (an astounding result within the

34 *Environmental Regulations and Housing Costs*

mediation field) and property owners complied with these written agreements in more than 70 percent of them (an equally astounding level of agreement and compliance within the mediation of other types of disputes). While the CMDR experiment focused on code violations, this model could easily apply to development permit issues and could be institutionalized within a local government or university.

The next chapter moves to an assessment of how implementation of environmental regulations has changed over time—from the time they were first introduced broadly in the 1970s and into the 2000s.

THREE

Excessive Costs and a Comparison of Historical Changes in Environmental Regulations and Approval Processes

To establish a baseline for the analysis, this chapter reviews the state of local environmental regulatory and residential subdivision permitting processes at the beginning of the modern environmentally sensitive epoch of planning—the mid-1970s. Two baseline continua were developed from previous studies: environmental costs and procedural review timelines. This chapter examines research completed in 2002 that addresses many of the same procedural issues. Notably, the research found that the incidence of residential subdivisions requiring zoning relief increased from 33 percent to about 45 percent, and on average it appeared that the typical time to process a residential subdivision between 1975 and 2002 increased from fifteen months to seventeen months. Processing time increased, but it has increased by only two months or about 13 percent, despite a consensus that regulatory processes have become vastly more complicated since the 1970s. Available research is simply unable to ascribe any part of this relatively small increase in processing time to locally applied environmental regulations. The cost and process continua are broad, national average benchmarks and may bear little resemblance to particular regions or unique local conditions. They also apply mostly to new, suburban density, single-family detached, residential subdivisions in "greenfields" and not to complex, mixed-use, mixed-type housing; urban/suburban infill; or redevelopment sites. However, the continua provide a basis for comparison of current research both nationally and in particular markets.

THE BASELINE

The purpose of the baseline is to establish parameters of the residential development review and approval process existing at a particular point in the past, and then use the baseline to compare the current situation. The baseline period selected is the mid-1970s, roughly a generation or thirty years prior to when the research leading to the book was undertaken. This period was selected for several reasons. First, it comes at the early stages of national and state interest in improving environmental quality. The federal Environmental Protection Agency (EPA) was launched in 1970 with several states forming their own versions of the EPA around the same time. Second, the period comes at the beginning of several state efforts to engage in statewide land-use planning processes through local government efforts—principally California, Colorado, Florida, and Oregon. Third, the period marks a watershed in efforts to change development patterns (especially residential development patterns), characterized by a move away from low-density, single-use approaches to mixed-use and cluster development. Such publications as the Real Estate Research Corporation's *Costs of Sprawl* (1973) and the National Association of Home Builders's (NAHB) *Cost Effective Site Planning* (1976a) were especially prominent. And, fourth, numerous "model" development codes and subdivision manuals were published, such as the American Bar Association's *Model Land Development Code* (1976) and the American Society of Planning Officials' (now American Planning Association) *Model Subdivision Regulations* (Freilich 1973). These efforts helped launch the current regulatory environment. One of the techniques researchers use to assess change is to establish baseline conditions at the beginning of a change and compare current conditions against that baseline. The mid-1970s seems to be an appropriate period in which to create the baseline. Baseline conditions for the nation as a whole are constructed for costs and processes.

COSTS

The baseline is composed of cost and process elements. Fortunately, the NAHB's *Cost Effective Site Planning* (1976a) provides an important baseline for the costs associated with building comparable residential products available between the mid-1970s and mid-2000s. The NAHB analysis created prototypes of single-family developments for traditional and cluster or modern configurations, showing substantial savings in development costs, plus increases in amenities that enhance the value of residential developments. The baseline cost condition used here is that for the "typical standards" for a subdivision of four dwelling units per acre. The total share of the cost per lot assigned to environmentally related costs is about 15 percent (table 3.1).

Table 3.1 Distribution of Subdivision Improvement Costs, 1975

Cost Category	Cost	Share
Clearing and grubbing	$381	6.1%
Grading streets	$392	6.3%
Street pavement	$731	11.7%
Grading, seeding lots/right of way	$768	12.3%
Sanitary sewer	$923	14.8%
Water distribution	$531	8.5%
Curbs and gutters	$679	10.9%
Driveways	$700	11.2%
Sidewalks	$212	3.4%
Street trees	$306	4.9%
Storm drainage	$619	9.9%
Total	$6,242	
Environmentally related costs	$925	14.8%

Figures in 2005 dollars using data from *Engineering News & Record*'s twenty cities fourth-quarter index. *Source:* National Association of Home Builders (1976a, 135).

How do improvement costs, especially those related to environmental regulations, compare with finished lot prices? The Urban Land Institute's *Residential Development Handbook* (1990) estimates the average finished lot price for 1975 at $10,055 (the unweighted average of the thirty markets reported). Improvement costs are estimated to be about 62 percent of finished lot prices with environmentally related costs at about 9 percent of the finished lot price, as seen below:

$$\frac{\text{Improvement Costs per Lot}}{\text{Finished Lot Cost}} = \frac{\$6{,}242}{\$10{,}055} = 62.1\%$$

$$\frac{\text{Environmentally Related Costs per Lot}}{\text{Finished Lot Cost}} = \frac{\$925}{\$10{,}055} = 9.2\%$$

Data from the mid-1970s do not allow for the construction of a continuum of environmentally related costs per lot. In statistics, a normal distribution of variation in measurement assuming a randomly selected population would have about two-thirds of all cases distributed on both sides of the mean. If environmentally related costs in the mid-1970s had a mean of around 9 percent, and assuming a normal distribution about the mean, about two-thirds of all cases would fall between 6 percent and 12 percent. Based on this approach, a range is constructed here with low, normal, and high categories as follows:

<6% of Lot Cost	6–12% of Lot Cost	>12% of Lot Cost
Low	Normal	High

PROCESSES

For information on processing subdivision approvals, the research is aided by analysis by Ben-Joseph (2003), who compares changes in various subdivision regulatory features and procedures between 1976—based on a survey of developers by Seidel (1978)—and Ben-Joseph's replication of that survey in 2002. It is interesting to note that, during the twenty-six-year period from 1976 to 2002, the mean time to process subdivision approvals increased only two months, from fifteen to seventeen (table 3.2). The mode length of time to process subdivision approvals remained the same in both

Table 3.2. Average Time to Receive Residential Subdivision Approvals According to Developers, 1976 and 2002

Survey	Less than 7 Months	7 to 12 Months	13 to 24 Months	More than 24 Months	Mean Months
1976	14.5%	27.5%	47.0%	11.0%	15
2002	6.4%	28.0%	45.0%	20.5%	17

Mean months calculated by authors based on six months, nine months, eighteen months, and thirty months, respectively, for the categories of less than seven months, seven to twelve months, thirteen to twenty-four months, and more than twenty-four months. *Source:* Figures for 1976 are from Seidel (1978), and 2002 figures are from Ben-Joseph (2003).

surveys, thirteen to twenty-four months, but the distribution of subdivisions approved in less than seven months in 1976 was halved by 2002, while those approved in more than twenty-four months nearly doubled.

However, an increasing percentage of residential subdivision approvals also require variances, special exceptions, and/or rezoning decisions in addition to plat approval. As seen in table 3.3, the incidence of securing

Table 3.3 Incidence of Developers' Application for Zoning Relief, 1976 and 2002

Percentage of the Time Developers Applied for Zoning Relief	Percentage of Developers, 1976 (%)	Percentage of Developers, 2002 (%)
Almost never	49.5	14.1
5% to 10%	5.3	11.3
11% to 25%	6.1	8.5
26% to 50%	10.2	11.3
51% to 75%	3.9	15.5
More than 75%	31.6	36.6
Weighted Average Incidence	33.1	45.7

Weighted average incidence calculated by authors based on 0 percent, 7.5 percent, 18 percent, 38 percent, 63 percent, and 80 percent for each category of percentage of time applied for zoning relief, respectively, multiplied by the incidence for 1976 and 2002, respectively. *Source:* Ben-Joseph (2003).

Table 3.4 Developers' Estimate of Approval Time for Zoning Relief, 2002

Procedure	Time Required	Percentage of Developers
Variance or special exception	<1 month	0.0%
	1–2 months	28.6%
	3–4 months	32.9%
	4+ months	38.5%
	Mean	3.9
Rezoning	<1 month	0.0%
	1–2 months	6.8%
	3–4 months	23.3%
	4+ months	69.9%
	Mean	5.1
Unweighted Combination	Mean	4.5

Weighted average incidence calculated by authors based on 0 months, 1.5 months, 3.5 months, and 6 months for each category of percent of time applied for zoning relief, respectively, times the incidence for 2002, respectively. *Source:* Ben-Joseph (2003).

zoning relief (variances, special exceptions, and/or rezonings) rose from about 33 percent in 1976 to about 46 percent in 2002, an increase of nearly 40 percent.

How much time this adds to the overall entitlement process is unknown. Sometimes the zoning relief is processed as part of an overall package of land-use decisions, but other times the zoning relief entails a separate process. The only study that may address this is Ben-Joseph's, but an inference may be made here.

Table 3.4 shows developers' representation of the time it took to secure zoning relief in 2002. On average, a zoning relief decision takes four to five months to process, but because of due diligence, developers likely know in advance if their proposal will require zoning relief and thus anticipate the process in their decision about whether to proceed.

Therefore zoning relief is already included in the residential subdivision approval estimates reported in table 3.2.

The overall increase by two months between 1976 and 2002 is essentially equivalent to the mean unweighted combination zoning relief approval months in table 3.4 times the incidence of projects needing zoning relief in 2002 from table 3.3, or about 2.1 months.

| <7 months | 7–12 months | 13–24 months | 24+ months |
| Expedited | Accelerated | Normal | Delayed |

LIMITATIONS AND CAVEATS

The cost and process continua presented here have important caveats. First, these are broad, national average benchmarks that may bear little resemblance to regions or unique local conditions. Areas rich with diverse but fragile habitats, such as much of Southern California and many parts of Florida, may require higher-level assessment than other areas with a narrower range of habitats and/or more resilient environments such as much of the Piedmont region in the Southeast or the Great Plains that span the distance from Canada to Texas. Second, the continua also primarily apply to new, suburban density, single-family, detached, residential subdivisions in greenfields, and they do not apply to complex, mixed-use, mixed-type housing; urban/suburban infill; or redevelopment sites. Single-use, traditional residential subdivisions on greenfields in the Piedmont region and Texas may very well face relatively fewer regulatory hurdles and may more efficiently address environmental concerns than do complex projects in fragile landscapes that might also require environmental remediation. Thus, these continua need to be refined for different regions and for different kinds or scales of developments, and such is beyond the scope of this research. Nonetheless, the approaches developed and applied in this research may inform future research on how to construct continua relevant to different conditions.

THE COST OF EXCESSIVE REGULATIONS

Our research did not examine the issue of whether the monetary costs of environmental regulations are excessive, but research conducted for HUD by NAHB's Research Center (2007) provides insight into this question.

The NAHB study notes that subdivision regulations are a significant tool by which local governments manage and shape housing development. Those regulations specify how plats or site plans should be prepared and go on to establish infrastructure requirements, such as those for streets, sidewalks, water and sewer, drainage, curbs and gutters, street signs, and landscaping, among others. Subdivision regulations may also require trees, utility easements, and dedication of land or fees in lieu of land for parks and recreational areas and/or public school facilities. Subdivision regulations aim to enhance the public health, safety, and general welfare of the community.

However, the costs of the subdivision requirements are a significant share of the cost of building new homes. If the costs are indeed *excessive*, they can be considered regulatory barriers to affordable housing because the local requirements are greater (and, hence, more costly) than those necessary to provide for the health and safety needs of the community. To determine whether subdivision requirements are excessive, HUD commissioned the NAHB to conduct a nationwide study. The purpose of the study was to develop a national estimate of the costs of excessive subdivision regulations on single-family detached housing built in subdivisions. This is the type of housing most closely associated with the idea of homeownership in America.

The NAHB study involved four elements: (1) collecting regulatory standards from a nationally representative sample of jurisdictions for the selected subdivision and related zoning rules; (2) establishing benchmark values and unit costs for each requirement based on an expert panel; (3) producing cost estimates for excessive regulation based on the benchmark costs; and (4) creating a national estimate of the costs of excessive subdivision regulations. Similar to ours, the NAHB study focused only on single-family residential subdivisions.

The NAHB ran two principal models. The first, an *aggregated* model, assumed that the geographic distribution of regulatory standards for subdivisions do not vary by census region or by metropolitan statistical area status within the nation. Excessive costs were thus summed for the entire nation assuming no variation in cost factors and home prices. The second, a *disaggregated* model, assumed that excessive subdivision regulatory costs would vary by census region and urban and rural status within them.

Separate analyses were done for each sample of communities in each region and urban and rural status, and then summed. The disaggregated model may provide a refined view of the cost of excessive subdivision regulations. It is also important to note that the NAHB study used conservative assumptions about costs, using lower cost figures when in doubt. The study results should thus be considered conservative estimates.

The NAHB estimates that excessive regulation raises the cost of housing from 3.7 percent (disaggregated model) to 4.9 percent (aggregated model). Excessive lot size (density) regulations were the largest share of the increase at 65 percent. Excessive lot widths accounted for 9 percent of the increase. Minimum floor area requirements made up 17 percent of the higher costs. Table 3.5 summarizes these findings.

Table 3.5 Estimates of the Excessive Subdivision Regulatory Cost Barriers for All Building Permits Issued for Detached Single-Family Dwelling Units in the Nation, 2004

Cost Estimates Variable	Aggregated Analysis, Share of Excess Cost Burden		Disaggregated Analysis, Share of Excess Cost Burden	
	Figure	Percentage	Figure	Percentage
National cost of excessive regulation	$19,215,338,860		14,603,018,827	
Lot size	$12,552,280,392	65.3%	11,137,670,615	76.3%
Lot width	$1,811,355,507	9.4%	1,551,371,592	10.6%
Front setbacks	$797,956,481	4.2%	743,335,966	5.1%
Floor area	$3,291,995,430	17.1%	872,800,196	6.0%
Pavement	$223,586,056	1.2%	96,777,852	0.7%
Sidewalk	$216,734,720	1.1%	36,107,707	0.2%
Sidewalk width	$50,334,294	0.3%	21,564,900	0.1%
Off-street parking	$76,312,500	0.4%	73,915,367	0.5%
Open space	$194,783,479	1.0%	69,474,632	0.5%
Per single-family dwelling unit	$11,910		$9,051	
Mean new home price	$244,000	4.9%	$244,000	3.7%

Source: Adapted from NAHB (2007).

The NAHB study is unique because it was able to reasonably define and estimate excessive costs. Our study reports total costs associated with environmental regulation. The two studies together can provide an overarching perspective.

CONCLUSION

The total costs associated with environmental regulation have not changed much over the past three decades even though those regulations have certainly increased in number, rigor, and requirements. Moreover, using NAHB's open space measure—the only one directly related to environmental regulation—it would appear that excessive environmental regulation accounts for only about 0.5 percent (disaggregated model) to 1 percent (aggregated model) of the excessive cost burden. Put differently, the share of the total sales price of the home attributable to excessive open space regulation would range from 0.02 percent ($43) to 0.05 percent ($121) in the disaggregated and aggregated models, respectively. Two other factors, lot size and setback requirements, may also be considered forms of excessive environmental regulation. If all three factors are assigned fully to excessive environmental regulation, the share of the cost burden from these would rise to 71 percent in the aggregated model and 82 percent in the disaggregated model. Thus, home prices would rise by 3.0 percent ($7,407) to 3.4 percent ($8,395) in the disaggregated and aggregated models, respectively. This is slightly less than what we found in the case study presented in the next chapter and information provided by the focus group convened in Tucson (see chapter 6), but roughly comparable to the experience of focus groups convened in Dallas and Denver (see chapter 6).

FOUR

Case Study
Washington, DC, Metropolitan Region

This chapter presents the Washington metropolitan area case study, which consists of detailed studies of six residential development projects by regional and national developers building new, market-rate housing across the case study area. Three points of interest emerge from the case study:

1. *Nearly all cases required zoning relief, and the overall average time-to-approval was twenty-four months. This is at the top end of the "normal" range of the processing continuum discussed in chapter 3.*
2. *Environmentally related costs per finished lot, based on an estimate of the market clearing price of a finished lot to builders, averaged 4.7 percent.*
3. *All developers indicated that, for the kinds of residential subdivision projects included in the case study, the typical improvement cost per lot is about $75,000. This includes all site preparation and infrastructure improvements plus the permit processing time, overhead, and cost of financing.*

From 1995 to 2005, the Washington, DC, metropolitan region became one of nation's most expensive places to purchase a home. Economic and job growth throughout the region has spawned substantial demand for new development, especially for new housing within the suburban counties and cities that surround the District of Columbia. While these communities share a robust regional housing market, metropolitan Washington, DC, includes three distinct models of local government, two traditionally different state environmental regulatory systems (Maryland and Virginia), and several distinct and extensive land development review processes. Given these regulatory variations and its strong regional housing market, metropolitan Washington, DC, provides an ideal laboratory to explore the ways in which environmental protection permit and regulatory systems may affect suburban housing affordability.

It is important to note that the case study time period occurred when the national and regional housing markets were at their peak in prices: the mid-2000s. The latter part of the first decade of this century saw increasing foreclosure rates and falling home prices in suburban and exurban areas, although the closer-in areas saw little change in housing prices. In booming markets, the time it takes to review development proposals may be increased because regulatory systems are clogged. Also, in such times, there is a tendency by local government to add conditions because (A) developers are anxious to meet market needs and may be more prone to accepting conditions simply for the sake of securing entitlements in a hot market; and (B) local governments may perceive that with housing prices escalating rapidly the cost of additional conditions is relatively small. In economic downturns, local governments may be more prone to expediting development applications because there may be fewer of them and governments may be less prone to adding conditions for fear of driving desired development elsewhere. The case study should thus be seen as a reflection of a very strong market that may have slowed review processes while adding costs that may be unusual in a normal to slow market.

The case study compares the environmental regulatory systems of Maryland and Virginia and two adjacent counties (Montgomery and Fairfax), which are separated by the narrow band of the Potomac River. The case study examines how land development processes differ between the two local jurisdictions and states, how the differences affect environmental compliance and reviews, and how much time it takes home builders to obtain the final development approvals for standard subdivisions. Fortunately, a local developer granted access to a number of projects completed in the region and this access enabled the research team to investigate the effects of jurisdictional and regulatory differences from within the uniformity of a single firm in a single market.

We began this research with two presuppositions: (1) that environmental regulatory costs and approval periods would be higher generally in the metropolitan Washington, DC, area than for the nation as a whole in the 1970s; and (2) that costs and time would be higher in Montgomery County, Maryland (being a national example of growth management in addition to being located in a state that mandates high levels of environmental protection), than in the Virginia jurisdictions (not having any notable growth management efforts and located in a state with few state-level planning mandates).

We were not entirely right on either account. First, as a whole, the cost of environmental regulatory compliance is not much different in this region during the 2000s than national costs as reported by literature thirty years earlier. While this region is at the upper end of the continuum presented in chapter 3, the permitting times were mostly in line with expectations based on national research (table 4.1). Second, although Montgomery

Table 4.1 Average Project Sales Price, Environmental Costs, and Approval Times

County	Project	Average Sales Price	Environmental Costs Per Unit	Environmental Costs as a Percentage of Sales Price	Review Time (in months)
Fairfax	Phased	$748,852	$5,500	0.7%	22
	Single phase	$821,900	$12,000	1.5%	18
Montgomery		$670,042	$5,500	0.8%	28
Loudoun	Phased	$749,833	$2,900	0.4%	22
	By-right	$790,233	$16,500	2.1%	27
Prince William		$626,900	$8,500	1.4%	29
Unweighted Average		$734,627	$8,483	1.2%	24

Table 4.2 Fairfax and Montgomery Counties Compared

Category	Fairfax County	Montgomery County
Population 1990 (total)	818,584	757,027
Population 2000 (total)	969,749	873,341
Population 2005 (estimated)	1,006,529	927,533
Median household income in 2004	$88,133	$82,971
Single-family detached homes in 2004	194,453	184,085
Attached residential units in 2004	177,945	168,634
Total housing units in 2004	380,637	353,051
Median new home sales price, 2005	$807,266	$759,933
Median new home sales price, 1997	$389,747	$343,295

Source: Authors' analysis of data from U.S. Bureau of the Census 2000 for Fairfax County, Virginia, and Montgomery County, Maryland.

County had slightly higher permitting periods than the Virginia jurisdictions, the fact that its new housing prices were slightly less indicates the delay has little, if any, effect on prices (table 4.2).

CASE STUDY METHODOLOGY

The research team enlisted the support of regional home builders to conduct an inventory of the direct costs associated with the environmental and development review processes incurred in completing four residential subdivisions in Fairfax County, Virginia, and Montgomery County, Maryland. In addition, cost information was gathered for three projects in two adjacent Northern Virginia counties (Loudoun and Prince William). Because of the long-standing environmental regulatory systems, comprehensive land-development processes, and staff capacities in Fairfax and Montgomery counties, the research team focused their case study comparison and cost calculation on the regulatory systems and projects in those counties. The additional projects provide additional cost data beyond those two counties, but in the same regional housing market.

BOX 4.1 Research Goals and Hypotheses

The goal of the case study is to generate insight into the impacts of environmental regulations (and the systems used to support them) on the housing industry and specifically on the cost of housing units. The following are the case study hypotheses.

1. **Environmental Compliance Costs.** Drawn from the academic literature, the research team investigated two hypotheses relating to environmental compliance costs:
   - Environmental compliance costs include costs for additional environmental plans and studies and costs for physical measures for mitigation, restoration, and protection, and that these combined costs are a significant percentage of the costs of development and the price of housing.
   - The compliance costs of physical measures for environmental mitigation, restoration, and protection carry a higher cost commitment than the preparation or implementation of plans to protect these resources.
2. **Costs of Environmental Review and Approval Processes.** Drawn for the academic literature, the case study investigated three hypotheses relating to development review processes:
   - Increased levels of environmental regulations require more time and resources for development review and permit approvals.
   - The longer it takes to navigate the development review process, the greater the costs to the home builder. These costs are transferred to the customer in the form of higher housing prices.
   - Environmental regulations are more effective and less costly when the administrative processes are streamlined and provide greater clarity and certainty to both developers and the staffs of reviewing and approving agencies.

The Fairfax/Montgomery case study examines three main areas:

1. **Environmental Regulatory Systems.** A survey of relevant and applicable state and local environmental regulations (statutes, ordinances, policies, and guidelines) imposed on the projects, such as erosion con-

trols, stream buffers, tree inventories, open space set-asides, and the like.
2. **Local Development Review Processes.** A careful evaluation of how the local development processes interface with the environmental regulatory systems, especially tracking how long it takes (from application to entitlement) and how many decision steps (such as zone change, plan amendment, and subdivision approval) are involved.
3. **Developer Costs.** An inventory of typical costs incurred by the home builder, such as engaging the services of environmental consultants and installing erosion control measures and stormwater infrastructure.

Information for the case study was collected from interviews with local elected officials and their planning staffs; review of planning documents and approved final plans acquired from a home builder active in the metropolitan region; online research from each county's Web site; and interviews with local builders, developers, and engineers. The builders provided access to final construction plans and documents for seven project sites, six in Virginia and one in Maryland. The research team surveyed and conducted inventories of each project to gather information regarding environmental regulations, general characteristics, and special requirements pertaining to environmental situations on the site. Interviews with the developers and their environmental and design consultants were used to gather information about the process and costs associated with the projects. Online municipal data were used to acquire information about project timing and requirements.

PROFILE OF METROPOLITAN WASHINGTON, DC

The metropolitan Washington, DC, region has experienced, and continues to experience, significant growth in recent years. The metropolitan statistical area (MSA) grew from 4.1 million residents in 1990 to 4.8 million in 2000 (Woods and Poole Economics 2007). There were an estimated 5.1 million residents in the MSA as of 2005, with the Metropolitan Washington Council of Governments (MWCOG) forecasting it to reach 6.6 million by 2030 (MWCOG 2006a). This growth has been generated in part by a robust employment market, which is fed by both federal government and private-sector jobs. Nearly 125,000 new jobs have been added in the region since 2000, raising the number of employed persons in the MSA to 2,677,815 (MWCOG 2006a).

As a result of this growth, the housing market in the metropolitan Washington region is strong, with a high demand for residential units in all categories. According to the *Metropolitan Washington Annual Regional Housing Report*, there were an estimated 27,420 permits issued for single-family and multifamily residential units in 2005 (MWCOG 2006b). This figure is divided between an estimated 18,523 permits for single-family residential units and 8,897 permits for multifamily residential units. Between 1998 and 2005, nearly 157,000 single-family residential units were constructed in the Washington region. Although permit activity fell by about half for the metropolitan area as a whole during the latter half of the decade, as compared with activity in the first half of the decade, the region continued to grow and is expected to surpass 5.5 million by 2010. The Washington metropolitan region includes the following locations (as shown in figure 4.1):

- Washington, DC
- Virginia
  - City of Alexandria
  - Arlington County
  - City of Fairfax
  - Fairfax County
  - City of Falls Church
  - Loudoun County
  - City of Manassas
  - City of Manassas Park
  - Prince William County
- Maryland
  - Frederick County
  - Montgomery County
  - Prince George's County

The report also revealed the metropolitan region experienced a 130 percent increase in average homes sales prices between 1998 and 2005,

52   Environmental Regulations and Housing Costs

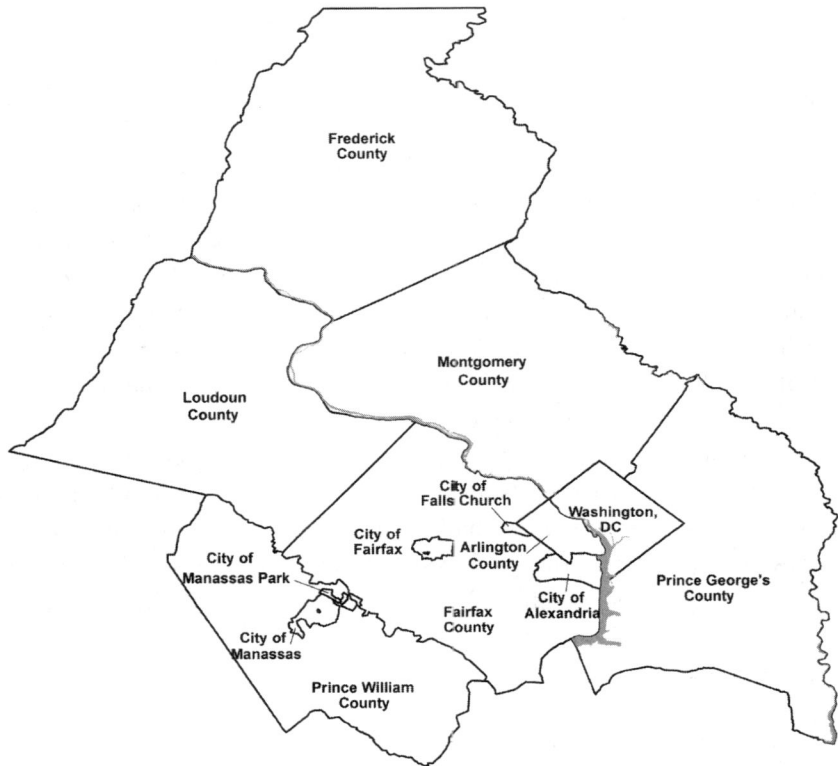

Figure 4.1   Metropolitan Washington, DC

a figure that incorporates single-family detached and attached homes as well as condominium units. This figure is supported by the area's marked increase in average home sales price—from $205,964 in 1998 to $472,536 in 2005 (figure 4.2). In addition, from 2000 to 2005, the average number of days a home spent on the market decreased from forty-six days to twenty-three days, indicating a practically insatiable demand for the region's residential units.

The U.S. Bureau of the Census, which tracks building permit activity annually for single-family and multifamily units, reveals that regional permitting activity decreased and increased, respectively, between 2000 and 2005 (U.S. Bureau of the Census 2008a). During this same time period, the average number of construction permits for single-family and multi-

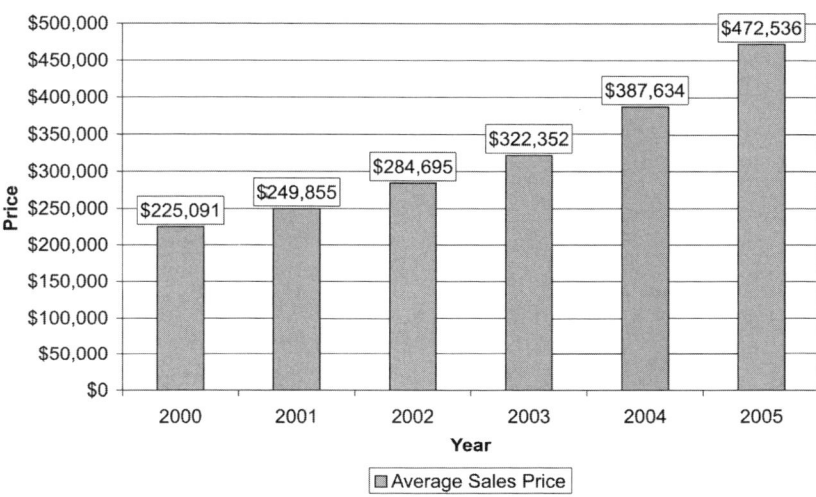

Figure 4.2 Regional Home Sales Price, Study Period 2000–2005. *Source:* Authors' analysis of data from Metropolitan Regional Information Systems, Inc.

family units was nearly 30,000, with multifamily units accounting for between one-quarter and one-third of the building permits issued. The census does not track whether the permitted units are to be owner- or renter-occupied. Figure 4.3 illustrates the number of single-family and multifamily building permits issued from 2000 through 2005.

The housing market in the Washington metropolitan region has been strong for a number of years. The market did slow during the latter half of the decade, attributable to the subprime "meltdown" along with tighter mortgage credit. The area continues to grow, though, and it is anticipated that by the end of the decade excess inventories would be mostly gone. Housing prices would be expected to rise as supply is expected to lag demand, but whether they will rise to pre-meltdown levels is uncertain ("Changing Seasons, Changing Markets" 2006). With a steady source of employment in the government sector and a strong regional technology sector, the area's housing slowdown is not expected to last. Indeed, the region is forecast to add an average of 50,000 new residents annually through 2030 (MWCOG 2007).

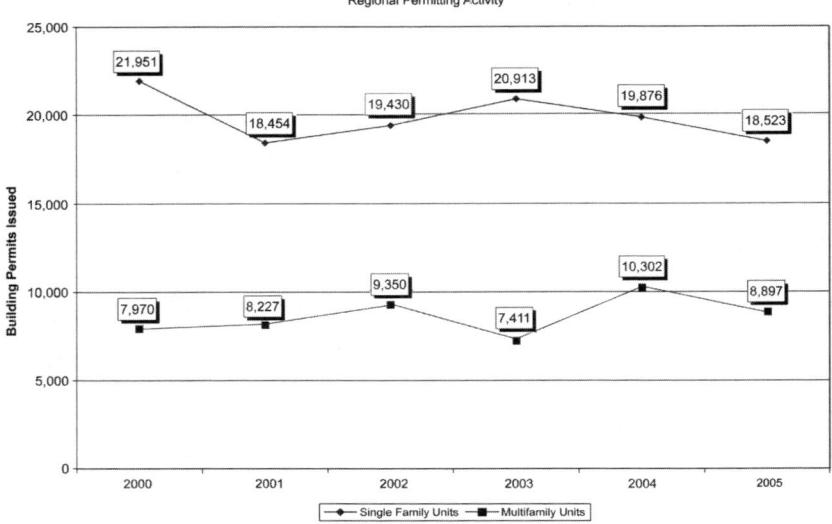

Figure 4.3 Regional Permitting Activity, Study Period 2000–2005. *Source:* U.S. Bureau of the Census. Data for 2000 through 2005 accessed August 12, 2008, from http://www.census.gov/const/www/C40/table3.html.

Finally, the study area is situated entirely within the Chesapeake Bay watershed. The Chesapeake Bay is a major natural asset unique to the Washington metropolitan region. Environmental regulatory issues that arise in connection with this important natural resource include stormwater management, sedimentation and erosion controls, impervious surfaces, air pollution, tree cover, and open space preservation.

PROFILE OF FAIRFAX COUNTY, VIRGINIA, AND MONTGOMERY COUNTY, MARYLAND

Fairfax County, Virginia, and Montgomery County, Maryland, employ two very distinct institutional approaches to governance and land development. In fact, it would be difficult to find such contrasting styles in another metropolitan area. Officially part of the Washington, DC, metropolitan statistical area (MSA), Fairfax and Montgomery counties now share similar trends in demographics, population growth, development pressures, and high-end housing markets. These suburban counties, separated only by the Potomac River, historically have varied considerably in governance structure and state-level environmental regulatory review requirements.

Fairfax County operates in a Dillon's Rule state, which means that its local powers are strictly limited by what the Virginia legislature expressly says they can do. By contrast, local governments in Maryland enjoy a greater level of autonomy and wider range of powers. Virginia law has a deep tradition of and high respect for the interests of private property owners, making it historically more conservative when it comes to state and local environmental regulations, land-use planning, and zoning powers. In recent years Maryland has promoted itself as one of the nation's leaders in smart growth and land-use planning. Compared with neighboring Virginia, Maryland has a stronger state environmental regulatory system that shares significant implementation responsibilities with county governments. With the advent of federal and Virginia state regulations aimed at reducing pollution in the Chesapeake Bay, Fairfax County's environmental approaches have started to resemble those of Montgomery County and the state of Maryland.

Fairfax County, Virginia, and Montgomery County, Maryland, are counties representative of the broader environmental and affordable housing challenges facing the region. Table 4.2 provides a general comparison of the demographic and housing characteristics of the two counties. Their proximity to the District of Columbia has helped these counties evolve from bedroom suburban communities into localities with strong economic development and regional employment attractions. Their respective approaches to the increased residential development pressures are indicative of the challenges each faces in preserving the environment and providing affordable housing.

Virginia's Dillon's Rule structure limits the ability of local governments to directly regulate or control the activities of developers and builders when it comes to environmental protection and affordable housing needs. For example, developers are encouraged and offered incentives to participate in Fairfax County's affordable housing program, but state law does not expressly empower the county to enact a local ordinance that would mandate affordable housing set-asides. Municipal law in Maryland allows Montgomery County to play a more active role in land-use management, preparing and enforcing area master plans, affordable housing requirements, and environmental regulations. In fact, Montgomery County requires developers of housing projects that exceed a predetermined threshold of units to provide a certain percentage of affordable housing units within the development.

Fairfax County, Virginia

Many of the demographic and economic characteristics of the two counties are similar—like Montgomery County, Fairfax County has about 1 million residents. Also like Montgomery County, Fairfax has experienced double-digit population growth in the past ten years, and housing prices and household income are well above the national average.

Where the counties differ is in land-use policy and regulation based on their governing structures. The Fairfax County government, which is guided by an elected board of supervisors and a chairman at-large, tends to be more advisory than regulatory in its approach, whereas Montgomery County is very involved in land-use decisions and growth patterns. Fairfax County has a relatively sprawling growth pattern compared with Montgomery County. An extensive network of transportation corridors in Fairfax County has allowed for dispersed suburban development, whereas Montgomery County has developed more or less along the Metro rail corridors. Since 1970, Fairfax County has not developed as much land around Metro stations in contrast to Montgomery County, as Fairfax development has tended to cluster around highway exits, causing it to be a fairly decentralized area with no "county core" (Mid-Atlantic RESAC 2006).

Demand for housing in Fairfax County has remained fairly high in the county—the homeowner vacancy rate was 0.7 percent and the rental vacancy rate was 4.9 percent in 2004, lower than the national average (U.S. Bureau of the Census 2006). Between 2000 and 2003, Fairfax County grew at a rate of 4 percent, as compared with a 1 percent growth rate in Montgomery County (MWCOG 2006c). Housing prices also have steadily increased. The median housing unit market value in 2004 was $415,418, an increase of 13.6 percent since 2003, significantly higher than the national value of $151,366 (U.S. Bureau of the Census 2006). Most housing units in Fairfax County in 2004 were single-family residences according to the U.S. Bureau of the Census (2006). In 2005, the median sales price of a new single-family home was $807,266.[1] The existing single-family home resale price in 2005 was $615,000.[2] Both new and resale prices fell from 2005, the peak year for the decade, but by the end of the decade they had begun to rise. The median household income in 2005 was $158,000 (in 2004 dollars) (Woods and Poole Economics 2007). But, because of the national economic downturn in the latter half of the decade, the county's median household income is expected to fall to about $145,000 (also in 2004 dollars). In Fairfax County, where providing affordable housing units as a part of a development project cannot be required, the Affordable Housing Partnership Program works with nonprofit and for-profit housing development organizations to develop and preserve affordable residential units in the county.[3]

The regulatory structure of the state limits the environmental and affordable housing regulations the county is able to develop and enforce. Therefore, the county follows the traditional state and federal guidelines set forth for stormwater and wetlands. Fairfax County also seeks to protect rural space by allowing one house per five acres in the Occoquan area, and the county has a conservation easement partnership in place. The Virginia Chesapeake Bay Preservation Act, enacted in 1988, also influenced the county's environmental regulatory structure. Additionally, the county adopted the Chesapeake Bay Ordinance in 1993 in compliance with the Chesapeake Bay Preservation Act. The ordinance established Chesapeake Bay Preservation areas, including Resource Protection areas and Resource Management areas, to protect water quality. The ordinance has been successful in protecting water resources for the county, which received the Chesapeake Bay Program's Local Government Advisory Committee "Gold" Partner Community designation in 1997 and 2003.

Montgomery County, Maryland

Montgomery County, Maryland, is a large county adjacent to and northwest of Washington, DC. Like Fairfax County, it is home to more than 900,000 people of diverse races and backgrounds—and it is growing.[4] The elected county executive oversees a large governing body that offers its residents a strong public schools system, jobs, and attractive suburban neighborhoods and rural areas for living.

Almost half (48 percent) of Montgomery County residents live in multifamily housing.[5] Existing—as opposed to new—homes (including attached and detached types) are a most affordable option for housing in the county. Existing single-family home prices have seen an increase at a rate of 1.1 percent since 1991 as compared with a 2.5 percent annual increase for new residential units.[6] The median sales price of a new single-family home in 2005 was $759,933.[7] The median resale price for existing single-family homes was $500,000 in 2005.[8] For all single-family homes—attached, detached, new, and existing—the median sales price was $440,000 in 2005.[9] The county's median household income in 2005 was $82,187 (U.S. Bureau of the Census 2006).

Montgomery County, which has a mandatory affordable housing requirement for new residential development projects over a certain number of units, leads the metropolitan region in building affordable housing. The county was recognized as a pioneer in affordable housing dating back to the 1970s. Between 1976 and the benchmark year for this study, 2005, 11,647 moderately priced dwelling units (MPDUs) were constructed.[10] In 2003, 29 percent of households (approximately 98,000) in the county fell below the household income cap to qualify for the MPDU program, which is set at 65 percent of the county median income (Montgomery County Department of Park and Planning 2004).

The county also has a long-standing tradition of being a regional leader in environmental protection, placing high importance on open space, farmland preservation, and natural resource protection. Developed in 1994, Montgomery County's Special Protection Area (SPA) program strives to protect streams with existing high-quality and sensitive environmental resources relating to water quality by closely coordinating water quality protection measures with land-use controls (Montgomery County Department of Environmental Protection 2002).

Montgomery County also was one of the first localities in the nation to create a program using Transfer of Development Rights (TDR) to protect agricultural land. The voluntary program, which was created in 1981, has preserved more than 40,000 acres (American Farmland Trust 2001). The program enables property owners in "sending areas" to transfer their development rights at one unit per five acres to a "receiving area" through a sales process. The owner can choose not to participate in the program but in doing so is permitted to develop units only at a density of one unit per twenty-five acres. The program helps to direct growth to appropriate areas while maintaining the agricultural activities in the western portions of the county.

In both Fairfax and Montgomery Counties, the different county and state governmental structures affect the land development process and subsequent environmental and affordable housing issues in each locality. The following sections further highlight the development processes and environmental regulations in each county.

RELEVANT ENVIRONMENTAL REGULATIONS AND PROGRAMS

Federal and state environmental policy essentially shapes the environmental regulatory systems found in the Washington, DC, metropolitan region. Broad policy goals of protecting water and air quality in the name of public health and of preserving natural resources and habitat guide federal, state, and local policy makers in enacting the federal laws, state statutes, and local ordinances that govern the region. Federal and state policy goals generate federal, state, and local regulations. The hierarchy of responsibility is complex, with multiple federal, state, and local agencies claiming overlapping responsibility for the implementation of the regulations. Federal and state environmental regulators may further adopt guidelines that govern the environmental review process. These intergovernmental dynamics have a significant impact on the implementation of environmental regulations and ultimately on the compliance costs incurred by home builders.

The policies and regulations generated for implementation by developers may originate from federal, state, or local agencies or from a partnership among various entities in a region. Federal policies such as the Clean Water Act stipulate that states must develop their own regulations for meeting the requirements. States also may decide to regulate, or encourage the regulation of, environmental resources through such measures as forest conservation acts. Local governments may respond to state acts or, given the authority, develop regulations of their own. Unique environmental features also may propel interstate agreements leading to state mandates and local legislation. The following section discusses federal, state, and local environmental regulations influential in the Washington metropolitan area.

The regulatory framework in the case study area features the interplay among federal, state, and local regulations. The area's unique natural resource, the Chesapeake Bay, also has led to the creation of a regional alliance that influences state and local regulations.

Special Regional Environmental Protection Programs—Chesapeake Bay Program

The Chesapeake Bay program is a good illustration of the environmental hierarchy that can develop around state and federal policies and laws. Different government agencies active at state and local levels and a layering of regulations help to implement the policies established in this federal and state environmental protection program. Although this case study focuses on metropolitan Washington, many of the same approaches and policies are applied in states and larger metropolitan areas, such as the Carolina coastal areas, Florida, California, selected areas of the Great Lakes, and the Pacific Northwest, that have sensitive water systems. Appendix B offers a detailed review of the approaches and policies applied to the case study and may be instructive to similarly affected areas.

Environmental Regulatory Programs Common to Fairfax and Montgomery Counties

Although the case study includes several Virginia jurisdictions, the principal players in the metropolitan Washington, DC, market are Fairfax and Montgomery counties. Details of their environmental regulatory features are outlined in appendix C. This section outlines their common elements. The next section reviews their development approval processes.

Water
Both states have regulatory systems for protecting water resources to meet federal requirements. These state regulatory systems, which may be sup-

plemented with local laws, establish guidelines for the protection of wetlands and other bodies of water, stormwater management, and floodplains.

Wetlands. Issues regarding wetland protection and mitigation have an impact on water quality, development practices, and mitigation costs.
- Delineating and permitting is required on all but the smallest projects.
- Mitigation is required when a project is found to be in violation of a permit or to have violated the law requiring the project to acquire a permit before beginning construction.

Stormwater Management. Set to protect water resources from degradation, stormwater management regulations seek to control water quality and quantity.
- Water quality is controlled by erosion and sedimentation controls as well as other best management practices designed to reduce or eliminate pollutant levels in the stormwater runoff.
- Water quantity also is controlled by best management practices but is designed to mitigate flooding, and thus property damage, at downstream locations by controlling the quantity and rate of discharge from development sites.

Floodplain Regulations. Like stormwater management, floodplain regulations seek to prevent the loss of life and property by regulating development in areas subject to flooding.

Environmental Protection Areas

These locally developed guidelines can be used to protect water resources as well as wildlife habitat. Both Fairfax and Montgomery counties, through riparian protection areas (RPA) or SPA designations, have established local regulatory systems guiding development in environmental protection areas.

Environmental Quality Corridor (EQC) System. Fairfax County developed this system to identify, protect, and enhance an integrated network of ecologically valuable land and surface waters in the county.

Habitat Preservation

Federal and state laws can mandate the protection of critical habitat areas for threatened and endangered species. The preservation of habitat is one of the main methods of enforcing the protection of these species.

Threatened and Endangered Species. Field surveys, sometimes limited to certain times of the year, are used to establish the presence of threatened and endangered species and to identify the resources to be protected.

Open Space Preservation

The protection of open space helps to preserve and protect habitat for all floral and faunal species, a benefit recognized by local governments, which may require minimal percentages of project sites to be dedicated for preservation.

Forest Preservation

Forest cover provides stormwater runoff management and wildlife habitat, among other environmental benefits, which has prompted many localities to pass forest and tree preservation ordinances.

Cultural and Historical Resources

Preserving the connection to history in the physical environment helps us to better understand human activities. The relationship between history and the environment plays a vital role in how environmental regulation requirements are met.

Archeological Studies. Localities often require developers to complete phase I, II, and III archeological surveys to identify, conduct an inventory of, and preserve or document historic resources present at the site.

Table 4.3 summarizes the broad range of environmental regulations in the metropolitan Washington region.

Based on the tasks performed by the environmental consultants in the case study development projects, the research team identified the following categories of relevant federal, state, and local environmental laws and policies. Each task listed in table 4.4 follows the chronological process of an environmental consultant's general work plan. Developers and their consultants may develop a systematic method for meeting these regulations, often directed by state and local requirements. Consultants familiar with these regulations often are employed by developers to mitigate the time delays and confusion involved with meeting the requirements. The following reviews major categories of environmental regulations identified in the study:

Table 4.3 Environmental Regulatory Acts

Governmental Body	Environmental Element	Regulatory Act	Oversight
Federal	Water	Clean Water Act	Wetlands, stormwater
	Endangered species	Endangered Species Act	Threatened and endangered species and their habitats
State	Water	Virginia Erosion and Sediment Control Law, Virginia Stormwater Management Law, Code of Virginia Wetlands Policy, Code of Virginia Standards for Use and Development of Wetlands	Wetlands, stormwater, erosion and sediment control, floodplains
		Maryland Economic Growth, Resource Protection, and Planning Act of 1992, Maryland Nontidal Wetlands Act	
		Chesapeake Bay Preservation Act (VA) Maryland Critical Area Program of 1984 (expanded 2002)	Chesapeake Bay
	Forest and trees	Code of Virginia Tree Replacement, Maryland Forest Conservation Act of 1991	Forest and trees preservation and conservation
Local	Water	Fairfax County Code Erosion and Sediment Control, Fairfax County Code Wetlands Zoning Ordinance, Code of Montgomery County Erosion, Sediment Control and Stormwater Management Regulations	Stormwater, wetlands, floodplains, erosion and sediment control

Table 4.3 Environmental Regulatory Acts (*continued*)

Governmental Body	Environmental Element	Regulatory Act	Oversight
Local		Fairfax County Code Chesapeake Bay Preservation Ordinance	Stormwater, wetlands, stream corridors
		Code of Montgomery County Erosion, Sediment Control and Stormwater Management Regulations, Water Quality Review for Development in Designated Special Protection Areas (MD)	High-quality watersheds
	Forest and trees	Fairfax County Code Subdivision Provisions, Code of Montgomery County Forest Conservation Regulations	Forest and tree preservation, conservation and cover
	Noise	Fairfax County Code—Noise, Code of Montgomery County Noise Regulations	Noise reduction for residential developments
	Cultural resources	Code of Montgomery County Forest Conservation Regulations	Archeological and cultural resources
	Threatened and endangered species	Code of Montgomery County Erosion, Sediment Control and Stormwater Management Regulations	Threatened and endangered species and their habitat

Source: Authors' synthesis of environmental regulations.

Table 4.4 Fairfax/Montgomery Case Study Environmental Regulations

Water	Cultural Resources	Forest and Tree Resources	Species
Background research	Archeological study	Tree Preservation	Background research for threatened or endangered species
Wetland delineation	Cultural resource designation	Forest conservation	
County RPA requirements			
SPA requirements			
CWA permitting: sewer, stormwater, streams			
County stream outfall analysis			
Mitigation and CWA permit modifications			
Regular stream and sewer monitoring			

Source: Authors' synthesis of environmental regulations.

- **Background research** includes preliminary assessment of probable wetland locations and environmental elements regulated by the county; this research is used to estimate the potential environmental resources on the site.
- **Wetland delineation** involves mapping the location of the wetlands on the site. This phase involves a review process by the U.S. Army Corps of Engineers (COE). Wetland delineation costs are dependent on the amount of wetland present on the site.
- **Section 404 of the Federal Clean Water Act (CWA) Permitting for Wetlands Development** for a site may involve acquiring an individual or a

general permit. The permit application involves a review by the Army COE. Depending on the property conditions, the regulatory review by the COE might proceed quickly under a nationwide permit or require special hearings for individual permits. Any changes to a project may require modifications to be made to the original permit or a new permit may be required. The following categories of permits may need to be applied to comply with CWA requirements associated with wetlands. Mitigation is required for impacts as a result of a project or violations of permits. Specific permits and related procedures include:

- **Nationwide Permit #39:** This permit covers residential, commercial, and real estate development activities that will not result in the filling of more than a half acre of wetlands.
- **Nationwide Permit #43:** This permit covers stormwater management facilities and is required for projects with more than one acre of disturbance.
- **Joint Permit Application:** This application consolidates the application process for local, state, and federal agencies regarding activities affecting wetlands and waters in the Commonwealth of Virginia. These agencies include:
  - U.S. Army Corps of Engineers
  - Virginia Department of Environmental Quality
  - Virginia Marine Resources Commission
  - Local Wetlands Boards
- **Individual Permit:** An individual permit is required in place of the general permit when the project will have significant impacts on wetlands and waters of the United States. Section 404 rules require an individual permit when:
  - The project is located in or adjacent to prime wetlands, tidal wetlands or buffer zone, sand dunes, or bogs
  - The wetland is an exemplary natural community
  - Threatened or endangered species are present
  - Greater than 20,000 square feet of wetlands, surface waters, or banks are impacted
  - Major docking systems are constructed or modified
  - More than 20 cubic yards are dredged in public waters
  - Greater than 200 linear feet of a stream, river, lake, pond shoreline, and/or bank is disturbed

- **Preconstruction Notification:** A preconstruction notification must be filed if the project will result in the fill of more than 1/10 acre of wetlands.
- **Permit Modifications:** Permit modifications are required whenever a project undergoes a change in the scope of work. In addition, if there is an increase in the amount of wetland impact, a new permit is required.
- **Section 402 of the CWA Permitting for Stormwater Discharge** also involves state and local agencies. These agencies enforce construction and separate municipal storm sewer regulations aimed at improving water quality. This section of the act regulates erosion and sediment control and is enforced at the state and local levels.
- **Archeological and Cultural Resource Surveys** involve preliminary scoping of the site's previous historical and cultural assets. All projects require a Phase I survey to assess the site for the potential presence of any cultural resources. Phase II and III surveys are required only when significant resources are discovered. These surveys are specific to identified locations on the site, generally not to the entire project area.
  - **Cultural Resource Designation:** This involves the preparation of a National Historic Register application, which requires an intense survey and documentation process of the resource.
- **Threatened or Endangered Species Assessment** may need to be completed for all or a portion of a project site. A preliminary assessment is conducted if it is suspected that threatened or endangered species may be present. If such species are identified on the site, a more intense study and preservation plan is completed.
- **Mitigation and CWA permit modifications** may be needed to accommodate changes to the approved project or impacts to wetlands resulting from approved or unapproved construction.

DEVELOPMENT REVIEW PROCESSES

It is during the development review process that environmental regulations are enforced. Each local jurisdiction develops review processes consistent with state and federal requirements. These processes also are influenced by state enabling legislation, allowing more regulatory control in Montgomery County and a proffer system in Fairfax County.

Elicited by new state and federal requirements, changes in local environmental regulations and their enforcement have affected the development review process for residential development in recent years. According to development professionals working in the field, the development review process in the early 1990s did not require the level of detail needed for approval in more recent times.

Fairfax County Development Process

Development review in Fairfax County can involve either a by-right or a rezoning application. Each application is required to meet a series of criteria for approval regarding environmental regulations. The process for preparing by-right or rezoning applications is similar, but a rezoning application often is associated with proffers agreed to by the developer.

Several Fairfax County and outside reviewing agencies may be involved with the development approval process. This process provides an opportunity for these agencies to review the project's conceptual compliance with environmental and other regulations. These agencies include:

Fairfax County Government
- Department of Planning and Zoning
- Department of Public Works and Environmental Services
- Planning Commission
- Department of Transportation
- Board of Zoning Appeals
- Board of Supervisors

Outside Agencies
- U.S. Army Corps of Engineers
- Virginia Department of Environmental Quality
- Virginia Department of Transportation
- Virginia Marine Resource Commission
- Utility companies

To gain approval for a development application, a layout plan must be prepared by a certified architect, landscape architect, engineer, or land surveyor licensed in the Commonwealth of Virginia, and the plan must include information, such as boundaries of the property; locations, dimensions, and height of existing and proposed structures; ingress/egress from a public street; parking, proposed landscaping, and screening; stormwater management facilities; and the presence of any floodplains or environmental quality corridors (EQC).[11] A preapplication meeting is recommended at which staff will meet with applicants to identify any environmental, land-use, or transportation issues early in the development process.

The applicant completes a natural resource inventory during the development application process. This inventory identifies and maps:

- Wetlands
- Threatened and endangered species
- Floodplains and EQCs such as RPA or RMA
- Existing vegetation
- Soils

The natural resource inventory identifies environmentally regulated components of the site. Wetland delineation guides the project layout and is used in acquiring the necessary permits. The identification of threatened and endangered species and their habitat designates areas where development will be prohibited or limited. Forest stands and specimen trees may be mandated as part of a tree preservation plan or a forest canopy cover requirement. Floodplains, stream corridors, and associated riparian buffers may be included as part of an EQC or RPA. In areas where scenic or natural features exist that deserve protection and preservation, these assets must be delineated on the plan and the applicant must submit a statement indicating how these areas will be protected and preserved.[12]

By-Right Development Process

If the land development project is by-right, meaning it is being done in conformance with the existing zoning regulations, plan review and acquisition of a building permit generally is less complicated. Before submitting a plan for review, the developer or applicant must check on covenants and deed restrictions, comply with building codes, and create a grading and building plan that conforms to county requirements. The following steps illustrate the development review process for a by-right application.

1. An accepted application is transferred to the Zoning Permit Review Branch where the grading plan is reviewed.
2. The application is then transferred to the Department of Public Works and Environmental Services Permit Branch. At this stage, the plan goes through various environmental review processes including:
   - the conservation agreement
   - grading
   - soils
   - conformity to the Chesapeake Bay Ordinance
3. If the project will be on a septic or well system, the Health Department also reviews the plan.
4. The Building Plan Review Division reviews the plan for adherence to building codes.
5. Approval for the project may be issued once all of the departments have reviewed and signed off on the plans and the required fees have been paid.

Throughout the building phase of the project, inspectors from the Environmental and Facilities Inspection and Residential Inspections divisions visit the site to make sure the approved building and site plans match what is being built. They also make sure all environmental regulations and agreements are being followed. A land ombudsman also is assigned to projects located near RPAs, floodplains, or wetlands to ensure that the developers are adhering to the special county requirements regarding these areas.

Rezoning Process and Additional Review Requirements

A developer may seek a rezoning application upon completion of a development project in Fairfax County. The following is an overview of Fairfax County's Rezoning Process—from the time an application is filed to the time of the Board of Supervisors Public Hearing.[13]

1. The applicant files an application.
2. Application submissions are reviewed by the Building Plan Review Division. When all zoning ordinance submission requirements are met, the application is accepted and distributed to various county agencies for review.

3. The application is scheduled for a Planning Commission public hearing and is assigned to a county staff coordinator.
4. The applicant is contacted by staff regarding initial staff comments—this is called prestaffing.
5. The applicant submits application revisions related to prestaffing comments.
6. So-called staffing of the application occurs when the applicant is contacted by staff about final staff comments.
7. The applicant submits revisions related to the staffing comments.
8. The final submission deadline (six weeks before the Planning Commission public hearing) occurs when the staff report is published based on information received to date.
9. Staff send the applicant notification letter(s) to adjacent property owners thirty days before the hearing. The applicant must mail these notices (postmarked at least fifteen days before the hearing date) to adjacent property owners.
10. The staff report is published two weeks before the public hearing.
11. The Planning Commission public hearing is held.
12. The application is scheduled for a public hearing in front of the County Board of Supervisors.
13. Staff send the applicant notification letter(s) to adjacent property owners thirty days before the Board of Supervisors public hearing. The applicant must mail these notices (postmarked at least fifteen days before the hearing date) to adjacent property owners.
14. The Board of Supervisors public hearing is held. At this stage, the permit may be approved, denied, or approved with conditions. (Appeal may be made to the Board of Supervisors and, ultimately, through the state court system.)

When the project is not a by-right development, conditions of approval often are included in the staff report prepared during the process. These conditions, called proffers, may include locations of improvements, landscaping, or additional requirements for meeting environmental conditions present on the site. These proffered conditions become binding with the approval of the application by the Planning Commission, Board of Supervisors, or Board of Zoning Appeals.[14]

The developer also may need to complete an archeological survey of the site during the rezoning application process to identify culturally significant resources present on the site. The survey is contracted for and financed by the applicant, but the Building Plan Review Division must approve it. Based on this survey, additional studies, preservation, and mitigation may be required. The applicant also must submit a statement identifying any known environmental contamination that may exist on the site, such as the size and contents of any underground storage tanks and the presence of hazardous or toxic substances. This requirement also includes the identification of any proposed hazardous material usage or storage on the site.[15]

The applicant must also develop preliminary stormwater management plans as part of the application process. The goal of these plans is to scientifically identify pre- and postconstruction runoff quantities to ensure the postconstruction runoff is equal to or less than the preconstruction quantities. In addition, the application must include a narrative describing best management practices to be employed on the site and outfall abatement techniques used to meet adequate outfall requirements to prevent stream erosion and scouring.[16] Outfall regulations are designed to mitigate adverse impacts of development on stream corridors by establishing requirements for pre- and postconstruction monitoring to demonstrate that no degradation has occurred.

The identification, inventory, and avoidance of these regulated areas during the development review process can create more expense for the rezoning of a development site than in years past. This expense comes in the form of time and direct expenditures for meeting the requirements. However, should the developer continue with the project, much of the planning and data acquisition expenses do not have to be repeated in later stages of site design approval.

The Influence of Tree Preservation Regulation on Development in Northern Virginia

Tree preservation regulations are different from wetland or stormwater regulations because they are not a derivative of a federal environmental policy. In Virginia, state enabling legislature has allowed local jurisdictions to develop canopy coverage ordinances and a tree preservation ordinance

Table 4.5 Virginia Code Tree Canopy Requirements in Localities of More Than Seventy-five Persons per Square Mile

Zoned Land Use	20-Year Canopy Coverage
Business, commercial, or industrial	10%
Residential (20 units per acre)	10%
Residential (10 to 20 units per acre)	15%
Residential (less than 10 units per acre)	20%

Source: Code of Virginia Section 15.2-961 (n.d.).

for Heritage, Memorial, Champion, and other specimens of trees. However, owners of the properties on which the trees are located have the option to not participate in the tree preservation ordinance.

The Code of Virginia (Section 15.2-961) allows any locality with a population density of at least seventy-five people per square mile to adopt an ordinance providing for the planting and replacement of trees during the development process. Minimum canopy coverage requirements are to be based on a twenty-year coverage calculation and applied at different percentages based on zoned land uses (table 4.5).

In localities where ordinances have not been passed or where these density requirements have not been met, the proffer system may be used to direct developers to provide tree preservation plans. Using the proffer system, a developer may agree to meet the localities' forest canopy or tree preservation requirements set during the rezoning phase of a project in exchange for changes in density requirements. The calculation used for determining the requirements of the tree preservation plan differ among municipalities, with some requiring that the calculation be based on forest cover and with others using calculations based on the disturbed acreage of the project.

Tree preservation plans identify areas where localities seek to maintain or improve existing forest stands. These existing or proposed areas are generally associated with riparian buffers, stream corridors, or other areas of contiguous forest cover. The tree preservation plan preparation process, which may include a reforestation component, generally involves:

- A site inventory
- Identification of tree preservation areas
- Mitigating issues that may have an adverse effect on identified tree preservation areas

Preservation plans may require the developer to remove submarginal forest cover and replace it with species deemed to be of higher environmental quality. The removal of trees deemed to pose a safety hazard to humans also may be required as part of the preservation plan. In addition, the ordinance or proffer may require the developer to work with the municipal urban forester to identify desirable species.

Reforestation can be a component of the forest canopy or tree preservation plan. The areas typically targeted for reforestation are riparian buffers. The process involves:

- Initial planning
- Site preparation
- Planting of seedlings and/or larger caliper trees
- Mowing and herbicide application
- Deer browse control
- Monitoring and replacement

Reforestation projects generally require a three-year monitoring period. After one year, the survival goal is typically two-thirds of the planted seedlings. In instances where large caliper trees have been installed, maintenance costs to ensure their survival are typically higher when compared with areas where seedlings have been planted because of the higher costs associated with replacing large caliper trees.

Montgomery County Development Process

With a Home Rule Charter in effect, Montgomery County plays a stronger role—compared with Fairfax County—in orchestrating development. The county combines multiple guiding regulations, such as area master plans and SPAs, to guide development patterns.

Area master plans, which are subarea plans within the county's general plan, are documents prepared by the county planning board, with input from various agencies, government officials, and citizens. These plans incorporate current and future development trends pertaining to housing, transportation, stormwater management, preservation of historic and agricultural resources, and environmental resources, among other items. Each plan outlines the locations for land uses, zoning, and provides guidance for the future placement of public facilities. Plans are subject to approval after a public hearing, adoption by the Maryland-National Capital Park and Planning Commission (MNCPPC), and, as implementing elements, are incorporated into the general plan.[17] Developed in 1994, Montgomery County's SPA program strives to protect streams with existing high-quality and sensitive water quality resources by closely coordinating land water quality protection measures with land-use controls (Montgomery County Department of Environmental Protection 2002).

A variety of Montgomery County and outside reviewing agencies can be involved with approving permits for development projects.[18] These include:

Montgomery County Government
- Department of Public Works and Transportation
- Department of Fire and Rescue Services
- Office of the County Attorney
- Department of Environmental Protection
- Department of Finance
- Board of Appeals

Outside Agencies
- Utility Companies
- State Highway Administration
- Washington Suburban Sanitary Commission
- Assessments Office
- USDA, Soil Conservation District
- Maryland-National Capital Park and Planning Commission
- Historical Preservation Section and Commission

During the subdivision and development process, the MNCPPC (through the Montgomery County Planning Board and the Montgomery County Department of Permitting Services) is the lead reviewing agency.

This quasi-governmental agency is responsible for coordinating reviews and negotiating compromises when conflicting requirements or interests arise. MNCPPC, through the planning board's Department of Park and Planning's development review division, is charged with ensuring that the proposed development complies with the recommendations of the area master plan and the requirements of the following:

- Zoning ordinance
- Subdivision regulations
- Annual growth policy
- Adequate Public Facilities Ordinance
- Forest conservation regulations[19]

The Department of Permitting Services (DPS), through the land development division, which reviews water quality related to construction practices, is responsible for approving the conceptual stormwater management plan for the development.[20] DPS is also responsible for the coordination of approvals from other agencies, such as MNCPPC, on permits issued by the department.[21]

The county's use of an area master plan usually eliminates the need for a rezoning process because the intended land-use characteristics for the site already have been determined. In special circumstances, such as when area master plans compete or errors in a plan are discovered, rezoning may be allowed. Generally, Montgomery County's subdivision review process involves the following:

1. It is recommended that developers create an optional pre-preliminary plan to obtain advice from the planning staff or board, which should ensure that plans conform to county regulations.
2. Preliminary plan approval requirements include, but are not limited to, the submission of a stormwater management concept plan, sewer and water conceptual plan, preliminary site layout of lots and streets, preliminary forest conservation plan, natural resources inventory, and a preliminary grading plan.[22]
3. Site plan approval requirements include, but are not limited to, more detailed information for the requirements from the preliminary plan,

a landscape plan, a forest conservation plan, and a sediment control plan.[23]
4. Final construction plan approval requires the submission of the final site and grading plan and final landscape and lighting plan as well as other final development plans.
5. Requirements for the record plat, which allows building permits to be issued, include, but are not limited to, submission of the previously approved plans from both the preliminary and site plan reviews.[24]

The Montgomery County Department of Park and Planning's development review division, which is responsible for coordinating the timely review of proposed development projects, also sends notice to any affected homeowner associations. A development review staff member is assigned to each case for evaluation. The staff member coordinates input from the department's environmental and transportation staff and the Development Review Committee (DRC). DRC is an interagency task force composed of representatives from public agencies and utilities, such as PEPCO, the State Highway Administration, and the departments of Permitting Services, Environmental Protection, Public Works, and Transportation. The DRC meets regularly in meetings that are open to the public but are not public hearings. Once the Montgomery County planning board receives the staff evaluation, it approves, approves with conditions, or denies the project. Record plat approval, after which a building permit can be issued, is granted after board approval of the preliminary, site, and final construction plans.

HOUSING AFFORDABILITY IN FAIRFAX AND MONTGOMERY COUNTIES

Now let us examine the key housing indicators in both counties. Notably, the median sales prices for single-family homes in Montgomery County are lower than those in Fairfax County for both new and existing units (table 4.6). It is possible the difference between the median values in the two counties is even greater than the figures shown in table 4.6, because the figures for Fairfax County include attached units, which typically are sold for a lower price than detached units.

Table 4.6   Median Sales Price for Single-Family Homes, 1997–2006

Year	New	Existing
Fairfax County[a]		
2005	$807,266	$615,000
1997	$389,747	$203,000
Montgomery County[b]		
2005	$759,933	$500,000
1997	$343,295	$230,000

[a] Price for single-family detached and attached
[b] Price for single-family detached

To address housing affordability needs, both counties have roughly comparable programs. First, note that "affordable housing" is a term that can mean different things to different people. The term can refer to housing that individuals can qualify to buy, housing for low-income households, or it may be considered any housing built with government assistance. Montgomery County's Housing Policy, contained in Chapter 25B of the County Code, defines an affordable housing unit as "any dwelling unit constructed for sale or rent at a price equal to or less than that provided in Chapter 25A, (the Moderately Priced Dwelling Unit [MPDU] Ordinance), and any assisted elderly housing" (Maryland-National Capital Park and Planning 2001). Fairfax County's comprehensive plan defines affordable housing as that which is affordable to households with incomes that are at or below 70 percent of the MSA median household income.[25]

Under the Fairfax County Zoning Ordinance, the county may provide a density bonus (up to 20 percent) for developers who elect to incorporate affordable dwelling units (ADUs) in eligible projects in certain districts. The program was established to provide dwelling units affordable to households earning 70 percent or less of the median income for the Washington, DC, MSA (in 2004, this would have been households earning approximately $50,000 or less). The ordinance is applicable only to projects affected by a rezoning or a special exception or a subdivision of fifty or more dwelling units at a density of greater than one per acre within an approved sewer service area.[26]

As mentioned earlier, Montgomery County also has a requirement to provide affordable housing units as a part of any new residential development project consisting of twenty or more units. The program requires that the developer make a certain percentage of units affordable for households earning 80 percent or less of the county's median household income, or approximately $66,000 or less in 2004. The required percentage of MPDUs ranges from 12.5 percent to 15 percent of the total projected units, although if a density bonus is awarded, projects are required to develop more than the 12.5 percent minimum requirement.[27]

In addition, Montgomery County has a Green Tape Process for Affordable Housing for projects in which at least 20 percent of the units are designated affordable. This Green Tape Process enables the project to receive expedited application review, modified application forms, and expedited construction and utilities permit processing. The process also dictates improved interagency communication and the creation of a geographic information systems (GIS) map showing overlays of affordable housing projects.

RESIDENTIAL SUBDIVISION PROJECTS REVIEWED

The developers working with the research team provided seven projects for review. Of these, six were in Virginia (with three in Fairfax County, two in Loudoun County, and one in Prince William County) and one was in Montgomery County, Maryland. These projects were reviewed by the research team for the environmental regulations and affordable housing provisions they were required to meet, either outright or through a proffering system. This section describes these requirements, as well as the time and known financial costs associated with their development. Using available information, the following will be highlighted for each project:

- General project characteristics
    - Site acreage
    - Units developed
    - Type of application
    - Time needed to complete the development review process

- Affordable dwelling units developed
- Proffers and conditions of approval
- Environmental regulations and required reviews
- Estimated costs pertaining to compliance with environmental regulations
  - Percentage each regulation represented of the overall environmental compliance cost
- Timeframe for acquiring the required environmental permits

Case Study Methodology

The research team used a twofold process for categorizing the environmental regulatory costs. First, it held a meeting with representatives of the firm responsible for the completion of the environmental regulatory related components for each of the projects. The representatives identified and provided background on the activities involved in the steps completed for each element of the project. Second, the research team grouped these steps into larger categories and evaluated the costs associated with these categories against the total environmental regulatory related costs. This comparison was done to provide an indication of the impact each category had on the total environmental regulatory cost pertaining to natural resource inventory and mitigation.

Limiting Factors

The process for identifying the environmental costs for each project was limited by a number of factors. Although many of the consultants were more than willing to talk about the development process and the associated environmental regulations, it was often difficult to acquire hard cost numbers pertaining to their fees for meeting these requirements. The research team also had difficulty maintaining consistency among the consultants' different accounting practices, especially regarding the different tasks associated with meeting the regulations. In some cases, the consultants provided a lump sum number that may have included meeting many different environmental regulations; in other instances, consultants provided a detailed cost breakdown identifying specific processes and time commitments.

In addition, it would have been useful if the research team had identified the development costs and the land costs for each project, because it would have enabled the team to more accurately evaluate the effects of environmental regulations on housing affordability. Development costs can be categorized as those associated with consulting services and construction, and they typically include:

- Consultant fees
- Site surveys
- Tree preservation planning
- Wetland and natural resource inventories
- Archeological surveys
- Permitting fees
- Design and engineering

Land costs can be categorized as costs associated with acquisition of the property, the carrying cost of the property during the review process, and the opportunity costs that may have been lost as a result of the enforcement of environmental regulations. For the case study, development costs were more readily identified but, due to differences in accounting practices among the developers' consultants, the team was unable to isolate all of these costs for each project.

In addition, although changes in development plans were probably generated early in the process, these iterations were lost to the final site plan. Although consultants were found to be very helpful in discussing the process of meeting environmental regulations throughout the development process, information regarding early plans submitted and changes to these plans resulted in little or no feedback about loss of lots or site plan restructuring that may have decreased the development potential due to environmental constraints.

Fairfax County Projects

The developers provided information for three projects in Fairfax County. Two, which have been grouped together, were separate phases of a large development project and one was a stand-alone, single-phase project.

Phased Development Project

This project, which was completed in phases, developed nearly 300 acres and proposed approximately 700 new homes on an infill site. Due to the increasingly scarce supply of greenfield parcels, many projects in the county are finding themselves located on more challenging infill sites. As one consultant said, "all the low-hanging fruit has been picked." One challenge of developing infill sites is that they sometimes involve remediation actions as a result of past uses. In this project, environmental contaminants were identified and removed as part of the development process. This project required a zoning change; in other words, it was not a by-right development. As a result, a set of proffered conditions was agreed upon during the approval process. The rezoning process was for the entire site, after which site plan approvals were sought for each phase.

The rezoning process took approximately eight months. During the rezoning process, proffers pertaining to the site's development and environmental conditions were agreed to by the developer. These included stream monitoring for impacts on an RPA, the procurement of an offsite conservation easement, and the installation of best management practices (BMPs) for improving stormwater runoff quality. The proffers also included the completion of Phases I, II, and III archeological studies on the site.

In addition, the approvals for the site plans for each of the phases of the project took between ten and eighteen months. Both phases were required to be submitted at least two times because previous submissions were denied. The total project development time for each phase was approximately eighteen to twenty-six months. Table 4.7 shows the environmental regulations triggered by site conditions.

Each phase of the project was required to meet certain environmental regulations, either determined by federal, state, or local requirement, or agreed upon during the rezoning process. During each phase, for example, separate portions of the site were dedicated as open space. Other regulations applied to the entire site and required coordination of both overall and phase-specific requirements. For instance, an overall wetland permit was required as well as permits for specific activities pertaining to the different phases of the project not covered under the overall site permit.

The developer was required to submit a tree preservation plan as part of the proffering process that provided for the preservation of trees larger

Table 4.7 Phased-Project Environmental Regulations

Regulation/Review	Federal	State	Local
Wetlands permitting	X	X	
Stormwater		X	X
Wastewater collection and treatment		X	X
Other nonpoint water quality			X
Erosion and sediment control		X	X
Resource protection area			X
Open space set-aside			X
Tree preservation			X
Landscaping			X
Noise attenuation			X
Archeological review			X
Proffers for environmental measures			X
Water distribution			X
Soils/geotechnical report			X

than a certain diameter within a specified distance of identified grading and clearing limits and environmental quality corridors. This plan, however, could not alter the number or reduce the size of the proposed dwelling units.

The project, because it required a rezoning, was eligible and elected to include ADUs. One phase incorporated approximately twenty units, although under the guidelines of the ordinance, a minimum of nearly 100 units were to be provided by the conclusion of the entire project. Table 4.8 shows the project's known or estimated costs relating to environmental regulation compliance.

As noted earlier, the total project development time for each phase was between approximately eighteen and twenty-six months. These rezoning and site plan approval processes occurred concurrently with the environmental permitting required. The approval of the development plans required the permits shown in table 4.9 to be acquired before construction could begin.

Table 4.8 Phased-Project Environmental Costs

	Cost	Percentage of Improvement Cost[a]
Preconstruction		
Wetland delineation	$68,500	2%
RPA delineation	$7,500	<1%
EQC delineation	$2,000	<1%
Environmental contamination remediation	$400,000	10%
Archeological investigation	$84,000	2%
Tree preservation plan	$5,500	<1%
Wetland permitting	$65,000	2%
Construction		
Stormwater management ponds	$1,000,000	25%
Erosion and sediment control	$1,700,000	42%
Noise attenuation	$380,000	10%
Postconstruction		
Wetland mitigation	$155,000	4%
Outfall mitigation	$93,500	2%
Total environmental regulatory compliance cost	$3,961,000	7%
Total project cost for land[b]	$53,000,000	
Average environmental regulatory cost per unit	$5,500	7%
Average lot cost per unit	$75,000	

[a] Percentage of total known environmental regulatory compliance costs.
[b] Cost for finished lot, does not include construction cost for dwelling unit.

The amount of time needed to acquire the necessary permits associated with the CWA as it is enforced by the state was relatively short compared with the entire length of time it took to receive approval for the project. In any case, a developer must have these permits in hand before beginning construction, which prompts many developers to undertake the application process concurrently with other approvals to minimize time delays. In other words, if sought concurrently with other approvals, securing environmental permits adds little time, if any, to the process.

Table 4.9 Phased-Project Environmental Permitting

Permit	Approval Time (in months)		
	COE	DEQ	VMRC
Individual (site)	3	3	4
Modification (site)	1	1	Not available
National Wetland Permit #39	2	Not required	Not required
Individual (utility)	2	Not required	3
Modification (utility)	3	Not required	6
Temporary access road	1	Not required	5
National Wetland Permit #39 (phase)	2	Not required	Not required
Individual (phase)	1	Not required	Not required
Modification (phase)	1	Not required	Not required

The homes in the completed development have been listed at prices ranging from approximately $400,000 to $1,000,000.

Single-Phase Development Project

The other project in Fairfax County was a single-phase development on an approximately fifty-acre site. A mix of nearly 100 single-family attached and detached dwelling units were developed, approximately 10 percent of which were ADUs. The project set aside approximately 30 percent of the site as open space, which was above the county requirement of 25 percent. This project took longer to receive rezoning approval (approximately eleven months) than it did to receive entitlement, which required roughly eight months. The development phase of the project took approximately nineteen months, from completing the necessary reviews, to applying for the rezoning, and to receiving final site plan approval. Table 4.10 shows the site conditions that triggered environmental regulations.

The developer was required to submit a tree preservation plan as part of the proffering process that provided for the preservation of specific quality trees or stands of trees to the maximum extent feasible. This plan, however, could not alter the number of units, reduce the unit size, significantly alter their lot location, or require the construction of major retaining

Table 4.10 Single-Phase Environmental Regulations

Regulation/Review	Federal	State	Local
Wetland	X	X	
Stormwater		X	X
Wastewater collection			X
Erosion and sedimentation control		X	X
Open space set-aside			X
Tree preservation			X
Landscaping			X
Noise attenuation		X	X
Archeological review			X
Water distribution			X

walls. These proffers also required including language in the homeowners' association documents stipulating the proper use by residents of areas where tree preservation was required, including the conditions that must be met to allow residents to remove trees.

The site had minimal wetland disturbance and required only a preconstruction notification for its permitting activities. The project also required the construction of a noise attenuation wall, which necessitated additional permitting and landscaping requirements. A Phase I archeological study also was required. Table 4.11 shows known or estimated costs relating to the project's environmental regulation compliance.

As noted, the rezoning application and approval process for the site plan's entire project was completed in approximately nineteen months. The rezoning and site plan approval processes occurred concurrently with the required environmental permitting. The approval of the development plans required the permits shown in table 4.12 to be acquired before beginning construction. The only permit required for this project pertaining to wetlands was a preconstruction notification.

As with the phased project, the amount of time needed to acquire the necessary permits associated with the CWA as it is enforced by the state was relatively short compared with the entire length of time it took to

Table 4.11 Single-Phase Environmental Costs

	Percentage of Cost	Improvement Cost[a]
Preconstruction		
Wetland delineation	$10,500	1%
Background environmental research	$1,500	<1%
Archeological investigation	$4,000	<1%
Wetland permitting	$2,500	<1%
Construction		
Stormwater management ponds	$150,000	14%
Erosion and sediment control	$225,000	20%
Noise attenuation	$666,000	61%
Postconstruction		
Wetland mitigation	$39,500	4%
Total environmental regulatory compliance cost	$1,099,000	14%
Total project cost for land[b]	$7,500,000	
Average environmental regulatory cost per unit	$12,000	14%
Average lot cost per unit	$75,000	

[a] Percentage of total known environmental regulatory compliance costs.
[b] Cost for finished lot, does not include construction cost for dwelling unit.

Table 4.12 Single-Phase Environmental Permitting

	Approval Time (in months)		
Permit	COE	DEQ	VMRC
Preconstruction notification	1	Not required	Not required

approve the project. Once again, because the developer sought the necessary approvals and environmental permits concurrently, compliance with environmental regulations added minimal costs and time to the overall process.

The homes in the completed development have been listed at prices ranging from approximately $775,000 to $875,000.

Montgomery County Project

The project reviewed for Montgomery County developed approximately 250 dwelling units, practically evenly split between attached and detached residences, on nearly 125 acres of land located in an SPA. The development provided 12.5 percent of the units as MPDUs, the minimum percentage required of all new residential projects in the county. Approximately 40 percent of the site was dedicated as open space.

The preliminary approval for the project took approximately nine months. Approval for the site plan and completion of the record plat, which initiates the building permit process, averaged about eighteen months. The review process for each of the phases was done concurrently, so the overall planning process, from preliminary plan to record plat approval, took approximately twenty-eight months.

The site conditions necessitated adherence to several environmental regulations (table 4.13).

Due to environmental limitations of the site, the percentage of attached units was increased above the limitations set in the county's general plan. The forest conservation plan, established using county guidelines, was one of the regulations instigating this change. The developer faced further site challenges because of conflicting regulations regarding stormwater management in the SPA and master plan. They rectified this conflict by granting the project a waiver from the swale requirement but also preventing the installation of any stormwater management facilities inside of the environmental preservation areas. Additionally, in an effort to minimize the overall impact of environmental disturbance, the county required that the project be phased. This necessitated the preparation and approval of erosion and sedimentation control plans for each phase of the project.

The project received preliminary plan approval before the developer acquired the property. After acquisition, the developer reconfigured the

Table 4.13 Montgomery Project Environmental Regulations

Regulation/Review	Federal	State	Local
Wetlands permitting	X	X	
Floodplains			X
Stormwater			X
Erosion and sediment control			X
Resource protection area			X
Resource water protection			X
Open space set-aside			X
Tree preservation			X
Landscaping			X
Reforestation			X

preliminary plan design to better fit the home product to the site. These changes were done without altering the approved preliminary plan development envelope. While modifying the approved preliminary plan and seeking site plan approval, the developer simultaneously began the production of engineering plans. The timing of these tasks increased costs, because changes made during site plan approval had to be reengineered.

SPA development guidelines required the developer to install multiple stormwater BMP facilities to mediate development impact on the high-quality water resource. These facilities were required to be oversized to accommodate more stormwater volume as compared with similar installations outside of an SPA. The stormwater BMPs also were required to be installed in a series. The intention behind such requirements is to create backups in the event that if one BMP facility fails, the others would be able to handle the additional loading. To fulfill this requirement, the developer installed a number of at-grade stormwater BMP facilities under parking lots and other site elements. These stormwater accommodations increased costs for the developer, but this approach was chosen in order to maximize the site's building potential.

In addition, the county required a forest preservation plan as a part of this project. The plan required reforestation to take place along the riparian buffer of a watercourse present on the site. This reforestation process included a five-year monitoring period with a 100 percent survival rate of the plantings. In addition, the plan required that a stand of existing forest be preserved, which decreased the amount of density that could be achieved on the site and thus required a master plan waiver. This density waiver, a result of environmental regulations, meant additional homes were not constructed on the site.

As a component of the final construction plan approval process, the construction was required to be completed in three phases in an effort to minimize the amount of disturbance to the site at any one time. The required phased construction schedule added costs, because in some instances earthwork had to be done multiple times. The additional costs could have been avoided or minimized if a phased project construction schedule had been required from the outset, because the developer could have balanced each phase of the development. Table 4.14 shows known or estimated costs relating to environmental regulation compliance of this project.

The research team was unable to ascertain environmental permit timeframes for this project. The homes in the completed development have been listed at prices ranging from approximately $450,000 to $800,000.

Projects in Neighboring Virginia Counties

Information about three additional projects was provided by the participating developers, but the projects were not used in the case study because they were located outside of Fairfax and Montgomery counties. Case study information on these additional projects, located in Loudoun and Prince William counties, does not include the time it took to acquire any necessary rezoning approvals.

Two projects were evaluated in Loudoun County. One project was a by-right development, meaning there were no rezoning conditions of approval developed. The other project was part of a larger development and included numerous rezoning proffers.

By-Right Development Project
The by-right project in Loudoun County consisted of roughly 200 detached units developed on approximately 200 acres of land. The project set aside more than 40 percent of the site as open space. The project was divided into phases, and only one phase was provided for analysis. This phase de-

Table 4.14 Montgomery Project Environmental Costs

	Cost	Percentage of Improvement Cost[a]
Preconstruction		
Natural resources inventory	$15,000	1%
Wetlands delineation	n/a	
Wetlands permitting	n/a	
Forest conservation plan	$75,000	5%
Construction		
Stormwater management	$850,000	59%
Site demolition and construction preparation	$260,000	18%
Erosion and sediment control	$250,000	17%
Total environmental regulatory compliance cost	$1,445,000	7%
Total project cost for land[b]	$22,000,000	
Average environmental regulatory cost per unit	$5,500	7%
Average lot cost per unit	$86,000	

[a] Percentage of total known environmental regulatory compliance costs.
[b] Cost for finished lot, does not include construction cost for dwelling unit.

veloped roughly fifty detached residential units on approximately forty acres, of which 20 percent was set aside as open space. The project was part of a larger preliminary plan approval that included approximately six additional phases. The project was in review and approval processes for nearly twenty-seven months. The site conditions necessitated adherence to several environmental regulations (table 4.15).

The site involved background research, archeological study, wetland delineation, CWA permitting, and mitigation. The site survey costs of the wetland delineation are not reflected in the categories. This project required phase I, II, and III archeological surveys to be completed. No proffers were required as this project was a by-right development. Table 4.16 shows known or estimated costs relating to environmental regulation compliance of this project.

Table 4.15 By-Right Project Environmental Regulations

Regulation/Review	Federal	State	Local
Wetlands permitting	X	X	
Stormwater		X	
Wastewater collection		X	
Erosion and sediment control		X	X
Open space set-aside			X
Tree preservation			X
Landscaping			X
Archeological review			X
Water distribution		X	X
Soils/geotechnical report			X
Reforestation		X	X

Table 4.16 By-Right Project Environmental Costs

	Percentage of Cost	Improvement Cost[a]
Preconstruction		
Wetland delineation	$22,500	<1%
Background environmental research	$6,000	<1%
Archeological investigation	$63,000	2%
Environmental contamination remediation	$400,000	13%
Wetland permitting	$46,500	1%
Construction		
Stormwater management ponds	$1,400,000	44%
Erosion and sediment control	$880,000	28%
Postconstruction		
Wetland mitigation	$343,000	11%
Total environmental regulatory compliance cost	$3,161,000	22%
Total project cost[b]	$14,325,000	
Average environmental regulatory cost per unit	$16,500	22%
Average lot cost per unit	$75,000	

[a] Percentage of total known environmental regulatory compliance costs.
[b] Cost for finished lot, does not include construction cost for dwelling unit.

Table 4.17 By-Right Project Environmental Permitting

	Approval Time (in months)		
Permit	COE	DEQ	VMRC
Joint permit application	6	7	Not required
National Wetland Permit #43	2	Not required	Not required
National Wetland Permit #39	2	Not required	Not required
Modification	1	7	Not required
Modification	4	11	Not required

As mentioned, the approval process for the site plan's entire project was completed in approximately twenty-seven months. The preliminary plan, construction plan, profiles review, and record plat approval processes occurred concurrently with the environmental permitting required. The approval of the development plans required the permits listed in table 4.17 to be acquired before beginning construction.

As with the other projects reviewed, the amount of time needed to acquire the necessary permits associated with the CWA as it is enforced by the state was relatively short compared with the entire length of time it took to approve the project. Nevertheless, a developer must have these permits in hand before beginning construction, which prompts many developers to undertake the application process concurrently with other approvals to minimize time delays. Once again, because the developer sought the necessary approvals and environmental permits concurrently, compliance with environmental regulations added minimal costs and time to the overall process.

The homes in the completed development have been listed at prices ranging from approximately $675,000 to $975,000.

Phased Development Project

The other Loudoun County project is part of a phased development plan to create approximately 300 units on nearly 200 acres that required rezoning

Table 4.18 Phased-Project Environmental Regulations

Regulation/Review	Federal	State	Local
Wetlands permitting	X	X	
Floodplains	X		
Stormwater		X	X
Wastewater collection			X
Wastewater treatment		X	X
Erosion and sediment control		X	
Open space set-aside			X
Tree preservation			X
Landscaping			X
Archeological review			X
Water distribution			X
Soils/geotechnical report			X

approval. The phase of the project provided for the case study creates approximately 100 detached units. As a part of the rezoning process, the developer agreed to proffer cash to the county's Affordable Housing Trust Fund in lieu of providing affordable dwelling units in the project. The project took approximately twenty-two months to receive entitlement from the time it entered the rezoning process. The site conditions necessitated adherence to several environmental regulations (table 4.18).

The rezoning process required for this project resulted in numerous proffered conditions of approval, many of which were influential in bringing additional environmental regulations into play. The construction of a recreation facility along a watercourse required additional permitting from federal, state, and local agencies. The developer also agreed to have an outside agency prepare an environmental management plan to promote sustainable resource management through sound environmental planning, construction, and management of the project. This plan was to include management plans for numerous environmental resources and issues related to the site.

A number of project proffers related to tree preservation and forest cover. The developer agreed to complete an afforestation plan, preserve at least 80 percent of the identified tree preservation areas, maintain a minimum acreage of trees in an identified area of the project, and complete a riparian buffer planting plan to preserve and protect water quality and wildlife habitat while enhancing aesthetic value.[28] At least 50 percent of the new trees must have the capability to reach a 2-inch diameter 4.5 feet from the ground within seven years. Complying with these proffers involved the guidance of a certified arborist or landscape architect, and at this time of this writing plans were to be approved by the county's urban forester.

The project also initiated proffers relating to archeological resources present on the site, including the completion of a phase I survey prior to any grading and, if required, phase II and III surveys. In addition, some of the cultural resources present on the site were to be preserved and enhanced by the developer, including the completion of the process for listing resources eligible for the National Register of Historic Places. The developer also agreed to open space and riparian buffer proffers.

Table 4.19 shows known or estimated project costs relating to environmental regulation compliance.

The permitting for the wetland regulations associated with this project was completed before the developer purchased the site. The costs associated with the permitting process, as outlined above, resulted in the developer paying a higher price for the land because this work had already been completed. The developer was still responsible for any mitigation costs associated with the permits.

The completed homes in this development have been listed at prices ranging from approximately $525,000 to $1,000,000.

Prince William County
The final case study project is in Prince William County. It is part of a phased development to create nearly 200 homes on approximately 100 acres, although one-third of the site will be preserved as open space. The phase evaluated for the case study planned to develop between sixty and seventy detached units on approximately thirty acres, while preserving nearly ten acres as open space. The developer agreed to proffer a cash contribution to the county's Housing Preservation and Development Fund. Prince William County requires that rezonings be consistent with the comprehensive plan. If a rezoning application is necessary, which was the case

Table 4.19 Phased-Project Environmental Costs

	Percentage of Cost	Improvement Cost[a]
Preconstruction		
Wetland delineation	$78,500	6%
Background environmental research	$500	<1%
Archeological investigation	$122,500	11%
Cultural resource designation	$32,500	3%
Environmental contamination remediation	$85,000	7%
Tree preservation plan	$14,000	1%
Wetland permitting	$25,000	2%
Construction		
Stormwater management ponds	$100,000	9%
Erosion and sediment control	$445,000	39%
Tree preservation plan implementation	$200,000	18%
Archeological resource management	$35,000	3%
Total environmental regulatory compliance cost	$1,138,000	5%
Total project cost for land[b]	$23,775,000	
Average environmental regulatory cost per unit	$3,800	5%
Average lot cost per unit	$75,000	

[a] Percentage of total known environmental regulatory compliance costs.
[b] Cost for finished lot, does not include construction cost for dwelling unit.

for this project, a developer must request to amend the comprehensive plan; such amendment requests are accepted in January of each calendar year. The project required approximately twenty-nine months to receive approval. The site conditions necessitated adherence to several environmental regulations (table 4.20).

The endangered species requirement is a unique element of this study. This project required a study for endangered species because preliminary assessment revealed a potential presence of such an element, but additional study did not reveal any such species.

The project proffers included certain agreements that had environmental implications. These proffers included cash contributions by the

Table 4.20 Prince William Project Environmental Regulations

Regulation/Review	Federal	State	Local
Wetlands permitting	X	X	X
Stormwater			X
Wastewater collection			X
Erosion and sediment control		X	X
Endangered species	X	X	
Open space set-aside			X
Tree preservation			X
Landscaping			X
Noise attenuation			X
Archeological review			X
Water distribution			X
Soils/geotechnical report			X

developer for environmental monitoring, more stringent erosion and sedimentation control plan guidelines, and additional landscaping requirements. The proffers also agreed to stipulate that the developer was to preserve and protect identified tree preservation areas to the greatest extent practical and feasible. An archeological study and resource preservation proffer also was part of the approval conditions. Table 4.21 shows the known or estimated project costs relating to environmental regulation compliance.

As noted earlier, the rezoning application and approval process for the site plan's entire project was completed in approximately twenty-nine months. The joint permit application required for the project was completed before the submission of the project for rezoning approval. The rezoning and site plan approval processes occurred concurrently with the required modified environmental permitting (table 4.22).

Once again, because the developer sought the necessary approvals and environmental permits concurrently, compliance with environmental regulations added minimal costs and time to the overall process. The completed homes in this development have been listed at prices ranging from approximately $575,000 to $675,000.

Table 4.21 Prince William Project Environmental Costs

	Percentage of Cost	Improvement Cost[a]
Preconstruction		
Wetland delineation	$16,000	<1%
Background environmental research	$1,500	<1%
Resource protection area	$3,000	<1%
Endangered species research	$6,000	<1%
Archeological investigation	$8,500	<1%
Environmental contamination remediation	$220,000	12%
Wetland permitting	$19,000	1%
Construction		
Stormwater management ponds	$300,000	16%
Erosion and sedimentation control	$863,000	47%
Archeological resource management	$65,000	4%
Noise attenuation	$215,000	12%
Postconstruction		
Wetland mitigation	$117,000	6%
Total environmental regulatory compliance cost	$1,834,000	11%
Total project cost for land[b]	$16,125,000	
Average environmental regulatory cost per unit	$8,500	11%
Average lot cost per unit	$75,000	

[a] Percentage of total known environmental regulatory compliance costs.
[b] Cost for finished lot, does not include construction cost for dwelling unit.

Table 4.22 Prince William Project Environmental Permitting

	Approval Time (in months)		
Permit	*COE*	*DEQ*	*VMRC*
Joint permit application	3	2	Not req'd
Modification	1	1	Not req'd

Projects Summary

The case study was based on information provided to the research team by experienced, national developers working in the local market for many decades. Each of the development project studies provided useful information on costs and delays associated with environmental regulations, including:

- General project characteristics: site acreage, units developed, type of application, time needed to complete the development review process, affordable dwelling units developed, proffers, and conditions of approval
- Environmental regulations and reviews triggered
- Estimated costs of compliance with environmental regulations, cost per unit, cost as a percentage of housing price, cost as a percentage of land, and development costs
- Timeframe for acquiring the required environmental permits. (Although the study sought to estimate the cost of delays, this could not be done. One reason is that projects actually gained value during the review process. A second is that it was difficult to ascribe delays specifically to environmental regulations as opposed to other reasons.)

Seven development projects were included in the case studies, two in Fairfax County (one was a two-phase project where data were aggregated), one in Montgomery County, two in Loudoun County, and one in Prince William County.

- Fairfax 1: Two-phase (accounting for two of the seven projects reviewed), 700-unit development on a 300-acre infill site. Rezoning required; twenty-two months to approval. Up to 100 affordable dwelling units (ADU) were proffered. Home prices range from $400,000 to $1,000,000.
- Fairfax 2: 100-unit development on a fifty-acre greenfield site with 30 percent open space and twenty ADUs. Rezoning required; eighteen months to approval. Home prices range from $775,000 to $875,000.
- Montgomery: 250 units on 100 acres; twenty ADUs. Rezoning required; twenty-eight months to approval. Home prices range from $450,000 to $800,000.

- Loudoun 1: 200 units on 200 acres; 40 percent open space. By-right development that still required twenty-seven months for approval. Home prices range from $675,000 to $975,000.
- Loudoun 2: 300 units on 200 acres; proffered cash to Affordable Housing Trust Fund in lieu of providing ADUs. Rezoning required; twenty-two months to approval. Home prices range from $525,000 to $1,000,000.
- Prince William: 200 units on 100 acres; one-third preserved as open space; proffered cash to County's Housing Preservation and Development Fund. Rezoning and amendment to comprehensive plan required; twenty-nine months to approval. Home prices range from $575,000 to $675,000.

Table 4.23 compares the characteristics of the six project studies, and gives total environmental compliance costs and their breakdown by specific environmental area, as well as time to approval, proffers, and various indicators of compliance cost. These indicators include environmental compliance cost per lot and cost as a percentage of land and development cost. The research team was impressed by the finding that the percentage of environmentally related costs to total improvement costs was less than half the figure estimated for 1975 (see chapter 3). In fact, in relation to finished lots, prices were generally on the low end of the cost continuum established in chapter 3, and in only one of the case studies were the costs in the "normal" range. One reason for this finding may be that land and house prices are so high in this market that environmentally related costs are simply not a large percentage of the total. The focus groups and other case studies reported in later chapters will further inform this theory.

The assessment also found that on average the time to approval was at the high end of "normal," although three cases were in the "delay" category and none were in the "accelerated" category. Two of the three "delayed" cases are interesting.

The developer for the Prince William project indicated that planning and other staff at Prince William County are overwhelmed by rapid growth in that county and look to how other counties—especially Fairfax—handle such issues as environmental concerns. Through some delay, the staff would use ad hoc approaches to condition final development approval on

Table 4.23 Comparing Seven Project Studies

Feature	Fairfax 1	Fairfax 2	Montgomery	Loudoun 1	Loudoun 2	Prince William	Average
Land-Use Decision	Rezoning	Rezoning	Rezoning	By-Right	Rezoning	Rezoning; Plan Amendment	
Acres	300	50	100	200	200	100	
Units	700	100	250	200	300	200	
ADUs	20–100	20	30		AHTF		
Percentage of open space		30%		20%			
Environmental Compliance Cost (in millions)	$3.96	$1.10	$1.52	$3.16	$1.14	$1.83	
Percentage of erosion/sedimentation	42%	20%	15%	28%	39%	47%	32%
Percentage of stormwater	25%	14%	54%	44%	9%	16%	27%
Percentage of remediation	10%		20%	13%	7%	12%	11%
Percentage of wetlands/ESA	8%	5%	5%	13%	8%	8%	7%
Percentage of tree/forestry	<1%		5%		19%	<1%	4%
Percentage of noise attenuation	10%	60%				12%	13%

Table 4.23 Comparing Seven Project Studies (*continued*)

Feature	Fairfax 1	Fairfax 2	Montgomery	Loudoun 1	Loudoun 2	Prince William	Average
Land-Use Decision	Rezoning	Rezoning	Rezoning	By-Right	Rezoning	Rezoning; Plan Amendment	
Percentage Other	4%	1%	1%	2%	18%	5%	5%
Environmental cost per unit	$5,650	$11,000	$6,000	$15,800	$3,800	$9,150	$8,600
Environmental cost share of land plus development cost	1.9%	3.3%	2.3%	5.3%	1.2%	3.6%	2.9%
Imputed lot cost[a]	$187,250	$205,500	$167,500	$187,250	$197,500	$156,750	$183,500
Environmental cost share of finished lot cost	4.7%	3.0%	5.0%	3.6%	8.4%	1.9%	5.8%
Approvals	Concurrent	Concurrent	Concurrent	Concurrent	Concurrent	Concurrent	
Time to approval	22	18	28	27	2	29	24
Proffers	Stream monitor; BMPs; archeological review; off-site conservation easement	Tree preservation	None in MD	None for by-right	Tree preservation; forest cover; archeological; one review; open space	Funds to monitor, E&SC, tree preservation; on housing fund	

[a] The builders also built homes, so the finished lot price is not provided directly. This figure is based on a 25 percent finished lot-to-home sale ratio, which is conservative and will have the effect of increasing the relationship of environmentally related costs to finished lot cost.

BOX 4.2 Quick Lessons from the Case Study

- Water issues dominate but a large number of other issues can affect specific projects.
- Typical costs for environmental compliance are about 3 percent per unit.
- Concurrent reviews are critical to avoid long and uncertain delays.
- About twenty-four months is typical of the time for approval, even when rezoning is involved.
- Uncertainty prevails in negotiated approvals needed for rezoning.
- Retaining environmental specialists trusted by local jurisdictions can develop good environmental information early and mitigate public concerns.

Fairfax-like environmental and other regulations; if Prince William County had the same regulations or regulatory approval processes, then the approval may have been given several months sooner.

The second interesting case in this regard is the one in Montgomery County. Although the case study included only one project from this county, the research team learned through online planning records and interviews that this case, which took twenty-eight months, required about a normal time period to approval for the county. Yet, the project's home sales and imputed finished lot prices were the second lowest of the six project studies and 10 percent lower than the overall average. The key to this outcome was that the developer for this project knew Montgomery County's processes and indicated it had anticipated much of the time-to-approval process from the outset as well as other costs. Presumably, because the developer knows the costs of environmental requirements and processing time, the land purchase price is reduced accordingly which has a moderating effect on housing prices (see chapter 2).

HOW DO THE COSTS ADD UP?

Remarkably, sales prices, improvement costs, and processing times were reasonably similar between the states and among the jurisdictions.

The study of seven subdivision projects highlights how jurisdictions can improve certainty and administrative efficiency when applying environmental regulations to residential development.

Results from the case study confirmed that home builders are likely to incur greater costs under more complex development reviews and more comprehensive environmental regulatory systems. However, the increased home builder costs in the case in Montgomery County did not translate into higher home prices compared with the projects in Fairfax County. For the projects reviewed, the average sales price in Fairfax County was nearly $750,000 for a new home, while the average sales price for the Montgomery County project was $670,000.[29]

By examining the costs from these typical housing projects in light of relevant state and local environmental regulations, the research team drew a number of important policy conclusions about the effects of environmental regulatory systems on suburban housing developments. While the original research methodology was more extensive, the Fairfax–Montgomery County case study still offers valuable insights regarding (1) the controlling influence of local government development review processes; (2) the relationship of environmental costs to housing affordability; and (3) the design and implementation of state and local environmental regulations. The research team also hypothesized about future research questions and set forth ideas about potential next steps that could flow from the case study.

Local development planning processes played a critical role in the implementation of state and local environmental regulations. How the local governments synchronized environmental and development reviews had a direct impact on the time, resources, and costs incurred by the home builder, especially in the early stages of the projects. A greater level of integration seemed to facilitate greater certainty and higher levels of trust during the negotiations among local government staff and the builder's consultants; thus, greater integration should result in less time to obtain approval and hence less cost to the home builder. The research team struggled with how to separate environmental regulations from standard planning and zoning regulations because the two systems are intricately integrated.

WHAT ARE THE COSTS OF REGULATORY COMPLIANCE?

One of the threshold inquiries in calculating total costs is determining the universe of direct and indirect costs associated with environmental regulations and when they occur before, during, and after construction. Based on our case study research, we found that these costs include:

- Preconstruction Costs
    - Background research and natural resource inventory
    - Wetland delineation
    - Environmental contamination remediation
    - Tree and forest conservation planning
    - Archeological investigation
    - Cultural resource designation
    - Permitting processes and approvals
- Construction Costs
    - Stormwater management ponds
    - Erosion and sediment control measures
    - Noise attenuation elements
    - Archeological resource management
- Postconstruction Costs
    - Mitigation
    - Wetlands
    - Stream outfall

Direct costs include those paid by developers to meet environmental regulations. These costs may include the cost of installing erosion and sediment control measures, stormwater best management practices, mitigation, and completing a wetland permit. Direct costs also include fees paid for the professional services needed to meet these regulations, either to employees or to consultants.

Indirect costs may be more difficult to identify. These may include the lost opportunity costs associated with environmental regulations or costs incurred due to time delays. Examples include the loss of all or part of the development site because of the presence of wetlands or endangered species habitat. Time also plays a role in the cost of environmental regulations, although this element was difficult to tease out in the case study. Developers participating in the case study indicate that the time it takes to acquire approval, partly due to environmental regulation review, has increased, and therefore adds landholding costs to a project. Market influences also may play a role, as land value may increase during the time it takes to review a project, especially in a hot market region. The study was unable to directly identify increased landholding costs or attribute costs to environmental regulations or to the overall review process.

The complexity of the issues and the local conditions often require developers to become dependent on outside environmental consultants for expertise and assistance in acquiring approval for a project. The additional cost of hiring an outside consultant to manage environmental regulatory issues may prevent smaller firms from entering the development market and could increase the costs of development for the larger firms that do not have staff able to provide these services.

The type and nature of the environmental costs will depend on the scope and nature of the regional and local environmental resources. For example, the protection of the water resources and water quality of the Chesapeake Bay are important environmental policy priorities for the region. In other parts of the nation, different but no less influential environmental protections are in place. In the case study, water resource regulations accounted for the majority of environmental costs in the subdivision projects reviewed. For the developers participating in the focus groups, environmental issues involving endangered species and habitat protection dominated concerns, as will be seen in chapter 6.

FIVE

Key Lessons from the Case Study

This chapter expands on the key lessons offered by the case study presented in chapter 4. We have organized the lessons into main categories that cover costs; specific elements of environmental regulations, ranging from stormwater to site remediation to wetlands permitting to the Endangered Species Act to forest cover and open space; special considerations such as noise and archeology; rezonings and voluntary requirements; time issues, including delays and uncertainties; regulatory and market factors affecting costs; predictable and unpredictable delays; the effects of politics on the approval process; expediting the approval process; and costs compared with benefits.

COST OF COMPLIANCE WITH ENVIRONMENTAL REGULATIONS

The seven case studies, of which two were phases of the same project, indicate that the cost of compliance with environmental regulations is not trivial, totalling $1.1 million to $4 million for the six developments. Of these costs, the study found that only a small amount (less than 5 percent) went to studies and permit fees, and nearly all of the expenditures were for controls and mitigation. While this cost seems high, when viewed as a percentage of the overall project land and development cost (1.2 to 5.3 percent), as a cost per home ($3,800 to $11,000), and especially as a percentage of home sales price (0.5 to 2.1 percent), the costs are very low.

In a high-priced market such as the Washington metropolitan area, developers are less concerned about actual environmental compliance costs than they are about the uncertainties and delays that can occur in the approval process. Before addressing this issue, let us look more closely at some of the compliance costs.

Environmental Regulatory Costs Depend on Special Environmental Site Conditions

When home builder costs are translated to a "per dwelling unit" ratio, the relationship between environmental regulations and suburban housing affordability seems tenuous. Based on a comparison of the case study projects, the environmental costs in Montgomery and Fairfax counties ranged between $5,500 and $12,000 per unit. The Montgomery County project, with its increased development approval times and added costs for stormwater management construction, was closer to $5,500. The single-phase project in Fairfax County was more expensive mainly due to the installation costs associated with the noise attenuation features. Considering all of the case study projects, the per dwelling unit costs of environmental regulations ranged significantly from $3,800 to more than $16,500 (for the by-right development in Loudoun County).

Another way of evaluating the wide range of costs is to take note of the special environmental conditions on the project site. Developer costs were substantially higher for the Loudoun County project because of the special environmental challenges of the site—development required extensive mitigation of wetlands impacted by the project. With fewer large tracts of land open for development in the Washington metropolitan area, developers now have fewer opportunities for housing development and will likely encounter more sites with important natural resources, thus increasing environmental costs. The scarcity of simple sites for new housing actually may drive the increase in home builder costs more so than increases from environmental regulations.

It is difficult to determine from the data how the costs of environmental regulatory compliance affect overall housing costs. It is unclear whether these environmental costs are added to the selling price of the house, inevitably increasing sales prices, or if these environmental costs are absorbed by the developer's profit margin or, perhaps more accurately, capitalized backward to the seller of land as a function of the due diligence process (see chapter 3).

Moreover, local developers informed the research team that the cost to finance the project ranges about 15 percent to 20 percent of all funds borrowed for the development before home construction actually occurs. However, because the developers do not secure the loans, the lenders have no recourse for collection if the project is not completed. A one-year delay on a $10 million loan carried for a project would thus cost $1.5 million to $2 million. In a very real sense, "time is money." If the review and approval schedule provided more certainty regarding timeframes, financing could be timed accordingly.

What Effects Do These Costs Have on the Price of Housing?
The case study research team was unable to determine the direct effects of the costs of compliance with environmental regulations on the price of housing. Overall, the price of housing in the Washington metropolitan region is robust, leading the costs of environmental regulation to be a minor player in housing price, which is determined by the market.

From a theoretical perspective, even if housing prices were to fall (as they have in the latter half of the 2000s), economic theory would require that land improvement costs associated with environmental regulations be capitalized backward into the price of land acquired for development. We thus focus on differences in prices between the states—Virginia and Maryland—to garner a general impression of environmentally related housing prices and supply.

With a comparable population in a metropolitan region experiencing nearly homogeneous growth pressure, the research team expected Fairfax and Montgomery counties to be similar in their housing prices and supply. However, the median price of a new home in Montgomery County consistently has been lower than the median price in Fairfax County, most recently the difference being nearly $50,000 in 2005. Montgomery County also has nearly 30,000 fewer housing units available than Fairfax County. Following the premise that increased environmental regulations and added time to receive approval would increase costs, it would be expected that Montgomery County would have higher home sales prices. Given the additional development costs to meet environmental regulations, either through extended review processes or increased design and construction requirements, Montgomery County should have a higher median sales price for new homes.

The results from projects in the case study were, in fact, the opposite. Fairfax County, with its quicker review processes, less restrictive environmental regulatory regime, and greater pool of housing from which to distribute residents, has an average new home sales price that is $80,000 higher than prices in Montgomery County for the projects reviewed. Clearly, factors other than environmentally related price effects are at work.

What Are These Costs Relative to Other Costs?

The costs incurred to comply with environmental regulations averaged 11 percent of the overall total project costs, not including the costs of constructing the dwelling units. Environmental regulation compliance generated costs ranging from 5 percent to 22 percent of the total project costs, not including the costs of constructing dwelling units. The Montgomery County project's costs associated with environmental regulations were 7 percent of the total project costs, while the by-right development's environmental compliance costs accounted for 22 percent of the total project costs, not including the costs of constructing dwelling units in both cases.

SPECIFIC ELEMENTS OF ENVIRONMENTAL REGULATIONS

Stormwater, Erosion, and Sediment Control

In the seven project studies, stormwater, erosion, and sediment control measures cost 59 percent of all environmental compliance costs, or about $5,000 per lot. An executive of a large, national builder shared with us his rule of thumb for stormwater costs in different states:

California—$9,000 per lot
Florida—$5,000 per lot
Texas—$1,500 per lot

Key Lessons from the Case Study   111

Water Resource Regulations Account for Majority of Costs
Because the Washington metropolitan region has strict controls—comparable to those in Florida—for protection of the Chesapeake Bay, compliance with water resource protection regulations accounted for nearly 66 percent of the overall environmental regulatory costs identified in the case study projects. These costs include preconstruction, construction, and postconstruction figures. The construction of noise attenuation features also represents an average of nearly 16 percent of the environmental regulatory costs, although these elements were present in only three projects. Environmental contamination cleanup, present in five projects, averaged 13 percent of the total environmental regulatory costs. The remaining environmental regulations, including cultural resources, endangered species, and tree preservation, represent less than 5 percent of the total environmental regulatory costs.

Site Remediation

Remediation was required for five projects and amounted to the next-highest compliance cost after stormwater and erosion and sediment control. Remediation is a catchall for a wide range of measures, including removing existing structures, old fuel tanks, drainfields, wells, and other hazardous or contaminated materials.

Wetlands Permitting

Surprisingly, the principal federal environmental regulations affecting land development—wetlands permitting and Endangered Species Act compliance—were relatively minor costs in the case study projects. All projects had wetlands delineation and permitting costs, and four projects required wetlands mitigation measures. Still, wetlands compliance costs ranged from $53,000 to $411,000 for each project. This translates to only 7 percent, or $300 to $2,000 per unit, of the total environmental compliance costs.

Table 5.1 traces the Fairfax 1 project wetlands permitting process and approval time. Although the sixteen months was required for the U.S. Army Corps of Engineers to approve various project phases, this time ran concur-

Table 5.1   Fairfax 1 Wetlands Permitting

Permit	Approval Time (in months)		
	COE	DEQ	VMRC
Individual (site)	3	3	4
Modification (site)	1	1	NA
National Wetland Permit #39	2	Not required	Not required
Individual (utility)	2	Not required	3
Modification (utility)	3	Not required	6
Temporary access road	1	Not required	5
National Wetland Permit #39 (phase)	2	Not required	Not required
Individual (phase)	1	Not required	Not required
Modification (phase)	1	Not required	Not required

rently with other permitting and did not add appreciably to the project delays.

Endangered Species Act

While all projects had to consider Endangered Species Act requirements, only one project (the one in Prince William County) had any suspected endangered species habitat. A $6,000 assessment did not find any such habitat.

Vegetation, Forest Cover, and Open Space

Local tree preservation, open space, and forest cover ordinances and proffered requirements were included in several projects. Tree and forest conservation were part of the Montgomery County project (which spent $75,000 on its forest conservation plan), and the Loudoun County 2 project (which spent $214,000 on tree preservation). In addition, two of the projects had open space set-asides.

Other Measures: Noise Attenuation, Archeological Studies

Of the developments studied, four projects required archeological studies and two required resulting resource management (up to $157,500 for the Loudoun 2 project). Fairfax 1 and Fairfax 2 required noise attenuation barriers (at costs of $380,000 and $666,000, respectively).

REZONINGS, PROFFERS, AND "VOLUNTARY" REQUIREMENTS BEYOND FORMAL REGULATIONS

By-right projects are rare—nearly all projects require rezonings. Rezoning applications open up a negotiated process with proffers as a big part of the process in Virginia. And proffers can add considerable environmental and other features to projects that go even beyond regulations. While they are officially "voluntary," proffers often become a required concession in the negotiated approval for rezoning. Although proffers are specific to Virginia, similar mechanisms are used whenever a rezoning requires conditions and concessions for a negotiated agreement.

TIME TO APPROVAL, UNCERTAINTIES, AND DELAYS

The Urban Land Institute (1979) set a rule of thumb for approval times: Approvals without zoning changes in areas with few regulations take six to nine months, and those in areas with many regulations take two to five years.

Our case studies in the Washington metropolitan region, however, did not follow this pattern. All cases were in jurisdictions with many complex regulations. The one by-right case took more than two years. All of the others involved zoning changes—one required a comprehensive plan change—and all required negotiations including open-ended Virginia proffers. Yet, they took eighteen to twenty-nine months for approval. All projects had concurrent review of different permitting and approval requirements, an approach that was crucial in minimizing delays.

One large developer gave its rule of thumb for Fairfax County: twelve months for rezoning, twelve months for site plan approval, and add twelve months if comprehensive plan revision is needed and not done concurrently. In Loudoun County, add another four months for rezoning.

Competing regulations enforced by different departments also can cause unpredictable delays and additional costs. Even with concurrent review, the process of rectifying competing regulations requires internal negotiations by different departments, delaying a developer's ability to move forward with design approvals until an agreement is reached among the departments. If this regulatory disparity is not identified until late in the design process, additional costs are incurred if completed designs need to be redone to meet the requirements of the departmental regulatory compromise.

What are excessive delays? Participating developers said they consider anything beyond twelve months if no rezoning is needed, and anything beyond twenty-four months with a rezoning, to be excessive delays. Some complex projects, such as Metro West, a transit-oriented infill development in Fairfax County, take longer, in this case forty-eight months. The project was complicated by the fact that a member of Congress opposed this mixed-use project, which was located at a federally financed heavy-rail transit station.

VARIOUS REGULATORY AND MARKET FACTORS THAT INFLUENCE ENVIRONMENTAL REGULATORY COSTS

Distinct Land Development Processes Can Directly Affect Environmental Regulatory Reviews

Montgomery and Fairfax counties review development using different planning processes. With fewer tracts of land available for development, Fairfax County relies on the rezoning of existing land for new housing developments. As a local government operating in a Dillon Rule state, Fairfax County uses the proffer system (a type of conditional zoning) to mitigate the potential environmental impacts of new development.[1] With a long tradition of comprehensive planning, cluster development, and open space conservation, Montgomery County relies on its comprehensive planning regime (comprehensive plans, master plans, and special protection area plans) to ensure that new housing developments have minimal environmental impacts.

Each county's development review process has its own nuances affecting the time it takes to garner approval and the level of involvement by agencies and developers. For the six developments studied, environmental regulations and review became a critical focus of the development review process. The research team hypothesized that additional environmental reviews would increase the involvement of the builder's environmental and planning consultants and hence take more time—and more time should translate into higher overall cost of housing in the respective county.

The research from these six projects has shown that the average cost per unit ($8,483) to comply with environmental regulations was slightly higher than 1 percent of the average home sales price of $734,626, with twenty-four months being the average review time for the projects. Projects with a longer review period did average a higher cost per unit but so did the projects with the two shortest review periods. The average sales amount for the projects with the two longest approval times averaged a lower sales price ($648,471) than the overall average. For projects with the shortest approval times (eighteen to twenty-two months), the average sales price was $773,528, nearly $40,000 more than the group. These results indicate that, during the study period, the sales price of homes were not influenced by the review time of the project. However, the study period occurred during a time when housing prices were rising at unprecedented rates largely because of historically low interest rates, rising incomes, increasing job opportunities, and overall greater demand for housing than there was supply in the case study area.

Indeed, we have found that, despite their differences, Northern Virginia and Maryland jurisdictions seem to be converging in the scope and management of environmental regulations. Interviews with home builders in these areas revealed that Fairfax County's environmental regulatory system is becoming ironically similar to Montgomery County. Although important differences still remain (e.g., the scope and breadth of their respective planning regime—comprehensive and master plan processes—devoted to environmental protection and open space conservation), the similarities between the two counties are striking when it comes to stormwater, stream erosion, and other water-quality regulations.

Part of this trend toward similar environmental regulatory systems is the unifying influence of the Chesapeake Bay Compact. During the 1990s the Commonwealth of Virginia made modest commitments to comply with the minimum requirements of the Bay Compact while Maryland (the state and its local governments) made the Bay's water quality a high policy priority. More recently several local governments in Virginia have adopted more comprehensive environmental regulations to address the Bay's decreasing water quality.

Increased Development Approval Time for Montgomery County Increases Home Builder Costs

Of the projects studied, Montgomery County's preliminary plan review process and Fairfax County's rezoning application process took roughly the same amount of time to complete. On average, the home builder spent approximately nine months in both counties to get the requisite approval during these critical first steps. However, during the site review and final construction plan approval process, the Montgomery County process was ten months longer compared with Fairfax County projects.

Results from the case study indicate that the home builder incurred additional out-of-pocket costs for the Montgomery County project. Moreover, the home builder no doubt incurred costs (e.g., property taxes and financing) for holding idle property while the project underwent plan review. While the research team was unable to document the holding costs for the projects, a savvy developer could minimize these based on due diligence assessments.[2]

Inconsistent Environmental Regulations Can Increase Costs

Most environmental regulatory systems have certain inherent competing environmental goals and objectives. Although seldom recognized explicitly, there are environmental policy benefits associated with the regulations, which may, for example, protect against stormwater runoff but also might reduce habitat or tree cover. Other conflicts might arise over the design of comprehensive and long-term maintenance and the operation of the onsite stormwater management system. Each of these environmental programs might be managed by two separate county departments. Resolving such inconsistencies takes time and resources to work through the negotiation with county planners and environmental engineers, all of which may result in a required redesign of a previously approved preliminary or master plan. With numerous and complex plan requirements, reworking one component often means revising other elements of the development plan.

Inconsistent environmental regulations and conflicts over different departmental interpretations can generate significant time and resource costs when compared with the original project design and engineering plans. In Montgomery County, for example, an area master plan was developed to require one form of development, eliciting a certain type of design solution to meet environmental regulations that conflicted with an environmental overlay district.

County executive and city/county managers, working with their planning directors, should devise a process for resolving conflicting policies among different county/city departments. Planning departments also should closely track and monitor the interpretations that arise with complex development proposals to ensure consistency, not only for the project in question but also for future development approvals.

Environmental Engineering Design Complexity Influences Compliance Costs

Home builders rely more and more on the abilities of their environmental consulting team to not only identify potential environmental problems on the site but also to design innovative plans that protect the environment. Environmental conditions on the site may demand more complex engineered and constructed solutions, such as underground stormwater retention and treatment facilities or extensive noise attenuation structures. With some complex projects the developer chooses a comprehensive approach that costs more to design and build, but in other situations the site necessitates extraordinary measures. However, as infill projects become more prevalent, these additional measures (e.g., tree preservation and outfall mitigation) are becoming the norm in suburban counties such as Fairfax and Montgomery. Given these existing realities, home builders and their teams of consultants and engineers will need to develop alternative methods for meeting these requirements, modify current construction practices, and improve their use of technologies to manage the costs for installation and compliance.

Infill Development Creates Additional Environmental Challenges to Mitigate

Increasingly, infill projects are becoming the norm in localities with few sites available for development. In the words of one interviewee, "all of the low-hanging fruit has been picked." Development of infill sites in the Washington metropolitan region presents additional challenges, such as tree preservation planning and environmental remediation. Montgomery and Fairfax counties each have special ordinances, extensive programs, and staff devoted to tree preservation. And, at certain infill sites, housing and tree preservation policies conflict. At times, the value of a specimen tree or area of forest canopy takes precedence over the development of additional housing units. In instances where increased density is not allowed on the site, the trade-off for tree preservation might encourage the development to locate someplace else, potentially fueling urban sprawl. These types of conflicts increase costs for the municipality because it has to provide and maintain public infrastructure in newly developing places when it could be maximizing those existing services at infill sites. If unchecked, problems such as these could hinder planning efforts seeking to better manage growth.

By limiting density and building more residences at sites under development, added pressure is placed in other locations to meet the rising demand for new homes. The higher costs of infill development affect housing prices because the expense is transferred to the units sold. When fewer units are developed, the per-unit sales price needs to reflect these increased costs. This unintended consequence could be mitigated by allowing for increased densities in areas where environmental regulations decrease the amount of developable land.

The potential for environmental remediation presents another infill development challenge. With the high cost of housing, Fairfax and Montgomery counties are exploring the construction of homes on former commercial and industrial lands. Many of these so-called greyfield and brownfield properties have sat idle or partially vacant for years. They often have large tracts of parking lots and storage yards that could easily be converted to residential uses. No doubt some level of environmental contamination exists on many of these sites, which would require a phase I and perhaps a phase II environmental assessment along with the eventual remediation. Further, if the state-approved environmental cleanup allows for some contamination to remain on the site in protective engineering caps, the developer and the local government will need to design a system of institutional controls to monitor the use and activities on the property for decades to come. Environmental covenants and overlay zoning are common approaches to managing these issues. Many home builders are just beginning to navigate the regulatory maze of brownfield redevelopment.

Within Fairfax County, the cumulative impact of stormwater flows presented special challenges for many infill developments. As a result of changes in local ordinances to comply with new Chesapeake Bay standards, Fairfax County required new development projects to have more extensive stormwater infrastructure than in the past to handle the cumulative flow from adjacent properties.

PREDICTABLE VERSUS UNPREDICTABLE DELAYS: DO MINISTERIAL DECISIONS CAUSE DELAYS?

When approval timelines are vague, the review process can bog down between, say, an erosion and sediment control plan approval and a preconstruction meeting. Delays are inevitable, but there's a difference between delays that are unpredictable because of vague timeframes and uncertain requirements, and predictable delays that are based on reliable timeframes and certainty in standards. Given the choice, developers would rather have predictable delays so that construction and financing needs can be scheduled appropriately.

APPROVALS TURN FROM MINISTERIAL TO POLITICAL, CREATING GREATER UNCERTAINTY AND MORE DELAYS

Developers are extremely concerned about the uncertainty caused by delays due to political conflicts and turf wars. The developers we interviewed stated that they would rather have more stringent environmental regulations that they could meet without question than the uncertainty of negotiated rezonings that are characterized by an uncertain political process.

According to developers, delays and added requirements caused by political uncertainty are exacerbated where review staff or elected officials do not have the expertise or time to understand the complexities of new environmental technologies. Some developers suggested that political figures and review staff are happy to ask for a long list of measures (e.g., low-impact development and filter systems) without necessarily understanding them. Developers perceive that these politically motivated demands and uncertain process environment pose the danger of increasing requirements, if not in formal regulations, then in negotiated rezonings. In the political process, environmental regulations are often not the driving factor for opposition and uncertainty, but they represent hot-button issues that can be—and often are—used by project opponents.

EXPEDITING THE APPROVAL AND NEGOTIATION PROCESS WITH GOOD INFORMATION AND ENVIRONMENTAL EXPERTISE

Good information up front is critical to getting off to a good start. It is important for developers to anticipate environmental concerns and address them first, rather than waiting for an elected official or citizens to raise them.

Retaining a respected environmental consultant to perform site studies and present information to staff and at public hearings is a critical strategy. The best way to comply with regulations and appease local staff, elected officials, and the public who may object on environmental grounds is to provide them with good environmental information and incorporate good environmental design. As a consultant admonished: Lead, don't follow.

BUILDERS CAN EMPLOY ENVIRONMENTAL CONSULTANTS AND BETTER ACCOUNTING PRACTICES TO REDUCE THE COSTS OF ENVIRONMENTAL COMPLIANCE AND DELAY

One method developers use to help reduce the costs of environmental compliance is to subcontract some of the work to environmental consultants familiar with the review process. These consultants, who likely have an established and respected reputation with state and local regulators, are familiar with a wide range of environmental regulations and can point out inconsistencies in the process and help to navigate the requirements, ultimately reducing costs. These environmental consulting firms have cornered a niche market by knowing the system and being familiar with the requirements and programs necessary to avoid delays and meet the needs of developers most concerned about navigating an uncertain process.

Second, developers can control costs by doing a better job of tracking environmental costs. More accurate, complete environmental cost data from home builders would greatly assist the home-building industry in understanding where improvements in the process are needed to help reduce expenditures. Although some of the case study projects provided a wealth of information regarding many of the development costs related to environmental regulatory compliance, this was due to the diligence of the developers and their environmental consultants. Implementing an industry standard for tracking such costs may enable developers to better understand how these costs affect projects. In addition, this information could be used to work with local and state regulators to create more efficient and effective environmental regulatory review processes.

A third cost-saving method for developers is the use of permit expeditors, who often reduce the time it takes to acquire approval, thus reducing landholding costs. Although developers pay expeditors for such services, these costs would likely be significantly less than the costs of paying additional taxes on land awaiting development.

Developers can also purchase a property for which part of all of the development review process has been completed to reduce environmental compliance and delay costs. For example, a developer could purchase property for which the preliminary plan or rezoning approval has already been completed, a step that requires that the majority of the environmental background data compilation and analysis be completed. Although developers may pay a premium for such properties, the costs associated with completing the background work and early approvals may be reduced in the long term.

Overall, many potential cost reductions in environmental compliance and delays greatly depend on the complexity of the project site (and, as discussed, complex sites are on the rise in the study region) and on the efficiency and effectiveness of the development team and its consultants.

THE COST OF ENVIRONMENTAL COMPLIANCE COMPARED WITH THE BENEFITS OF ENVIRONMENTAL PROTECTION

Gathering More Complete Environmental Data Earlier in the Development Review Process

Public reviewing agencies in Fairfax and Montgomery counties now require greater detail in the early planning phases of project development, including rezoning and preliminary plan submissions. Having more complete environmental information earlier in the process minimizes the potential for later surprises and extensive delays. Plans submitted for review and approval during these stages provide the home builder and the local government with a solid baseline of critical environmental data, such as the inventory of wetlands, threatened and endangered species, floodplains, forest stands and specimen trees, and quality of soils and water resources. These natural resource inventories can identify potential environmentally regulated elements of the site.[3] Wetland delineation guides the project layout and is essential in acquiring the necessary federal and state permits. The identification of threatened and endangered species and their habitats ensures that certain designated areas may be off limits for development or may require special mitigation measures. Local ordinances in Montgomery and Fairfax counties require a close look at forest stands and specimen trees that might eventually be protected through a tree preservation plan or a forest canopy cover requirement. Floodplains, stream corridors, and associated riparian buffers may become part of an environmentally regulated area, such as an environmental quality corridor or resource protection area in Fairfax County or a special protection area in Montgomery County.

Early gathering of environmental baseline data also can positively affect the design and layout of the project, thus potentially saving the home builder time and resources. Once the environmental features of the site are accurately identified, the developer's team can prepare a conceptual layout and identify potential strategies for mitigating or perhaps even avoiding any development impact on these resources.

As a project develops, the level of detail required early in the planning process facilitates a clearer vision of how the project will be completed. Wetland and other natural resource inventories combined with preliminary grading studies indicate the development potential for the site. Armed with the most accurate and current environmental data, local planners and environmental engineers gain a greater level of trust in opening the negotiations with the home builder and environmental consultants. In this scenario, all parties are in a much better position to identify potential environmental "hot spots" of the site and tailor potential mitigation measures or best management practices to mitigate any adverse development impacts. Moreover, during the early approvals, local governments may impose additional environmental measures, such as phase II or III site inventories, through rezoning conditions, proffering (in Fairfax County), or special protection area amendments (in Montgomery County).

In many respects the regional home building and environmental consultant communities seem to focus their energies more on gathering in-depth environmental data than on opposing new or expansive environmental regulations. This preventative approach might be an outgrowth of a maturing of the regional home building industry and their increasing understanding of and level of comfort with the overall objectives of environmental regulations.

Elusive Monetary Benefits Compared with Captured Costs

The environmental benefits associated with the costs highlighted in this report are elusive because they are difficult to define in monetary value. However, this complexity does not preclude the benefits of environmental regulations from being considered when weighing their average $8,500 cost per unit. The value of clean air, water, and a higher quality of life derived from environmental regulations, which often yield a higher return on developers' investment, is difficult to quantify.[4] Such difficult-to-quantify economic benefits include higher property values and lower long-term maintenance and remediation costs. More research must be done to quantify the environmental benefits produced by environmental regulations, such as stormwater management practices and wetlands mitigation. These benefits, however, may not be capitalized in the land and housing market until actors in the market—developers and tenants—can recognize, if not quantify, them as such.

In the end, compliance with environmental regulations is less costly than noncompliance. In Fairfax County, the expense of mitigating breaches of environmental regulatory compliance amounted to an average of 5 percent additional costs to the projects. In all projects where mitigation measures were required, either from a permit in violation or from a failure to acquire the necessary documents, the mitigation costs increased the project costs significantly beyond the normal costs associated with immediate compliance. In other cases, localities may be left footing the bill as developers default on their obligations to comply with agreements and regulations (Turque 2006).

SUMMARY PERSPECTIVES

Overall, it is difficult to show that environmental regulations add much to costs and procedural delays during the case study period (early to mid-2000s) compared with a generation ago (mid- to late 1970s). Although costs have risen nominally, they have remained stable in percentage terms. Also, the research team concludes that the timeframe for project approval has increased very little in spite of conclusive evidence that the regulatory processes have become more complex and demanding. Perhaps the development community, using technical and procedural experts combining more savvy market assessments and technological advances, has offset potentially adverse price effects at least in the case study example. More information on industry improvements is provided by the focus group assessments presented in the next chapter.

SIX

A View from the West

Findings from Denver, Tucson, and Dallas

This chapter reviews the information supplied to the research team from developers and builders in the markets in and surrounding Denver, Colorado; Dallas–Fort Worth, Texas; and Pima County (Tucson), Arizona. These markets were chosen because they allowed a reasonably concentrated view of a region that, by and large, has not had the same level of scholarly scrutiny as others have had.

Although cost analysis data were not made available to the research team in the detailed manner reported by case study participants discussed in chapter 4, the focus groups did provide sufficient information to allow the researchers to conclude that self-reported, environmentally related costs per lot in the three focus group markets were in the normal-to-low range based on the continuum of costs developed in chapter 3, and the costs were about in line with those found in case study projects. Costs varied in dollar amounts, certainly, but not in relative magnitudes given different markets.

In addition, the time-to-approval for focus groups generally can be described as "normal" based on experiences dating back to the 1970s, at which time it took between one and two years for the entire approval process including any zoning relief needed. Compared with the metropolitan

Washington, DC, case study, the focus group representatives indicated that their local governments on the whole appear to process applications a few months faster.

Although the participants in the three focus group markets shared similar frustrations about environmental regulations—particularly due to inconsistent interpretations by the Environmental Protection Agency (EPA), the U.S. Army Corp of Engineers (COE), and the Fish and Wildlife Service—the Tucson participants were more adamant that environmental regulations are a significant barrier to affordable housing. Because only about 15 percent of land in Pima County is privately owned, when a regulation is introduced that includes a land set-aside to protect endangered species or for other reasons, that regulation restricts an already small supply of land available for development. Thus, regions of the western United States, especially the Southwest, that are dominated by public lands have land markets significantly different from other areas of the country, and the effects of environmental regulations on land costs are likely to be more severe.

The focus group participants in each location quickly identified stormwater management as one of the most significant regulations affecting costs. Participants were very confident in estimating the costs, because achieving compliance with this regulation has become a somewhat standard practice. Generally, compliance with federal, state, and local stormwater requirements was reported to run about 4 percent to 5 percent of the total cost of a finished lot, which is comparable to the total percentage of finished lot costs represented by all environmental costs in the case study. In Dallas, the cost was as low as 1 percent.

Despite the heavy influence of federal environmental regulations in each market, regional and local regulations also affect development costs. Most of these regulations either are extensions of the federal regulations or are designed to protect a unique local resource. For example, the Tucson area developers cited protection of the saguaro cactus as a significant barrier or cost. In the Dallas–Fort Worth market, natural gas drilling platforms can place restrictions on development. Similarly, in Denver and Tucson, protection of ridges and slopes are regulated.

Generally, the research team found it difficult to determine if environmental regulations affect the total time required to obtain an approval in the focus group markets. Because most of the environmental regulations were evaluated as part of the overall approval process, isolating the impact of a single regulation was not possible. An exception was the Federal Emergency Management Agency (FEMA) map revision process under the federal floodplain regulations, which clearly adds extensive time to the process.

DENVER, COLORADO

The city and county of Denver are one of the few combined city-county governments in the United States. They are part of the Denver-Aurora Metropolitan Statistical Area (MSA) along with the counties of Adams, Arapahoe, Broomfield, Clear Creek, Douglas, Elbert, Gilpin, Jefferson, and Park. Both Douglas and Adams counties were listed in the top 100 fastest-growing U.S. counties between 2000 and 2004, according to the U.S. Bureau of the Census (see Woods and Poole 2005).

The Denver-Aurora MSA had a population of 2.3 million in 2005 (Woods and Poole 2005). By comparison, Denver County's 2005 population was 557,917. Although rapid growth of more than 18 percent occurred in Denver County from 1900 to 2000, a much slower growth rate of less than 1 percent occurred in the five years after 2000 (see Woods and Poole 2005). Most other counties in the MSA also experienced rapid growth in the 1990s.

Population growth in most counties, as in Denver, has fallen off since 2000. However, some counties such as Adams (which grew 14.8 percent between 2000 and 2005) and Douglas (which grew 41.9 percent in same period) continue to grow faster than the statewide average rate of 8.4 percent during the period 2000 to 2005 (see Woods and Poole 2005).

Metropolitan Denver Economic Development Corporation's (EDC) *Monthly Economic Summary* for July 2006 revealed a mixed view on the local economy. Job growth was stable at about 2.1 percent and the May 2006 unemployment rate of 4.3 percent was the lowest since 2001.

On the other hand, EDC reports record inventories of existing homes, although home sales were also up during the same period from 2005. Likewise foreclosures are running high, and only half of the city-county's eighteen economic indicators are positive (Denver 2006).

The area housing market included 20,751 permits in 2005, including 17,586 for single-family homes (U.S. Bureau of the Census 2008b). The 2005 median price for single-family homes in the MSA was $246,350 compared with $217,492 nationwide (U.S. Bureau of the Census 2008a).

For new homes, the area market has followed a pattern of strong escalation. In 2005, single-family detached homes in the Denver metropolitan area sold for an average of $329,967, an increase of about $80,000 from 2000 (Genesis Group 2008). Prices of attached homes rose by about $40,000 in the same period to $240, 814 (Genesis Group 2008).

Development in the region extends far beyond Denver into the surrounding counties, and is limited to the west by the Rocky Mountains. The region's big growth areas are north from Denver along I-25 and along the "ring" (Rt. 470) that forms a loop around the east side of the city. To the south, there is a gap in activity below Castle Rock until it picks up again near Colorado Springs.

Several of the Denver developers participating in the focus group indicated that they will soon be active in Colorado Springs. They also indicated that growth to the east will pick up, but is not as fast as the other areas around Denver.

A View from the West 129

The Development Process

The development approval process varies according to the jurisdiction. The counties generally are the authority governing development. We selected Denver County to describe the typical process. Keep in mind that the details of the approval process may be slightly different in other surrounding counties.

Local Approval

Information on the development approval process in Denver (city and county) is available at www.denvergov.org. For by-right development, the process begins with preliminary work completed by the applicant to determine if the property falls in a special district (e.g., historic, urban design, view preservation area, commercial corridor, or parkway/boulevard). Where a rezoning is required, the project is subjected to the rezoning process, which is discussed later in this chapter.

The development review includes three phases. During the concept phase, a case manager is assigned. This is followed by a formal phase and the final recordation phase. Each phase is described here, quoted from the city/county's Web site:

1. The concept phase of the site plan review process is designed to provide the applicant and the city with the opportunity to identify all significant and major issues (building location and footprint, orientation, site layout, access issues, required studies, and so on) that will affect the basic design and feasibility of the project. The county will also identify all public health and safety issues. Additional information or required studies necessary for the formal phase will also be identified at this phase. All concept phase conflict must be resolved at this stage. At the conclusion of the concept phase, the applicant and owner will receive a written summary of all comments and expectations, along with an "Authorization to Proceed to Formal Submittal." Both the county and the applicant may rely upon the work done and agreements entered into at this stage for all subsequent aspects of the process. However, if the applicant makes significant changes to their submittal in subsequent phases, the concept phase must be repeated.

2. The formal phase begins with a detailed schematic site plan and proceeds through to the final refinement and approval. This phase provides the county with the information, redesign, and actions required for final approval (i.e., technical data, drainage studies, transportation studies, design review compliance issues, and other requirements), which will enable the county to properly review and approve the project. The majority of engineering plans and studies are completed during the formal phase.
3. The final recordation phase concludes with the signing and recordation of the final plat.

Each phase is a distinct procedure involving the submittal of development plans and supporting technical documents, review team meetings, interagency review of the submittal, and a determination that the submittal is complete (including comments reflecting requirements and expectations for the next phase of the process). Timing for each phase is outlined below and does not include the amount of time required by the applicant to respond to the city's comments and requirements.

The development review process starts upon acceptance of the concept plan by the case manager. At that point, the case manager must schedule a review team meeting to occur ten to fifteen working days later. This is a concurrent review by all of the responsible county agencies. If there are disputes during the review team meeting, the case manager is charged with resolving these among the participants within three working days. Should disputes still exist, a two-stage appeals process must be conducted within twenty working days. Despite the presence of a process and timelines for the concept phase, the results of the concept approval are not binding for either the county or the developer.

Upon approval at the concept phase, a formal submittal is permitted. The formal submittal, including technical data, drainage studies, transportation studies, engineering plans, and similar information, must satisfy the case manager or risk being rejected. Concurrently, the responsible government agencies review the submittal. Fees based on the number of acres of the site are due with the formal submission. For example, a ten-acre site for a planned unit development (PUD) has a fee of $7,000.

A less stringent process is available for minor subdivisions, generally one acre or less in size. Fees for the minor subdivision review are $1,000.

During the review process, Denver staff also addresses requirements for stormwater quality and management. Local government staff enforces local standards and federal standards for sites less than five acres of land disturbance. A site larger than five acres requires a state stormwater permit.

By-right development is limited to county staff reviews for compliance with applicable codes and ordinances. The review team consists of representatives of the public works, parks, and planning departments.

Similar to the concept phase, the formal review phase has some timelines built into the schedule. However, in both the concept and formal phases, the timelines are goals rather than requirements.

The Rezoning Process

According to the developers participating in the focus groups, there is very little land in the Denver-Aurora MSA that does not require a rezoning. Most land outside of the city is zoned for agricultural use. If a developer is requesting a change in zoning, a PUD, or a variance, then a separate application to the planning board is required. Information from the county indicates that the zoning process must be complete before initiating development review. However, the developers we interviewed indicated that rezoning can occur concurrently with the development approval process and does not always result in delays.

Zoning applications are submitted first to the city/county planning department. After staff comments are addressed, the planning board reviews the plan. Finally, the county council must approve all zoning and rezoning applications. Because, as the developers indicated, there are few sites that are by-right development for residential use, the council basically has the final say on all land-use decisions affecting housing.

State Approval
The primary role of the state regarding development is to issue permits for stormwater management under the National Pollutant Discharge Elimination System (NPDES) process enforced by the U.S. Environmental Protection Agency (EPA). The Colorado Department of Public Health and Environment issues a permit upon submittal of an erosion and sedimentation plan by the developer.

Federal Approval

As noted earlier, the Colorado Department of Public Health and Environment, Water Quality Division-Stormwater program is responsible for enforcing EPA stormwater permits under the NPDES. For sites less than five acres, the local government in Denver is approved to administer the permit. Further, for small sites (again less than five acres) that can be shown to have minimal environmental impact based on a rating system employed by the state, developers can apply for a waiver of the state stormwater permit. However, the developers we interviewed believe that a state permit is always required.

Floodplain regulations also fall under the federal government's domain and require Federal Emergency Management Agency (FEMA) approval for development in the floodplain. However, Denver County typically enforces the floodplain regulations at the local level and handles the FEMA submission based on the developer's plans.

Developer Participants

Five high-volume developers/builders participated in the focus group study during August 2006. The participant developers produce from 150 to more than 1,200 building lots per year, primarily single-family housing lots.

Participants included one local volume developer who builds in all the local markets but is now working primarily in Aurora and Castle Rock; a national builder/developer active in all the surrounding areas, including Lowery, Fort Collins, Aurora, and Castle Rock; two regional developer/builders active throughout Denver and the surrounding counties; and a local development/building/management company involved in infill and new urbanist projects in the Denver area.

Summary of Developer Input

This section is based on the comments of the developer participants. There may be differences in their interpretations of the regulatory requirements compared with the actual county requirements. When discrepancies occur, we attempt to present the views obtained from separate interviews with members of the Denver County staff. The developers also discussed their experiences with the approval process and regulations in a general sense and noted that there are differences in some jurisdictions. Where these differences are relevant to our objectives related to environmental regulations, they are addressed in this section.

Major Environmental Regulations
The developers quickly identified three issues as the most significant environmental regulations in the Denver area—stormwater management, Endangered Species Act (ESA) requirements, and wetlands regulations.

Stormwater Management — This issue typically involves the county development department enforcing local stormwater and erosion and sediment regulations as well as the state health department enforcing NPDES permit requirements. A permit is required from the county as part of the local land development application process. A second permit is required from the state. The developers indicated that the county will often ask if the state permit is in hand before granting final local approval. Permit requirements from the state were viewed to be less difficult because they basically consist of the erosion and sediment plan that is typically required as part of the county application process.

ESA Requirements — Formal responsibility for enforcement of the ESA falls under the U.S. Fish and Wildlife Service (FWS), although the developers stated that the local jurisdictions require federal approval to be obtained as part of their review process. The county staff we interviewed indicated that they recommend having the federal approval but it is not a requirement.

Typically a letter of certification is requested from FWS and, if the site is not impacted by the ESA, the certification is granted with an expiration date, meaning that the developer must reapply from time to time to continue working at a site. The developers noted that their certification letters were as short as one to three years.

Typical restrictions surrounding the ESA include preservation of habitat and a surrounding buffer. In the Denver region, the Preble Jumping Mouse is the most often encountered endangered species. Other endangered species in the region include rare rats, orchids, toads, and migratory birds.

The developers' uneasiness with the ESA requirements seemed to be due primarily to the ever-changing nature and the unknowns in the process. The developers stated that they typically avoid land shown to be impacted by the ESA. However, even if they believe the site is free of endangered species, the ESA process allows later surprises that can stop or severely limit development after substantial resources have been invested in the property. The developers believe there should be more certainty at the beginning of the process to reduce the risk of losing their investment.

The changing nature of the ESA regulatory process also seems to be a large barrier to development. For example, when a developer reapplies for a certification letter, a different opinion can be issued seemingly arbitrarily by the FWS; these kinds of reversals can result in mitigation costs and lost lots.

Another murky issue is the inclusion of threatened species by the FWS. The developers claim there are no clear rules for threatened species and decisions from FWS appear arbitrary.

Wetlands Regulations — Wetlands regulations are enforced by the Denver region of the U.S Army Corp of Engineers (COE). For participant developers, the most frustrating issue they face regarding wetlands regulations is that the process seems to be somewhat subjective. The developers stated that they do not believe upland or isolated wetlands are covered under the federal statutes, but, apparently, the local office does.

Developers stated that the easiest way for them to secure approval from the COE is to hire a consultant who is well known by COE reviewers, and they noted that decisions often vary depending on the reviewer. When a ruling is made, a developer is typically given five years before a new certification letter is required.

Although technically not required, developers we interviewed submit every site to the COE for a determination, even if they and their consultants believed the site had no wetlands. Developers thought that not doing so would risk an adverse ruling later due to the subjective nature of the process.

The counties do not usually get involved in wetlands permit issues. However, the developers stated that the local jurisdictions typically will require the federal certification letter to be in hand during the review process. Like the ESA issues, the Denver County staff we interviewed indicated that they do not require COE approval, but they do recommend it.

Other Less Significant Environmental Regulations
A few of the local counties have their own environmental regulations, including those related to view preservation, tree planting ordinances, noise reduction, and light pollution. For the most part, the developers did not see these as difficult compliance issues because they happen rarely or because complying with them is not particularly costly.

Noise abatement is required only near certain districts affected by air traffic, and noise abatement is very rarely required for traffic or other sources. Some local jurisdictions are promoting methods to reduce light pollution, but, like noise, this is not a big issue yet.

Denver has a ridgeline or view preservation ordinance that limits building heights, but this rarely affects single-family housing. Aurora County is one of the few jurisdictions in the MSA with a tree-planting ordinance, but the developers stated they did not believe it was much of a burden. In fact, several developers said they plant more trees than required to make their homes more appealing to buyers. The one exception is when tree planting issues get expensive, such as when a county planner requires the planting of street trees in addition to requiring trees on individual lots.

Mineral Exploration Cleanup — This is not typically a regulatory issue for the developer, but more of a potential liability due to previous use of the land. All of the developers in the study had faced this issue before because much of the land near the Denver metropolitan area has been previously explored for oil, gas, or minerals. Previous exploration on the land is regulated by the Colorado Oil and Gas Conservation Commission (COGCC). The developers claim that the COGCC sets bonds on the exploration or mining operations that are so low that the companies often just forfeit the bond and walk away from the site. Thus, if a problem is discovered later, the builder or developer is stuck with the cleanup.

Due diligence on the part of the developer is the best protection against unknown mitigation costs. However, this is not a guarantee that future problems will not arise. Typically this would include relocation of gas lines or removal of asbestos pipes. If an extensive cleanup is necessary, then it is possible that the Colorado Health Department or EPA may become involved. This latter scenario is rare.

Floodplain Regulations — None of the participants discussed floodplain regulations during the initial meeting. One of the regional builder/developers later indicated that they have faced some floodplain issues but considered them to be minor.

Perceptions about Costs of Regulations

The developers identified stormwater management, endangered species, and wetlands as the regulations with the greatest potential cost impact. They have the best understanding of the costs associated with stormwater management (including erosion and sediment control), which they estimate to be around 4 to 5 percent of the total development cost (the cost to get from purchase through finished lot, not including house construction costs). This was independent of the type of development (greenfield, redevelopment, or infill). On a per-lot basis, the costs are in the range of $300 to $1,000 per lot.

The developers stated that they generally believe that wetlands and ESA compliance costs are too site dependent to provide a general range of costs. Much of the land in the region has no wetlands, so most of the costs are related to obtaining a certification letter from the federal government. One developer did estimate that his costs are typically about 2.5 percent each for wetlands and ESA issues. Another developer indicated that wetlands costs can be as high as 50 percent of development costs if mitigation is required.

For tree planting, the developers believed costs related to the regulations are less than 1 percent of costs per lot, or otherwise negligible.

Another way to assess costs is to compare local costs to the Washington metropolitan area case studies.

The developers believe the Washington metropolitan area costs are similar to those found in Denver for wetlands delineation and permitting (about 0.15 percent or less for each), but that the wetlands mitigation costs are too variable to compare to the Washington metropolitan area.

Likewise, the Washington metropolitan area experience with stormwater management and erosion and sediment costs are similar to those experienced by developers in Denver. They typically run about 5 percent of development costs for these items.

The costs of tree preservation in Denver, comparable to those found in the case study, are less than 1 percent. Most developers do more than the local governments require because the market expects it.

Approval Timeframe

The development process for by-right development generally takes nine to eighteen months depending on the jurisdiction. However, by-right development is rare in the Denver area, since most land outside the city is zoned agricultural. Rezoning or some variance is almost always required and can generally add three to eighteen more months to the approval process depending on the local jurisdiction and the complexity of the development. Some extreme cases have taken up to five years.

Stormwater management usually is part of the general application process so it does not add to the nine- to eighteen-month timeframe for a typical by-right development. If present, wetlands issues can add nine to twelve months, and ESA issues can add up to twenty-four months for approval, but each case is highly variable.

Developers try to get these processes moving concurrently to minimize delays. They could not give specific costs for delays, but indicated that they use a simple calculation based on their loan amounts and the interest paid on money borrowed.

The county staff we interviewed indicated that the time periods cited by the developers were probably accurate. One staff member noted that the Denver mayor is aware of the long timeframes and had proposed changes to speed up the process.

Other Looming Issues

Although not an environmental regulation, the developers cited a developing threat to the affordability of housing in the form of voter initiatives. Developers discussed the fact that citizens have a right to collect enough support to put the approval of zoning decisions on the election ballot. Op-

Discussion of the Denver Process and Regulations

Developers in the Denver area do not appear to face as many restrictions on development related to environmental regulations as developers in the Washington metropolitan market. However, they believe that many more environmental regulations are on the way and already are being discussed in the local regulatory environment.

Costs for compliance are similar to those identified in the case study projects. For tree preservation, the developers often voluntarily spend more than developers in Maryland and Virginia.

The participants indicated that compliance with most local environmental regulations is not a significant barrier. From a regulatory perspective, the unknowns and inconsistencies in federal regulations and decisions are the most worrisome environmental issues. They also noted that regulations can be an avenue for opposition groups to use to slow down development.

Projects requiring zoning changes caused participants even more concern. This concern was evident in their claims that a development application can take up to three years for approval of a project that requires rezoning.

Dallas–Fort Worth–Plano Market

The area of study for this location is defined as the Dallas–Fort Worth–Arlington, Texas, metropolitan statistical area (MSA). The primary growth areas identified by the participants generally falls within a triangle formed by the city of Dallas to the south and Plano and McKinney on the northern end. Growth is also healthy in the areas surrounding Fort Worth, although it is confined to a more compact area than in the Dallas side of the MSA.

Brief descriptions of some selected jurisdictions in the MSA are as follows:

- **Dallas:** In 2000, the city of Dallas had a population of 1.2 million (U.S. Bureau of the Census 2008b), making it the eighth-largest city in the nation. Although rapid growth of 18.1 percent (U.S. Bureau of the Census 2008b) occurred in Dallas from 1990 to 2000, a much slower growth rate of less than 2 percent occurred in the three years after 2000. Most other cities in Texas also experienced rapid growth in the 1990s.

The city of Dallas had 2.6 percent employment growth in June of 2006. The professional and business services sectors are responsible for most of the job growth taking place in Dallas. Meanwhile, the unemployment rate in June 2006 was 4.9 percent, just above the national average.

The housing market included 3,497 building permits (5,789 units) in 2005, of which 3,353 were for single-family homes (U.S. Bureau of the Census 2008a). The 2005 median single-family home price in the city of Dallas was $165,000 compared with $189,500 in Dallas County, and $217,492 nationwide (U.S. Bureau of the Census 2008b).

- **Dallas County:** In 2000, the county of Dallas had a population of 2.2 million (U.S. Bureau of the Census 2008b), tenth largest in the nation.

The Federal Deposit Insurance Corporation (FDIC) reported that Dallas County had a healthy 3.7 percent growth in employment for the first quarter of 2006. Meanwhile, the unemployment rate remained stable at 5.5 percent in the first quarter of 2006.

The housing market included 10,749 building permits (14,404 units) in 2005, including 10,520 for single-family homes (U.S. Bureau of the Census 2008). The 2005 median single-family home price for Dallas County was $189,500 (U.S. Bureau of the Census 2008).

- **Plano:** In 2000, the city of Plano had a population of 222,030 (U.S. Bureau of the Census 2008b). Although growth of 72.8 percent (U.S. Bureau of the Census 2008b) occurred in Plano from 1990 to 2000, the growth rate slowed to 9 percent in the three years after 2000. The city of Plano had just lower than 3 percent employment growth in May of 2006. Meanwhile, the unemployment rate in May 2006 remained steady at 4.9 percent, just above the national average.

The housing market included 1,409 building permits in 2005, of which 803 were for single-family homes (U.S. Bureau of the Census 2008a). The 2005 median single-family home price in the city of Plano was $162,300 (U.S. Bureau of the Census 2008b).

- **Fort Worth:** In 2000, the city of Fort Worth had a population of 535,000 (U.S. Bureau of the Census 2008b). Although rapid growth of 19.3 percent (U.S. Census Bureau of the Census 2008b) occurred in Fort Worth from 1990 to 2000, the growth rate slowed to 8.1 percent in the three years after 2000.

  The city of Fort Worth had less than 1 percent employment growth in May of 2006. Meanwhile, the unemployment rate in May 2006 remained steady at 4.8 percent, just above the national average.

  The housing market included 10,267 building permits (12,457 units) in 2005, of which 10,046 were for single-family homes (U.S. Bureau of the Census 2008a). The 2005 median single-family home price in the city of Fort Worth was $147,200 (U.S. Bureau of the Census 2008b).

Overall population growth in most Texas cities has slowed since 2000. However, some cities such as Plano (which grew 9.0 percent between 2000 and 2003) and Fort Worth (which grew 8.1 percent in the same period) continued to grow faster than the statewide rate of 6.1 percent over the first three years of the twenty-first century.

The Dallas–Fort Worth new home construction market has remained strong through mid-2006 despite the national downturn. According to the *Dallas Morning News* ("New Homes Extend Surge," August 24, 2006), the median new home price was $179,000 as of the second quarter of 2006.

The Development Process

Local Approval
Development in the area is almost all greenfield development, although infill plots are becoming more common in cities such as Plano. There is little redevelopment. This is mostly due to the large supply of land and the resulting choice that developers have in selecting a parcel of land to purchase.

Although jurisdictions vary in their requirements, they also have much in common in terms of the approval processes for residential development. According to the developer/builder participants in the study, all platting, zoning, and similar development issues are regulated by the city or other incorporated jurisdiction. In unincorporated areas, the county is the land-use authority. Exceptions to local control are discussed below for state and federal approvals.

For by-right development, the local city staff reviews the plan for conformance with local requirements and subdivision ordinances. The developers estimate this process takes about twelve months until approval is granted.

If a rezoning or variance is involved, then the process typically involves a planning staff review, a zoning commission approval, and city council approval. This stretches out the process for approval to about eighteen to twenty-four months.

There is no time limit on zoning decisions. However, Texas has a thirty-day statutory time limit for platting of subdivisions. The developers stated that they often face multiple delays beyond this time limit, but they said they risk disapproval if they do not agree to extensions when requested.

Responsibilities at the local level focus on conformance with zoning and subdivision ordinances, including the typical plat, streets, lot size, setbacks, landscaping, engineering, and similar requirements. A specific example of the process using Plano as an example is discussed in the next section. This information was provided during an interview with representatives from the city planning department and from information on the city's Web site.

Plano Approval Process

An application for a single-family detached residential development in Plano must first be submitted to the planning department. The process includes two steps that require a preapplication conference and a third final plat approval step.

Step 1 requires submission of a land study, general tree survey, conveyance plat, and stormwater management plan.
Step 2 adds a landscape plan and preliminary plat, as well as a specific tree survey.

Step 3 can be initiated only after public improvements are completed. This results in the final plat approval.

By state law, the plat approval must be granted or disapproved within thirty days. Plano (and most other jurisdictions) meets this requirement by granting a preliminary approval in the first stage of the process, but the approval is conditional on the pending engineering approval and completion of public improvements. This condition at least partially explains why the developers in this study estimated approval time at twelve months.

The primary objectives of the Plano review are to ensure compliance with the zoning and subdivision ordinances. This includes a SWPPP (stormwater pollution prevention plan) and a floodplain review. Plano officials enforce their own floodplain requirements but also submit the plan to FEMA for federal approval.

The Plano staff makes a recommendation for approval or disapproval to the City Planning and Zoning Commission, which meets twice a month to consider plat and zoning issues. Typically within this timeframe there is a markup and resubmission period before it goes to the commission for a decision.

Although there is no state requirement for a time limit on zoning applications, zoning applications in Plano follow a similar process as for plats. First the application must be submitted to the planning department. The staff provides a markup and the developer submits a corrected plan. Within about five weeks from a twice-monthly submittal deadline, the plan with staff recommendations is heard by the Planning and Zoning Commission. Unlike the platting process, the city council also must approve zoning applications.

The City of Plano has a schedule that shows about a two-month timeframe from submittal to a city council decision. Developers insisted that it takes much longer (as much as eighteen to twenty-four months) because they are often forced to withdraw applications at several points along the way and start over. However, none of the developers in this study spoke specifically about Plano and its processes.

State Approval

The state of Texas has limited involvement in land-use issues. The state's primary responsibility is to issue permits under the federal NPDES regulations for stormwater management and water quality. Although the state issues the permit for stormwater management, in many cases it is the local inspector that actually enforces the regulations.

The state stormwater management process consists of submission of an application that is used by the state to issue a permit. There are no plan reviews involved. The developer participants described this as more of a database than a permit process.

Federal Approval

Technically, the federal government regulates stormwater management under the EPA's NPDES program, the ESA through the U.S. Fish and Wildlife Service, wetlands management through the U.S. Army COE, and floodplains through FEMA. However, from the developers' perspective, stormwater management is the primary issue that has a large impact on a typical development in the Dallas area.

Arguably, there are few endangered species in the Dallas area. Given the abundant supply of land, developers typically avoid land with these issues and thus avoid interaction with the U.S. Fish and Wildlife Service on almost all projects.

Similar to the ESA issues, wetlands are not typically encountered in the Dallas area. One developer estimates less than 10 percent of sites are affected in any way by wetlands.

FEMA involvement is limited to sites in the floodplain, and developers indicated that complying with these regulations is not difficult. However, FEMA approval can hold up a site because the approval process is typically very slow.

Additional information on the local, state, and federal regulations and processes is provided in the following sections that cover input from the developers and local planning officials.

Developer Participants

Four participants were interviewed as part of the study during August 2006. Two of the participants are from the top ten largest builders in the United States, and they build several thousand homes in the Dallas market each year. Two other participants are from civil engineering/planning firms that support several of the other largest builder/developers in the area. One firm develops plans for about 1,200 lots annually and the other designs plans for around 4,000 lots. All of the participants deal primarily with single-family housing.

The participant activity is spread out in almost all of the incorporated areas in and surrounding Fort Worth and the Dallas-Plano-McKinney region.

Summary of Developer Input

This section is based primarily on the comments of the developer participants. Where there are differences in the developer interpretations of the regulatory requirements compared with information given by county requirements or planners, additional information from government sources is provided.

The developers discussed the approval process and regulations in a general sense and noted that there are differences in some jurisdictions. For example, depending on the jurisdiction, tree preservation regulations run from none at all to being very restrictive and costly.

Major Environmental Regulations That Affect Housing Development
The developers quickly identified two issues as the most significant environmental regulations in the Dallas–Fort Worth area—stormwater management and tree preservation. Other regulatory concerns, such as wetlands, floodplains, and endangered species were also raised but were viewed as much less significant than tree preservation and stormwater management regulations.

Stormwater Management — This issue typically involves the local planning department or development department's enforcing local stormwater and erosion and sediment control regulations as well as the Texas Commission of Environmental Quality's (TCEQ) enforcing the federal NPDES permit requirements. In addition, a separate permit is required from the state. The permit requirements from the state were not viewed as onerous because they basically consist of an application and a $100 fee to enter the development into a database.

The developer's design team will typically produce a SWPPP (stormwater pollution prevention plan) for the local jurisdiction, but it is not required to be submitted to the TCEQ.

Local inspections are performed in Dallas and Fort Worth by city staff. Plano is instituting a plan to administer stormwater management permits on behalf of the state. Currently, Plano and most other local jurisdictions have inspectors who will look over the site for general plan conformance and may ask to see that the state permit has been secured, but often the state or EPA inspectors are left to oversee field compliance. Because they have few inspectors, the end result is the developer must voluntarily comply with their SWPPP.

Without strict enforcement, developers generally file SWPPPs to create a paper trail to reduce the potential for liability. (Most cities also have a "mud in the street" ordinance that requires builders to keep the streets clean.) The cost to the developer for a typical SWPPP is about $300 to $400 per lot in erosion control, planning, and maintenance. The same amount can be expected to be incurred by the builder once home construction commences.

Tree Removal and Preservation — Trees are rare on the plains, so all cities in the area (with few exceptions) have ordinances requiring tree preservation and replanting. Some cities require an inch-for-inch replacement for all trees removed. Others limit protection to certain species and caliper of tree.

The most significant tree preservation cost to the developer is in surveying trees. This typically costs about $20 per tree. A recent project cited as an example spent $100,000 to survey a 400-acre site.

Tree surveying often needs to be done before the developer is granted approval to develop on the land. The process can take from one to three months prior to submission of a plan for approval.

If a developer cannot plant all the trees on the site, they can donate money to a tree fund or plant trees elsewhere (e.g., medians). However, Dallas is no longer accepting alternatives to site planting because the city is unable to meet water needs of street trees.

Other Less Significant Environmental Regulations

Wetlands "404" Regulations — The participants agreed that wetlands are not much of a problem because the area's concerns relate more to headwaters than to waters of the United States. Most developers stated that they do not apply for a determination from COE. They claim this would shut down development because of the excessive time it takes to receive an answer. The typical approach is to simply avoid any areas where there may be wetlands. Developers who do not go through the COE run the risk of repercussions, but participants indicated that they do not believe there are enough wetlands for this to be much of a risk. Local jurisdictions may include wetlands on their checklist, but they generally accept the developer's civil engineer's or consultant's report on wetlands.

At least one of the largest developers in the market takes a different route and submits every project to the COE. However, even in this case, very few sites end up having applicable wetlands or requiring mitigation or other action.

ESA Requirements — The TCEQ application for stormwater management requires a sign-off that the developer is compliant with the ESA. This is a self-certification process. The developers claim that endangered species are rare in this area and they do not incur cost or delays related to the ESA.

Floodplains — Although floodplain management may not technically have environmental protections as its main objective, this issue was raised by the participants not as one that necessarily raises construction costs for the developer directly, but as something that can delay the ability to start home construction for twelve months or longer once the lots are finished. This is not an issue for all development but only those where the floodplain has been delineated and a plan must be submitted to FEMA.

A "letter of map revision" generally must be secured to begin home construction. The path of the permit application to FEMA flows first to the local jurisdiction, which submits it to the FEMA regional office in Denton, which submits it to FEMA's Washington, DC, office. A contractor (Michael Baker Engineers at the present time) then makes a determination on the application. The time required can be nine months to one year, although several examples of up to two or three years were cited.

Cities often let developers move forward at their own risk in anticipation of FEMA's report. Floodplain rules are much more objective than they are for wetlands. Thus, the issue is not compliance (which is easy enough to do), but the time required to make this happen.

Septic Systems — Very few septic systems are used in the area. Typically, they require a one-acre minimum lot. State (TCEQ) and local jurisdictions regulate septic systems. However, most developers figure out how to get sewer to a site so they can build a denser development.

Natural Gas Drilling Regulations — Although not technically an environmental regulation in terms of its objectives, gas drilling regulations were identified as a smaller concern by developers. Gas pad sites seem to be popping up everywhere in the area. For example, a developer typically cannot buy a parcel of land in Fort Worth without a natural gas site. The state requires that development must stay 200 feet away from the wellhead, but cities can require up to 600 feet. Typically the state determines where drilling can occur and the railroad commission authorizes a permit, but the county or city enforces development restrictions. Gas wells can be developed after building starts (called a high-impact zone), but then it is the gas companies' responsibility to ensure that the setback requirements are met.

Developers may lose some lots because of gas drilling or they may have to discount others. However, generally, they know what they are getting before the land purchase and often have the choice to buy elsewhere.

Perceptions about Costs of Regulations

The participants believe that most environmental regulations can be avoided by selective purchase of land. There is enough land in the Dallas–Fort Worth area that problem sites can be avoided for now.

Developer participants stated that all their sites were affected by stormwater management regulations. Further, stormwater management costs were thought to be much lower than the 5 percent in the Maryland-Virginia area used as a benchmark for comparison. The participants estimated $300 to $400 per lot or less than 1 percent of total development costs (including land purchase price) were required for stormwater management compliance. This is also less than the estimates provided in a separate study involving Denver developers.

About 75 to 80 percent of local jurisdictions have tree preservation ordinances. The participants estimated that a heavily treed area could cost 3 percent to 5 percent of development costs, which is much greater than costs seen in the Maryland-Virginia and Denver areas. Much of the cost is in the upfront survey.

When wetlands are applicable, the developers agreed that the Maryland-Virginia study costs of less than 1 percent were consistent with cost in the Dallas region, but again stressed that wetlands regulations are rarely applicable. One large developer stressed that although wetlands do not affect many sites, there is typically a minimum $20,000 cost to conduct the upfront study to make this determination.

Other regulations were so rarely applicable that estimates were not provided. Floodplain issues may cause delays if FEMA does not review the plan quickly. No estimates were provided on these costs but they are basically the carrying cost of the development and land purchase costs.

Approval Timeframe

The development process for by-right development generally takes about twelve months and eighteen to twenty-four months when a rezoning is required.

The planners from Plano and Fort Worth both disagreed with the timeframes identified by the developer participants. The planners insisted that approval for a by-right development is thirty days as mandated by Texas law.

A likely explanation for the differences in opinion over approval time is the way each group views the term "approval." For a developer, approval is the point at which they can move lots or start home construction. The planners viewed plat approval by the planning commission as the approval. However, both sides acknowledged that the plat approval is not really final but subject to engineering approval and final plat recording.

The review of most environmental issues runs concurrent with the subdivision review or is a part of it, so time is not necessarily added to the schedule for these regulations. The one main exception is in obtaining a FEMA map revision for a floodplain.

In some cases, FEMA actually may increase the amount of available land for building because the FEMA determination is based on the planned site conditions after development. However, the developers cited the time for FEMA review as a potentially serious delay. Developers can proceed at their own risk after the local approval is given, but often they are forced to wait up to twelve months after local approval before they can start building homes. Depending on the market conditions (if the builder will buy pending FEMA approval), either the developer or the builder would have to carry the costs of waiting for FEMA approval. Again, it should be stressed that the floodplain regulations do not impact all sites.

Other Observations about Restrictions on Housing Development
The participants stressed that Texas is all about property rights and they have been slow to embrace restrictions on development. However, the rise in tree preservation ordinances and much discussion at the local level about "green building" has sent a message that more and more environmental regulations will be the norm in the future.

Discussion of the Dallas Process and Regulations

There do not appear to be as many environmental regulations that have a practical impact on residential development in the Dallas region as we found in the Maryland-Virginia or Denver markets, but many are on the way and being discussed in the regulatory environment. In fact, the market, with a few exceptions, is not highly regulated compared with the other parts of the United States.

Except for tree ordinances, stormwater management, and to a lesser extent, FEMA floodplain reviews, most environmental regulations were not considered significant problems for the participants in this study. Although some participants cited extreme examples where regulations have had a large impact on development costs, typically a developer can avoid most environmental regulations because there is a large supply of (environmentally uncomplicated) land that they can select for development.

Costs to comply with most environmental regulations are similar to those seen in the Maryland-Virginia study for major items, but again most are rarely applicable.

The developers also noted that there are many regulations on the horizon.

PIMA COUNTY (TUCSON), ARIZONA

Pima County, which includes the city of Tucson, is located south of Phoenix and extends to the United States–Mexico border. The county population in 2005 was about 925,000 (Woods and Poole Economics 2007). This compares with a population of approximately 6 million for all of Arizona. Although population growth in Pima County has lagged behind the 40 percent rate for Arizona in the period from 1990 to 2000, it has still managed a 26.5 percent increase in population during the 1990s (Woods and Poole Economics 2005).

On a base of 397,150 existing homes, the county issued 10,541 permits for new homes in 2004 (U.S. Bureau of the Census 2008a). About 75 percent of homes in the county are single-family detached units. The median sales price for all homes in the county for 2005 was $202,957 and the average was $238,058 (Bright Future Business Consultants 2006). For new homes, the 2005 average and median prices were $245,804 and $219,068, respectively (Bright Future Business Consultants 2006). This represents an increase of more than $85,000, or roughly 54 percent, over 2000 average new home prices.

The median household income was $37,454 (U.S. Bureau of the Census 2008b) in the county and $41,963 throughout Arizona. Unemployment in 2005 was at 4.6 percent, down from a peak of 5.6 percent in 2002 according to the (U.S. Department of Agriculture 2005).

Most development is on open or "greenfield" parcels. There is minimal infill or redevelopment in Tucson—most development is in the county.

The Development Process

The process for approval of a residential development in Pima County is similar to that of many jurisdictions around the country. There is a mix of local, state, and federal regulations and processes, although most activity is at the county level.

Local Requirements

For a by-right development where existing zoning has established a legal right to build at a certain density, the county staff reviews the application and the County Board of Supervisors (BOS) votes on an administrative action for final approval. For developments requiring zoning action, the county staff makes recommendations to the County Planning Commission. The commission then makes a recommendation to the BOS, who is responsible for final approval or denial. The staff and planning commission roles are advisory. The BOS can accept or reject their recommendations.

There are no statutory limits on the time for approval or denial of a development or zoning action. According to the county staff person we interviewed, the process typically takes about twelve months for a project that does not involve a rezoning action and an additional six months if rezoning is involved.

Applications are initially submitted to the Pima County Development Review Division. Although other agencies are also required to review the plans, the Development Review Division will frequently provide feedback to applicants on how other agencies' requirements may impact the development.

The county's development review division also reviews paving, grading, drainage, and sanitary sewer construction plans for new developments in accordance with the Department of Transportation and Flood Control District, the Wastewater Management Department, and the Department of Environmental Quality.

Development review coordinates with all other departments within public works when questions requiring policy interpretation arise.

County staff also addresses some federal issues. For example, the county requests that applications be submitted to the U.S. Army COE if wetlands are involved. The county also enforces stormwater management issues that overlap with federal and state regulations. However, the developer also must submit an application to the Arizona Department of Environmental Quality (DEQ) for stormwater management.

Developers must also submit an application to the Regional Flood Control District. This is a separate legal entity from the county, although the BOS members also oversee their activities.

The Regional Flood Control District reviews the development application for compliance with riparian zone regulations (a separate local ordinance) and county floodplain requirements. The Regional Flood Control District also submits the proposed plan to FEMA for compliance with federal floodplain regulations.

For developments requiring rezoning applications, the planning and zoning staff prepares comments, which are forwarded to the planning commission for their review and comments before going to the BOS for a final determination.

Currently, rezoning applications must also comply with the county's habitat preservation plan, which meets the intent of parts of a larger plan called the Sonoran Desert Conservation Plan.

State Approval

The primary role of the state regarding development is to issue permits for stormwater management under the NPDES process enforced by the EPA. The Arizona Department of Environmental Quality (DEQ) requires developers to submit an application before beginning development activities. Similar to other states, the primary purpose of this application is to record the project in the county's development database.

The state also has native plants requirements, and it is the developer's responsibility to secure this review and approval, similar to federal ESA permits.

Federal Approval

As mentioned earlier, the Arizona DEQ is responsible for enforcing federal stormwater permits under the NPDES.

Floodplain regulations are also under the federal government's domain and require FEMA approval for building in the floodplain. However, the Regional Flood Control District typically enforces the floodplain regulations at the local level and handles the FEMA submission based on the developer's plans.

The county representative was not sure if a builder could start construction without a FEMA letter of map revision. A staff member from the Regional Flood Control District clarified that a conditional letter of map revision from FEMA is required prior to issuance of building permits (for lots within the original floodplain limits). Before final approval of the map revision by FEMA, permits will be issued but lots must meet elevation criteria if within the original floodplain limits. The extent of the floodplain limits are often broader than what FEMA has identified, since the county has a stricter definition of the hundred-year floodplain than FEMA.

Each of the regulations or ordinances identified here is discussed in more detail later in this report.

Developer Participants

Input from the development community was obtained from six participants during a meeting on September 2006 at the Southern Arizona Home Builders Association (HBA) facility in Tucson and a follow-up interview with a developer who could not make the HBA meeting. Participants included one local developer with an active ninety-nine-unit inner-city development, two national builders who develop and build more than 1,000 homes each year in the Tucson area, a national builder who entered the market in the past eighteen months and currently has about 300 active building lots, a local building consultant who specializes in regulations and their cost impact, and the president and a senior staff member of the Home Builders Association.

The developer participants primarily develop single-family housing lots on greenfield parcels, although a couple have some smaller active infill sites.

Summary of Developer Input

This section is based on the comments of the developer participants. As noted for the previous focus groups, there may be differences in their interpretations of the regulatory requirements than as described in the county requirements. When discrepancies occurred, we attempt to present the views obtained from separate interviews with Pima County staff. The developers discussed the approval process and regulations in a general sense and, where relevant, noted regulatory differences among local jurisdictions.

This summary is not a comprehensive review of all environmental regulation. Rather, it is focused on the issues identified by participants in the study as having the most significant impact on residential development.

Major Environmental Regulations

The developers identified a series of the most significant environmental regulations in the Tucson–Pima County area. From the discussion, it was clear that the participants see stormwater management as a key issue. In fact, they tended to discuss multiple issues as if they were subsets of or arise out of the stormwater management regulations. From the developer's perspective, it was not important where the requirements originated, but rather that they are all issues that they have to address as part of their development plan. Thus, the discussion started with general remarks regarding the NPDES regulations to other federal regulations, including wetlands and endangered species, as well as local conservation regulations and stormwater issues. All of these issues are presented below as individual items along with hillside and ridge conservation, native plant preservation, and floodplain issues.

It is noted that the participants had a difficult time keeping the various regulations separate during the discussion, due to the significant amount of overlap among the various ordinances at all levels of government. The categories used in the following sections attempt to group regulations according to the perception of the developer participants.

Stormwater Management — This issue typically involves the county's enforcing local stormwater and erosion and sediment control regulations as well as the state DEQ's enforcing the federal NPDES requirements. Approval is part of the local land development application process, where a stormwater pollution prevention plan is required. However, a separate approval is required from the state. The developers indicated that the requirements from the state consisted of an application that puts them on record with the DEQ and submission of their stormwater pollution prevention plan. The state may conduct some periodic inspections.

The subject of riparian protection areas was also raised as part of the stormwater discussion. From a review and enforcement perspective, it is easy to see how the development community views this as part of the stormwater management regulations. However, it is triggered by a separate ordinance under the Sonoran Desert Conservation Plan, discussed later.

Species/Habitat Protection — For this discussion, the participants identified separate but related regulations from local, state, and federal agencies.

At the top of the list is the U.S. FWS process for enforcing ESA requirements. According to participants, the FWS currently list fifty-five species of wildlife or plants as endangered or threatened in Pima County.

Typically a letter of certification or permit is requested from FWS by the developer. The county requires FWS approval before local approval for a development is granted.

One twist in the enforcement of the regulations is the introduction of multiple federal agency requirements regarding the ESA. Although the primary responsibility falls on the U.S. FWS, the U.S. Army COE also has taken an active role in requiring FWS approval before they will take final action on a wetlands application. According to the Pima County representative, this is required of the COE by federal statute, even if it has not been common practice in the past.

In addition, the state has identified its own list of species that must be protected, which is enforced by the Arizona Department of Agriculture's Native Plants Division. Similar to the federal ESA, the developer is responsible for securing the state approval from the Native Plants Division.

The county also has an ordinance for native plants. According to the participants, the saguaro cactus is the most troubling of the protected species. A survey by a plant professional can be expensive. Further, the participants claimed they are required to move each Saguaro to a protected area and plant two new ones for each one that is moved, or set aside the land from development.

Wetlands — The wetlands regulations are enforced by the U.S. Army COE. The developer is responsible for determining whether or not it is necessary to submit a permit application to the COE. Typically, the developer relies on a report or advice from their civil engineering firm or a wetlands specialist to determine whether a specific site falls under the wetlands regulations. The participants stated that they are most concerned about inconsistencies and ambiguities in the way the COE makes determinations. They are aware of developers who have been "burned" because they believed their site did not have wetlands, or waters of the United States, but the COE later made a contrary determination.

Floodplain — Participants identified the regulations for floodplains enforced by FEMA as some of the more restrictive environmental issues in Pima County. Part of the issue is due to FEMA's process and part is related to the county's enforcement of floodplain requirements.

At the federal level, FEMA can take up to twelve months to provide a letter of map revision. The request cannot be submitted until the building pads are in place and at appropriate elevations. In the past, home construction could start but on an at-risk basis for the builder. Pima County (through the Regional Flood Control District) has instituted restrictions that limit the ability to move forward with construction even under an at-risk scenario. Participants stated that the county now only allows building in areas outside of the original floodplain until the FEMA approval is in place. However, a representative of the Regional Flood Control District clarified that construction can move forward if a conditional letter is provided by FEMA and the homes are elevated to meet the FEMA requirements.

Hillside Development Overlay Zone — This is a Pima County ordinance designed to protect ridge tops and steep slopes by restricting development in applicable areas.

Sonoran Desert Conservation Plan (Riparian Areas) — This is a comprehensive plan with many different objectives that overlap other regulations reviewed earlier. The builders identified two parts of the plan that significantly impact housing development. The first part is the actual restrictions placed on development in the form of conservation areas that must be left in a natural or undisturbed state. The second issue is the plan's objective of using public funds to purchase and conserve lands. This second issue was raised by the participants several times throughout the discussions because they believe it has a large impact on home costs by reducing the supply of buildable land.

A subset of the plan is the Conservation Lands System (CLS). This is applicable to residential developments that are being rezoned, waivers to the zoning ordinance, and to comprehensive plan amendments and specific plan requests. By-right developments are not covered.

Many of the requirements under the CLS are covered in other ordinances and regulations. The one specific and unique part of the CLS that was cited by the participants in this study is referred to as "Important Riparian Areas." This part of the CLS is triggered by floodplain use permits enforced by the Regional Flood Control District.

According to the CLS as amended June 21, 2005, the following is applicable regarding riparian areas: "At least 95 percent of the total acreage of lands within this designation shall be conserved in a natural or undisturbed condition" (Pima County 2005).

For the developer/builder participants, this basically equates to a total restriction on areas that are covered. The participants questioned the value of the definitions for riparian areas that are basically dry and isolated from other waterways or habitat areas.

Perceptions about Costs of Regulations

The developers identified stormwater management as the regulation with the greatest potential cost impact. They have the best understanding of the costs associated with stormwater management (including erosion and sediment control), which they estimate to be about 4 to 5 percent of the total development and construction costs, or about $4,000 per lot.

Stormwater management includes maintenance costs that the developer has to incur up through the completion of the very last house. In the past, these costs were much lower, but emphasis on maintaining structures and cleaning up after storm events has increased costs during development and construction activities.

The developers generally believe that the compliance costs for the other significant environmental regulations are too site-dependent to provide a general range of costs. For example, the cost of a survey for the saguaro cactus, which is basically required under the native plant protection regulations, depends on how many of these are on the site. Thus, they were not comfortable providing a general cost estimate for other regulations as they impact a typical site.

The HBA estimates that regulations of all types (not just environmental ones) add at least $40,000 to the cost of each finished lot. Despite the added cost to each lot to comply with individual regulations, a larger concern cited by the participants is the impact these regulations have on the available supply of land. For example, the participants cited a doubling of lot costs almost immediately following a FWS delineation in the 2000 timeframe that set aside approximately 1.2 million acres.

Approval Timeframe
According to the participants, the development process for by-right development generally takes about twelve months. Rezoning or some variance can generally stretch the process out to as long as two years, depending on the complexity of the development. For simple zoning issues, they can

sometimes stay within the twelve months required for a by-right development. These estimates are within the range of the Pima County representative's estimates of one year for a by-right development and six additional months for a typical rezoning action.

It is not apparent from the input we received that specific county environmental regulations greatly impact the schedule, as reviews are performed concurrently with other nonenvironmental regulations. This does not mean that the combined impact of the environmental regulations as a whole has not added to the time required for approval, but rather that we could not determine how much the schedule was impacted by one or more regulations. Because of the concurrent review and issues surrounding the scheduling of reviews, some local and state regulations may add to the approval timeframe while others may not. Federal floodplain regulations are the exception since the FEMA process for a map revision clearly extends the overall process.

Discussion of the Pima County Process and Regulations

Developers in the Tucson–Pima County area appear to face at least as many restrictions on development related to environmental regulations as developers in the Maryland-Virginia case studies. The impacts on development appear much more significant than effects seen in Denver and Dallas in terms of the complexity of the approval process and number of regulations.

Costs for compliance are similar to those found in the Maryland-Virginia case study, and those found for stormwater management regulatory compliance in Denver and Dallas. The developers generally believe that the compliance costs for the other significant environmental regulations are too site-dependent to provide an estimate for a typical project.

One outcome resulting from environmental regulations that is troublesome to the builders and developers is the impact on the supply of land for housing. Only about 15 percent of land in Arizona is privately owned—the rest is state, federal, or tribal land. Thus, land costs are particularly sensitive to set-asides or other conservation measures.

Last, it became evident in the interviews and discussions that the process and requirements in Pima County for residential land development are much more complex than in the Denver or Dallas areas. Neither the county officials nor the developers seemed to have a comprehensive understanding of the process. The county Web site is not particularly helpful—there is no master checklist one could use as a guide through the process.

The county has recognized the need for some clarity. A master checklist is under development. In addition, the county plans to use the Sonoran Desert Conservation Plan to consolidate the process for the regulations that now require multiple reviews and approvals.

DISCUSSION

Cost analysis was not made available to the research team in the detailed manner reported in chapter 4. However, the focus groups did provide sufficient information to allow the researchers to conclude that, on the whole, environmentally related costs per lot were in the normal-to-low range, and about in line with those found for the case study. Costs varied in dollar amounts, certainly, but not in relative magnitudes given different markets.

In addition, the time-to-approval can generally be described as "normal" based on experiences dating back to the 1970s, being roughly between one and two years for the entire approval process including any zoning relief needed (see table 6.1). Compared with the Maryland-Virginia region case study, the focus group representatives indicated that their local governments on the whole appear to process applications a few months faster.

The following section compares the three markets in terms of their differences and similarities relative to environmental regulations. Note that these discussions are based on the responses of the participants and are more qualitative than quantitative. Where appropriate, this section also discusses how the three markets compare with the Maryland-Virginia region. A general comparison of the regulations in each market is shown in table 6.1 and discussed in the following sections.

Overall Regulatory Environment

The Maryland-Virginia region would be viewed by most people as one of the more heavily regulated markets in the United States. Federal, state, regional, and local environmental regulations are abundant.

Table 6.1 Most Significant Environmental Regulations with Potential Impact on Residential Development Costs[a]

	Denver	Dallas	Tucson	MD-VA
Stormwater (including erosion and sediment control)	X	X	X	X
Remediation				X
Wetlands	X		X	X
Endangered species	X		X	X
Tree/forestry		X		X
Noise attenuation				X
Floodplain		X	X	X
Riparian areas			X	
Hillside/ridge preservation			X	
Average new home cost	$329,967	$179,000[b]	$245,804	$734,000
Typical time to approval (including zoning decision)	12 to 28 months	18 to 24 months	12 to 24 months	~24 months

[a] An "X" in the box indicates that the participants identified this as a significant environmental regulation. Other environmental regulations are present in each market, but were not identified as having a significant impact on costs.

[b] The average new home cost for Dallas was not available. This number represents the median price. See text for more details on housing costs in each area.

Source: Authors' compilation of pilot study research.

The views of the participants in the other three markets varied from one extreme to the other. In the Tucson market, the participants believe they are highly regulated in a manner that sharply increases housing costs. In Dallas and Denver, the participants believe the environmental regulations they face are not significant barriers to affordable housing. However, the Denver and Dallas participants see trends that point to increasing environmental regulation in the future. In both of these markets, there is no shortage of communities proposing new regulations, especially related to tree preservation.

Statements from the participants support their views that it is just a matter of time before the Dallas and Denver developers will be in a similar regulatory situation. For example, in the Dallas market, there is currently an abundance of land and it is relatively easy for a builder/developer to choose from among many sites when planning a development. Through due diligence, most developers are able to avoid properties that have potential environmental issues. As available and preferable land is used, however, the options will decrease and more and more environmental issues will come into play.

Although the participants in the three markets shared frustration over environmental regulations—particularly inconsistent interpretations by EPA, the U.S. Army COE, and the FWS—the Tucson participants were adamant that environmental regulations are a significant barrier to affordable housing. Their rationale was based on the cost of compliance combined with land supply effects. Only about 15 percent, or roughly 1,400 of Pima County's 9,186 square miles of land is privately owned. When a regulation is introduced that sets aside land for endangered species or other reasons, it restricts an already small supply of land available for development.

Environmental Regulations with Similar Effects in Each Market

One observation from participants in all three markets is that the federal regulations, in particular those related to the ESA, wetlands protection, floodplains, and stormwater management, are viewed as having the most significant impact on housing costs. State and local regulations were less frequently cited as concerns.

Even when state or local regulations were cited as significant barriers, they tended to be regulations that were related to the federal regulations. For example, some participants identified more stringent floodplain requirements than FEMA or state additions to the federal endangered species list.

It is difficult to compare items such as wetlands regulations, endangered species regulations, or tree preservation across jurisdictions because they vary widely in terms of the number of sites affected and the impact on each site. However, there do appear to be some similarities with floodplain and stormwater regulations.

Stormwater management regulations have been around longer than most other environmental regulations. Thus, the approach for addressing these issues has started to take on a degree of consistency in terms of interpretation of the regulations and the practices used for compliance. The participants in each location quickly identified stormwater management as one of the most significant regulations. They were very confident in estimating the costs for compliance because it has become a somewhat standard practice. Generally, compliance with federal, state, and local SWM requirements runs about 4 to 5 percent of the total cost of a finished lot (percentage of development costs). Dallas was the lone exception where stormwater management costs were estimated by the participants to be about 1 percent of development costs. Some of this can be expected because overall housing costs in Dallas are lower than in the other markets.

Although the amount of land that is affected by floodplains is highly variable, the response to floodplain issues was similar across the various markets. FEMA's process is viewed as a significant barrier due to the time it takes to obtain approvals. Compliance with the requirements is not the main issue, but rather the time it takes for FEMA to issue a letter of map revision. In each location, we were informed that FEMA will not begin the process until the plans are approved (i.e., final elevations are approved for each lot). Lots inside the original floodplain can be built upon, but only if the final map revision shows them outside of the new limits, or if the lots or buildings are elevated. Since the FEMA process takes up to twelve months, the developer is frequently put into a waiting mode until the map revision is approved. In some jurisdictions, developers can move forward at their own risk, but other jurisdictions have restricted this as an option for developers.

Local and Regional Differences

Despite the heavy influence of federal environmental regulations in each market, regional or local regulations also impact housing. Most of these regulations either are extensions of the federal regulations or are designed to protect a unique local resource. For example, the Tucson area developers cited protection of the saguaro cactus as a significant barrier or cost. In the Dallas–Fort Worth market, natural gas drilling platforms can place restrictions on development. In Denver and Tucson, protection of ridges and slopes are regulated. Likewise, there are regulations in the Maryland-Virginia market designed to protect the Chesapeake Bay from runoff.

All of the markets have various ordinances designed to protect trees or require tree plantings. However, these are somewhat unique to each area in that they focus on preservation of native species.

Overall Impact on Time-to-Approval

Generally, it is hard to determine if environmental regulations impact the time required to obtain an approval. But any additional regulations that must be addressed and reviewed undoubtedly add to time, effort, or cost, even if only minimally. Most of the environmental regulations are evaluated as part of the overall approval process, so isolating the impact of a single regulation was not possible. Only the FEMA map revision process under the federal floodplain regulations clearly adds extensive time to the process. Again, this is not to say that the other regulations do not add to the time required for approval, but rather that we were not able to determine the exact impact they have on the schedule.

Many factors cloud our ability to separate the impacts of a specific regulation on the schedule. For example, the rezoning process is in itself very time consuming in most jurisdictions and may be the most important factor in determining how long it takes to get an approval. When other reviews and approvals can take place concurrently, they may have little discernable impact on the overall schedule, even if they otherwise add to the developer's costs.

Attitudes toward Enforcement

The approach to enforcement greatly influences how an environmental regulation impacts the cost of housing. In Dallas, there seems to be less interest in enforcing federal regulations at the state and local levels. Thus, some jurisdictions do not place as much emphasis on compliance with the federal regulations, leaving it to the developers to make sure they have obtained all federal permits or approvals. Conversely, Pima County (Tucson) includes some federal approvals as a condition for local approval. When the local officials see a regulation as their responsibility to enforce, often local ordinances spring up alongside the federal regulations. Once it is part of their process, stricter interpretation and enforcement tend to follow. This may partially explain how developers in the three markets can have widely differing views of the impact of a specific federal regulation.

SUMMARY PERSPECTIVES

The research team came to two conclusions about information gathered from the focus groups. First, localities differ in the sensitivity of landscapes that may require environmental regulation. Some landscapes admittedly have few preservation concerns—at least fewer than those witnessed in the Washington metropolitan area case study. Dallas–Fort Worth and Denver, for example, do not have the kind of wetland and watershed sensitivities presented by the Chesapeake Bay. Tucson, on the other hand, has important habitat limitations.

Second, despite these differences in the substance of environmental issues to be addressed, the procedural timeframes are remarkably similar. Although some focus groups reported somewhat lower-end entitlement processing ranges than the case study, all had about the same upward limit (table 6.1).

Chapter 8 discusses the lessons that may be learned from this latest effort to assess the relationship between environmental regulations and housing costs.

SEVEN

The Benefits of Environmental Regulations and a Summary of Key Findings

This chapter outlines environmental regulatory benefits as they accrue to homebuyers, developers, and society at large. For the purposes of this research, we focused on the costs of environmental regulations but not on their benefits. However, we believe it is useful and informative to review some of the benefits to put regulatory costs in the proper context. This chapter concludes with a summary of key findings from our research and some recommendations for improvements.

THE BENEFITS OF ENVIRONMENTAL REGULATIONS

Environmental regulations benefit homebuyers in important ways such as preventing losses from erosion that may undermine foundations or setting development away from floodplains, thereby avoiding flood damage. These benefits save costs and may be translated into lower insurance premiums or psychological benefits. Habitat preservation can create general ephemeral benefits, such as exclusive enjoyment of unique landscapes, and these types of benefits can be capitalized as amenity value.

Overall, environmental regulations can enhance property values by providing environmental amenities and reducing impacts of new developments on existing neighborhoods through such measures as hazard mitigation and resource protection as well as tree preservation, landscaping, noise abatement, and other measures.

Society benefits similarly. By preventing or at least reducing home damage associated with natural hazards and disasters, society may reduce recovery payments to homeowners. By preserving endangered species, society maintains biodiversity with incalculable future benefits. More generally, environmental regulations can prevent adverse impact of land development on environmental resources deemed by public policy to have societal value, including water quality, air quality, natural habitats, open space, productive farmland, cultural resources, and others.

Developers also benefit. One advantage of environmentally related expenses such as erosion control and floodplain management is reducing buyers' sense of risk, possibly making buyers willing to pay more. For example, homes adjacent to or near protected open spaces are worth more than homes farther away; developers capitalize some if not all of these benefits in the sales price of homes. There is an indirect benefit in that developers may be able to reduce their long-term exposure to litigation that attempts to recover damages associated with environmental catastrophes.

Some environmental regulatory benefits may be efficiencies while others are amenities. Efficiency benefits occur when environmental regulations create savings recognized by the market. Not having to handle increased flooding on a site because of better upstream management can lower site development costs and thus increase the value of land and conceivably the value of the home by reducing worries about flooding. Amenity benefits are more subtle and relate to the extent that environmental regulations increase a community's overall appeal relative to competing communities. Sunding (2004a) notes that the effect of these benefits on land and/or housing prices have not been addressed in research but are likely quite real. The reality is that in some cases what appears to be a costly environmental regulation is in fact something that the market values. Although disentangling cost and benefit effect is beyond the scope of the research reported in this book, it is of vital importance.

The Benefits of Environmental Regulations and Key Findings   **167**

SUMMARY OF KEY FINDINGS

Regarding three types of costs (compliance costs, process costs, and reduced land for development), this project focuses on the first two. The third cost associated with reduced land for development resulting from environmental regulations could not be investigated within the constraints of this study because of the complexities of isolating factors affecting land costs. Among our key findings:

- Environmental regulatory compliance and delay costs are real and significant, but they are not a major factor in the increasing cost of housing compared with other land and development costs.
- Costs of compliance are about $5,000 to 15,000 (in 2006 dollars) per lot or unit in the DC market, comparable to Tucson, but apparently less in Denver and considerably less in Dallas.
- Stormwater management, erosion and sediment control, site remediation, tree preservation, wetland mitigation, and habitat preservation are important cost categories. Water issues (stormwater management and wetlands) dominate mitigation costs.
- Developers could do a much better job tracking environmental costs. If they had more concrete data on environmental costs it would greatly assist the home-building industry in understanding where improvements in the process are needed to help reduce expenditures. Indeed, through the course of our research we were aided immeasurably by a large-scale home builder that began to realize the internal accounting and decision-making benefits of tracking environmentally related costs systematically and was working toward modifying its national accounting protocols accordingly. Project delays for environmental approvals were apparent in the projects and markets studied. That said, the twelve- to twenty-four-month approval period was not atypical compared with historical norms for rezoning decisions, which are increasingly required for major developments. Concurrent permit reviews were important to minimize delays.
- Environmental compliance and expedited approval can be facilitated by the use of knowledgeable and trusted environmental consultants

- who can develop innovative compliance measures and communicate them to permitting agencies and the public.
- In certain markets with already limited buildable land (e.g., Tucson), ESA habitat conservation may limit land availability and raise land prices. There is no evidence from the study that wetlands permitting and mitigation affect land availability.
- Some state and federal mandates, such as FEMA map revisions and U.S. Army Corps of Engineers wetland review, caused delays that some developers thought were excessive. However, other projects showed that concurrent review by different jurisdictions and for different permitting decisions helped shorten overall review times.
- There are opportunities in many markets to reduce uncertainty for developers, to streamline the approval process, and to reduce costs while still protecting environmental resources (see chapter 8).

Regulatory Process Costs and Delays Are Not Substantial

Regulatory processes and costs vary widely across the nation because of differences in growth pressures and landscape conditions. Where there are few physical and environmental barriers to development, time-to-approval periods and environmentally related improvement costs are low relative to areas where there are physical or legal barriers (such as limited private land ownership) or important environmental limitations (such as wetland sensitivity, endangered species habitats, fragile or polluted waterways, and so on).

Yet, the study's results on time-to-approval and environmentally related improvement cost to total improvement cost ratios were mostly within the "normal" range on the process and cost continua (although the Washington market was at the high end of this range). Indeed the research team was impressed that, despite thirty years of what would seem to be ever-escalating environmental conditions and associated costs, there is little difference in time-to-approval periods and environmentally related costs as a share of total improvement costs between the mid-1970s and the mid-2000s.

There may be important reasons for this. With greater experience, environmentally related regulations may be clearer and more objective now than in the past and may have become part of the routine checklist of

The Benefits of Environmental Regulations and Key Findings 169

things to do as part of development preparation and review. In addition, technology may have improved to the point where many functions that once were very costly are now inexpensive in comparison. Also, decision makers and, to some extent, the public may be giving deference to experts to ensure concerns are addressed adequately—and in large part developers are turning to experts to act as an interface between them and review processes. Experts, in turn, seek solutions and build trust over time. Finally, administrative systems are probably much more efficient today than in the past in processing environmentally related conditions.

Recommendations for Improvement

Although costs and delays attributable to the environmental regulatory process do not seem to be substantial or increasing, there is room for improvement. The appendicies offer important details on current regulatory practices and suggest changes. These include examples of duplication of administrative review of environmental decision making even within the same jurisdiction (Montgomery County, Maryland, for example), unclear requirements, and confusing interjurisdictional responsibilities between state and local agencies, and federal interests such as those affecting the Chesapeake Bay.

The lessons and recommendations from this research project include a call for streamlining administrative review and implementation processes in a variety of ways drawn from recommendations in the existing literature. To this list, the research team adds a recommendation for clear and objective standards with expert review.

Clear standards are those that enable experts in the field to know what is meant by the standard—such as stormwater retention based on a one-year storm event extending one hour.
Objective standards would show how the stormwater retention may be achieved through design and choice of materials. Ideally, if the clear and objective standard is met, there may be no discretion by local decision makers to add further requirements that address the issue.
Expert review, provided by both the applicant and the local government, would also be available to ensure application of the standard.

A checklist of standards including a clear statement, means of compliance, and methods of analysis would help clarify standards and their technical basis for both developers and citizens. The use of clear and objective standards with expert review can ensure that public policy is achieved by addressing the environmental concern, reducing discretion (and related uncertainty) and the time to approval, and streamlining the process for both developers and decision makers.

In addition, an environmental cost audit could be used locally to help streamline the implementation of environmental regulations through best practices.

Closing the Knowledge Gap

Our research finds that we simply do not know enough about the relationship between environmental regulation and housing costs, at least in ways that can inform and improve administration. Therefore, to close this knowledge gap, we offer several suggestions for federal leadership.

HUD and other federal agencies should sponsor new research in this area to look at the broader national impacts of environmental regulation on housing affordability. Four avenues of research can help close these important gaps in understanding and lead to more informed regulatory processes, including:

1. Understanding the true costs of regulatory process barriers to the availability and affordability of housing
2. Understanding the effects of regulatory practices for areas in addition to regulation of building safety
3. Understanding lesser-studied aspects of regulatory processes, such as estimating the effects of citizen opposition to housing or the effects of fragmented regulatory structures
4. Understanding the balance among the economic, social, and environmental benefits of environmental regulations and the cost impacts on housing. Do the costs of regulations exceed the benefits they provide?

Research in each of these areas would close important gaps in information and create a more complete body of knowledge on the relationship between regulation—especially environmental regulation—and housing costs.

EIGHT

Assessment, Lessons, and Future Directions

This chapter examines the results of this new research in the context of what is already known in the literature. This chapter reviews the research findings and provides lessons and recommendations from this project.

Through project case studies, interviews, and focus groups, the research team found little evidence that either environmental compliance costs or costs of delay exceeded historic norms for time to approval or added significantly to overall project costs. There was some variation within these studies results, however, and because of data limitations it is difficult to generalize too far.

INTRODUCTION

The literature on regulatory barriers to housing affordability argues that land-use regulations, including environmental requirements, drive up the cost of development and thus the price of housing. Although there has been little empirical data to support this argument, it is, of course, true because health and safety improvements likely increase costs.

Some regulations take land out of development, increasing the price of the remaining available land. Other regulations call for additional expenditures for assessments and documentation, and these add to the cost of development. Still others require physical changes in projects, including impact measures and mitigation that also add to development costs. However, the literature largely fails to quantify these regulatory costs to determine if they outweigh the public benefits these regulations provide. If the costs outweigh the benefits, only then should they be regarded "excessive" or "unnecessary" as some have claimed.

The research reported in this book does not address the question of whether the costs of regulations exceed the benefits they provide, but it aims to shed light on the costs associated with environmental regulations, how those costs compare with land and development costs and housing prices, and how the related regulatory approval processes contribute to delays and financing costs in the development process.

The case study presented in chapter 4 investigated six large housing projects in the Washington metropolitan regional suburban market. Lessons learned from the case study were tested in three other major markets—Denver, Dallas, and Tucson—where focus groups with large builders and interviews with local officials provided a glimpse of the similarities and differences in those markets.

LESSONS FOR POLICY MAKERS AND PRACTITIONERS

The research leading to this book did not second-guess local governments' use of environmental regulations to guide development, and as such does not address the issue of what some may consider "excessive" or "unnecessary" environmental regulation. However, the research reported in this book offers important lessons on which to establish a framework for improving the implementation of environmental regulations.

This section, which is informed significantly by May (2005), will highlight insights from our research, focus groups, and case study that support May's observations and recommendations. Following May, the section considers two outcomes of regulatory implementation: (1) delays in construction and housing rehabilitation; and (2) added cost and procedural burdens that discourage actual housing development.

The research generally supports May's propositions that there are three broad procedural barriers involving environmental regulations:

1. *Regulatory approvals* entail delays because of cumbersome decision-making processes and duplication of regulations. These kinds of delays are of special concern to developers.

Assessment, Lessons, and Future Directions **173**

2. A *patchwork of administrative arrangements* results from the duplication of administrative structures and gaps in regulatory decision processes.
3. *Regulatory enforcement strategies and practices* are overly rigid and foster an unsupportive regulatory environment for housing development. (However, our research did not reveal major concerns about this issue.)

This section will focus on the first two implementation issues that arose from the development community following May's insights.

Although May suggests several broad administrative approaches to improving regulatory processes, one stood out as needed based on our research: regulatory and administrative process simplification. This includes steps to reduce duplication and procedural hurdles. In addition, May identified other improvements that seemed important among the developers participating in our study: (1) conflict-reduction and consensus-building approaches that are aimed at achieving agreement about affordable housing goals; (2) smart enforcement practices that reduce deterrents to housing development by fostering a supportive regulatory environment; and (3) facilitative reviews and inspection processes that speed up housing approvals and construction. As part of the cases studied in Fairfax and Montgomery counties, the research team identified potential opportunities for these dispute-resolution strategies to resolve conflicts over inconsistent interpretations and applications of environmental regulations by local government staff.

Regulatory and Administrative Simplification

Developers interviewed for this research echoed many of the approaches to regulatory and administrative simplification that May (2005) suggests, including one-stop permit shops, electronic permitting, and third-party certification, as discussed in chapter 2.

Participating developers also indicated the importance of conflict resolution and consensus-building efforts. It is not only regulators who can slow the approval process, but citizens acting to preserve their interests also can present a challenge by working to make the regulatory approval process more political than ministerial. Developers interviewed for this study believed that citizens with NIMBY (Not in My Backyard) opposition to projects often used environmental issues and regulations as a tool, not to protect the environment but to delay or obstruct a project they did not want. Conflict resolution and consensus-building methods could address this challenge.

Our research revealed another way to improve regulatory processes: establish clear and objective standards with expert review. The idea of having clear and objective standards is not new, but the extent to which such standards have been applied has not been studied. The concept is simple. *Clear* standards are those that experts in the field can easily understand—for example, stormwater retention based on a one-year storm event extending one hour. *Objective* standards would then show how the stormwater retention may be achieved through design, choice of materials, and so forth. Ideally, if the clear and objective standard is met there would be no discretion by local decision makers to add further requirements that address stormwater. *Expert review* provided by both the applicant and the local government also would be used. The use of clear and objective standards with expert review thus ensures that good public policy is achieved by addressing the environmental concern, making the process more transparent by reducing the amount of discretion in the decision-making process, and perhaps decreasing the time to approval. To our knowledge, only the state of Oregon requires this approach among all its jurisdictions. However, there has been no research comparing time-to-approval and condition-of-approval differences between Oregon's approach and that of other states.

POLICY CHALLENGES AND OPPORTUNITIES

What can be done by the state and/or local governments to ensure that environmental concerns are addressed reasonably and without significant delay in processing development approvals? Before suggesting some policy recommendations, it is important to note that our research did not find that review processes have added significantly to the approval period and we did not find that the general cost of environmental compliance is excessive—indeed, it is surprising that the review period is not much longer and the costs higher than in the 1970s. Of course, there are always local variations, anecdotes of processes and conditions of approval run amok, and stories about the occasional litigation that stymies projects sometimes for years and often with little improvement in outcomes. What can be done?

Federal and State Programs and Policy Reforms

The potential for improving the efficiency of local land development processes rests primarily with state and local governments and not with the federal government.

May (2005) offers a similar limited view of the federal role, but he does suggest some indirect ways in which the federal government may improve the efficiency and efficacy of environmental regulations and help reduce their potential effects on housing costs. One of May's suggestions is to conduct research to identify the sources of regulatory barriers and the means for addressing them. The U.S. Department of Housing and Urban Development (HUD) has begun doing this on a number of fronts, including sponsoring this study. Another suggestion is to gather and share information including examples of best practices for balancing environmental concerns with housing affordability, of which HUD's Housing Barriers Clearinghouse is a good example. A third suggestion May offers is the creation of demonstration programs, sponsored by local governments, that serve as exemplars of regulatory reform.

Federal as well as state policy makers also may consider a carrot-and-stick approach by attaching conditions to federal and/or state grants to local governments. However, as May (2005) suggests, the federal government has neither the political inclination nor budgetary support to take on such a centralized role, and this concept may not be worth pursuing accordingly. However, several of these ideas and suggestions could apply equally to state governments.

For example, the state of Maryland's Smart Growth program provides certain state infrastructure and technical assistance funds to local governments for specific types of projects that facilitate the principles and goals of smart growth. These priority funding areas essentially impose state conditions on state and local grants. A similar system could be devised to provide state funds to local governments in dynamic real estate markets, with the grant conditional on the local government's ability to institute a range of permit streamlining initiatives (e.g., technology upgrades and conflict resolution strategies).

Another potential state role would be to influence the housing elements of comprehensive plans. In states like California that require comprehensive land-use plans, the state could establish criteria for permit-streamlining approaches for local governments to integrate within their housing elements. Comprehensive planning and housing elements already establish affordable housing goals, so it would seem logical that they also could require the adoption of relevant permit streamlining strategies.

Several states provide matching technical assistance grants to local governments for certain planning tasks. For example, Wisconsin's Department of Administration annually provides about $3 million to local government to draft comprehensive plans. Likewise, states could provide local governments with technical assistance dollars to upgrade and retrofit their development permit systems. These state grants could establish a range of performance criteria for permit processing based on the size and capacity of the local jurisdiction—what might work in a large city with fast growth would be vastly different from an approach appropriate for a small, rural town or a city struggling with blight and abandonment.

Local Government Policies and Practices

Local governments also can play a role in reducing the costs associated with environmental regulation compliance. One approach would be to ensure continuity of regulations and to minimize regulatory overlap and conflict. Although some of these areas of conflict and overlap may be beyond their control—such as in instances involving compliance with state or federal regulations—local governments can work within their own systems to eliminate competing regulations. This type of review also may help identify conflicting state and federal regulations and could be used to encourage the respective agencies to reconcile differences. We have not come across such a system that streamlines both federal and state/local environmental regulations, and we recommend the creation of a pilot program to investigate this idea.

Local governments could help to reduce costs associated with environmental regulations and delays by taking affirmative steps to reconcile duplicative and conflicting environmental regulations. Our study found that regulatory delays could be minimized through collaborative review by multiple agencies. Delays also were reduced when developers sought multiple approvals concurrently. For example, table 5.1 shows that wetlands permitting required by three separate agencies would have required as long as thirty-eight months for review and approval if done sequentially, but took only sixteen months because it was done collaboratively and concurrently.

In Fairfax County, where the planners orchestrate environmental protection through the rezoning and proffer system, a builder in the case study received development approvals in roughly half the time of a similar-sized project in Montgomery County. Notably, rezoning and environmental reviews by planners in Fairfax seemed less contentious and adversarial. While Virginia and Maryland mandate similar environmental requirements in limited areas, such as wetlands and stormwater, Montgomery County seemed to have multiple departments setting and interpreting special environmental regulations, and this added time to the review and approval process (even if not to housing costs relative to other parts of the metro area).

In addition, local governments should develop specific environmental requirements for infill sites, especially in areas where "build out" will soon be or has been achieved. Infill sites often have more unique characteristics, making development more difficult and time consuming, and therefore more costly, under the environment regulations and review procedures. By creating regulations allowing for density bonuses, facilitating more efficient and effective infill projects, and streamlining the review process for infill sites, local governments can help developers reduce their overall project costs of environmental regulation compliance.

THE REGULATORY COST INVENTORY, BEST PRACTICES, AND INCENTIVES

So, what can we do to improve regulatory processes and the conditions they impose at least during the interim while new research is being conducted to fill in our current knowledge gaps? One approach involves conducting audit-like inventories of environmental conditions affecting sites. These inventories would include such elements as environmental assessments of brownfields and other developed sites to determine environmental remediation needs.

The idea of a regulatory cost inventory or audit would be a new application of the concept intended to assess the regulatory burden on the development process. The scope of the audit would be devised by a panel whose members would include those knowledgeable in comparative regulatory processes, housing and urban economics and finance, environmental engineering, landscape architecture, ecology/environmental analysis, and others who can inform the process. Like most audits, it would be intended to reveal the costs and benefits of the regulatory processes, with the goal of establishing a set of best practices and standards addressing each area of environmental concern along six dimensions noted below.

1. Cataloging the nature of particular environmental concerns in specific areas, including stormwater drainage, habitat preservation, tree preservation and enhancement, soil erosion and sedimentation, and so forth, that would be applicable to a wide range of residential developments and mixed-use developments that have housing components. For example, for most urbanized areas of the nation and many others, the national flood insurance program provides maps showing floodways and hundred-year floodplains. These maps are used to guide development decisions. In some parts of the country endangered habitats are shown; indeed, through remote sensing, some areas are beginning to map the habitats of endangered flora. Ideally, every jurisdiction would be able to map environmentally important areas so that everyone, from developers to planners to citizens, would know with reasonable certainty where those areas are. It is possible that some of the cost to develop the technical foundation for this mapping as well as its development and dissemination would be supported by the federal government, notably the Environmental Protection Agency (EPA), the Fish and Wildlife Service, and the National Marine Fisheries Service. Persons engaged in the process would be technical experts in each area and would provide the scientific and engineering background.
2. Identifying and specifying through descriptions, drawings/diagrams, and other means the appropriate range of development responses to each of the environmental concerns. Many but not all local governments provide technical specifications and drawings showing street, curb and gutter, sidewalk, and related subdivision and site development improvements. Some localities offer similar detail for onsite erosion control during construction and drainage, but many if not most do not. Fewer still provide sufficient technical specifications and drawings to provide developers with predictability in terms of cost and pro-

Assessment, Lessons, and Future Directions 179

cedural review in such areas as habitat and archeological preservation. These may be prepared through computer-generated graphics by engineers and landscape architects.

3. Framing the regulatory review process needed to address each concern, including the extent to which discretion in addressing each area of concern may be needed even if the design solution posed in the second step is posed by the developer, and determining the reasonable time needed to provide reasonable public review. Sometimes the best solution is simply not known and perhaps not knowable at least without extensive pioneering study, experimentation, and assessment. Such an approach may be appropriate under certain conditions, but in others—where the environmental risks may be judged to be small—providing "second best" clear and objective standards may be the wisest thing to do. Best standards may be developed over time through the experience gained in the meantime. Professionals appropriate for this task may include experts in public administration and the management of planning processes.

4. Determining where multiple environmental concerns may be addressed by the same review function, discipline, and group of design solutions. In some instances, individual projects are reviewed sequentially by different disciplines, sometimes with one or more disciplines waiting for others to complete their review. Conceptually, relevant disciplines would be assembled to review a development proposal with collective agreement on a comprehensive set of solutions. This task may involve a combination of technical, administrative, and process management experts.

5. Characterizing an overarching administrative process that implements the first four elements in a reasonably efficient manner that nonetheless accords discretion for unusual or complex cases. Integrating environmental review processes, even those of different levels of government, should be a goal. Perhaps the federal government could exert some leadership in helping design and implement integrated environmental review processes. This task may be a synthesizing exercise performed by public administrators and planning process managers.

6. Facilitating further streamlining of processes possibly through stronger federal involvement, such as incentives for states and localities to meet

federal guidelines of approval time-limits. This approach would elevate the discourse and response for process streamlining, but it may be hindered by practical and political limitations.

The work outlined above could lead to a publication on standards and guidelines similar to the *Time-Saver Standard* series of technical reference books for architecture, urban design, and planning (see appendix D). The publication, however, would include important auditing features that would allow local governments and others to assess current environmental regulatory processes and conditions in relation to the standards and thus identify areas for improvement.

The standards and guidelines would serve another important function—benchmarking. Local governments could use the guidelines to compare their procedures and requirements against the established standards. This type of review may result in changes that move current practices toward more efficient and efficacious outcomes, and may even create the opportunity for some agencies to advertise that their processes are better than the standards.

This approach need not wait for research to fully inform refinements or for reforms needed to reduce potentially adverse effects of environmental regulations, processes, and conditions on housing costs. The application of such standards could result in a kind of Leadership in Energy and Environmental Design (LEED)–based rating system (from platinum to lower grades) that ranks processes, and it may even induce some local governments to aspire to higher ratings. The ratings themselves could eventually be used by government agencies to allocate scarce resources on the basis of audit performance. HUD may wish to explore how such a system of standards and practices may be assembled, who should be involved, and how it may be used to inform local governments, states, and federal agencies, especially the U.S. Department of the Interior and the EPA.

RESEARCH QUESTIONS AND NEXT STEPS

As May (2005) notes, the existing research leaves important gaps in our understanding of how environmental and other regulations influence the time-to-approval process and especially housing costs. There are also important limitations in linking regulation per se—and in the context of this research, environmental regulations—with housing prices and housing affordability. On the one hand, most studies to date rely heavily on what developers report as their concerns, which can create bias in the survey outcomes. On the other hand, estimates of the costs associated with regulatory burdens are imprecise and, given their source (developers), perhaps biased. Some estimates appear to lump costs of administrative burdens together with legitimate regulatory conditions, which makes it difficult to fairly assign regulatory inefficiencies. Our experience with the case study confirmed many of these observations. However, we were surprised to discover that accounting practices for even a large-scale residential builder did not specifically track environmental costs and distinguish them from other development costs. Finally, it is difficult for the research team to generalize our findings to broader, national impacts on housing supply and affordability.

The following five avenues of research can help close these important gaps in understanding and lead to more informed regulatory processes. The first two are the most salient.

1. Understanding the true costs of regulatory process barriers to the availability and affordability of housing—Research on these topics is limited to case studies in selected jurisdictions and is based on particular housing types. Closing the existing knowledge gap requires systematic data collection for a sample of jurisdictions and development types across the country. HUD may be a logical sponsor for this.
2. Understanding the balance between the economic, social, and environmental benefits of environmental regulations and the cost effects on housing—Do the costs of regulations exceed the benefits they provide? Regulatory barriers do increase the cost of housing but they also provide benefits to the environment and society. Unfortunately, research that teases out the benefit and cost effects of such regulation remains elusive. Research is needed to assess the economic, social, and environmental costs and benefits of environmental and other regulations. HUD and the EPA may be logical sponsors of this inquiry.
3. Understanding the effects of regulatory practices for areas other than the regulation of building safety, and "green" regulations—Much of the current understanding of the effects of different regulatory pro-

cesses on housing production and prices is based on building regulation studies. Whether the insights from such research apply to environmental, land-use, and other forms of regulation is unclear.
4. Understanding lesser-studied aspects of regulatory processes—There has been little attention paid to estimating the relative effects of environmental regulations, nonenvironmental regulations, citizen opposition to housing projects, land and development costs, and other factors affecting housing affordability. HUD and the EPA could be reasonable sponsors of this area of research.
5. Research in each area would close important gaps in data—Comprehensive research in these areas could create a credible—rather than biased and anecdotally based—body of knowledge about regulation per se, particularly environmental regulation and housing costs. Such needed research may take years to accumulate, but it is necessary to move beyond the status quo in the meantime. While that research is conducted, communities could initiate the regulatory auditing process discussed earlier in this chapter.

THE CHALLENGE AHEAD

Continued population growth, climate change, sea-level rise, species extinction, and the once and future energy crisis would seem likely to dominate policy concerns facing the American presidency, Congress, the states, and the 80,000-some units of local governments in the coming years. Yet all these concerns have one thing in common: the environment. Environmental regulations are the tools that can manage humankind's impact on the planet and minimize adverse outcomes in all of the areas noted above.

There is also a sea change of sorts emerging in Americans's community design preferences. The conventional American suburb was designed in the 1950s to the 1970s catering to a situation in which half or more of suburban American households were raising children. Yet, during the next generation, only 15 percent of the net gain in demand for new housing will be associated with households raising children. Of course, there will be more children and more households with children over the next generation, but about 85 percent of the net gain in demand for new housing is expected to be among people who have already raised children, have yet to raise children, or will never raise children. The housing and community design demands of these changing demographics are not well known. Yet various market signals exist—from declining values of suburban fringe and exurban homes, to increasing value of homes (usually smaller ones on smaller lots) closer to cities, to the substantially increasing values of homes (often attached) near rail and bus rapid transit. The market is changing but the land-use regulations in many communities remain beholden to a past reality.

There is also a changing mood among the public. On the heels of the birth of the Environmental Protection Agency, one of its administrators, William K. Reilly, wrote in 1971:

> There is a mood in America. Increasingly citizens are asking what urban growth will add to the quality of their lives. They are questioning the way relatively unconstrained, piecemeal urbanization is changing their communities and are rebelling against the traditional processes of government and the marketplace which, they believe, have inadequately guided development in the past. They are measuring new development proposals by the extent to which environmental criteria are satisfied by what new housing and business will generate in terms of additional traffic, pollution of air and water, erosion, and scenic disturbance. (Nelson and Duncan 1995, 1)

Those words may be truer today than they were four decades ago. Where do we go from here? What is certain from our research is that by and large the development community understands the changing market but is frustrated in its attempts to "do the right thing." All too often, developers default to the cookie-cutter suburban template because they know they can secure necessary entitlements much more quickly that way than if they were to take the extra year or two or more to "do the right thing" to meet the changing needs of homebuyers while protecting the environment.

For their part, citizens and their elected officials are afraid of change, perhaps more now than ever before. In the face of these uncertain times, it seems that some developers, homebuyers, and localities would rather accept the certainty of lower property values than live with all the uncertainty required to successfully reshape the nation's existing communities into something more vibrant, sustainable, and receptive to emerging markets.

We have proposed several areas for further research that could be undertaken to both improve our understanding of the relationship between environmental regulations and housing costs, and to streamline development permitting processes in a way that is consistent with ensuring high-quality environmental outcomes from new development. If, and to what extent, these recommendations will be heeded is unclear. Moveover, we need to find better ways to engage citizens in reshaping the built environment. In many ways, this is the most difficult task of all. It is also the most essential.

CONCLUSION

We hope the suggestions offered in this book encourage local governments to clarify their environmental regulations, and offer more certainty regarding requirements and predictability in the review process. We conclude the book with a call for a new, better-informed perspective on the relationship between environmental regulations and housing costs. We also call for research quantifying the benefits of environmental regulation.

APPENDIX A
Literature Review References

Environmental Regulations Affecting Land Use and Development

1. American Planning Association. 2002. *Planning for Smart Growth: State of the States.* Chicago: Author.
2. Daniels, T. 2003. *The Environmental Planning Handbook.* Chicago: Planners Press.
3. Godshalk, D., T. Beatley, P. Berke, D. Brower, and E. Kaiser. 1999. *Natural Hazard Mitigation: Recasting Disaster Policy and Planning.* Washington, DC: Island Press.
4. Knapp, Gerrit. 2004. *Monitoring Land and Housing Markets: An Essential Tool for Smart Growth.* College Park, MD: National Center for Smart Growth.
5. Center for Best Practices Online. 2007. *Policy Academy on Coordinating Housing and Economic Development Best Practices and Lessons Learned.* Washington, DC: National Governors Association, Environment, Energy, and Natural Resources Division. Available at http://www.nga.org/Files/pdf/0701HOUSINGACADEMY.pdf.
6. Randolph, John. 2004. *Environmental Land Use Planning and Management.* Washington, DC: Island Press. Available at http://www.envirolanduse.org.
7. U.S. Department of Transportation, Federal Highway Administration. n.d. State Environmental Streamlining Practices Database. Available at http://environment.fhwa.dot.gov/strmlng/es6stateprac.asp.
8. U.S. Department of Transportation, Federal Highway Administration. 2002. *Environmental Commitment Implementation: Innovative and Successful Approaches.* Washington, DC: Author.

Studies of Environmental Regulations as Barriers to Affordable Housing

9. Downs, Anthony. 1991. Advisory Commission on Regulatory Barriers to Affordable Housing: Its Behavior and Accomplishments. *Housing Policy Debate* 2 (4): 1095–1137.
10. Kiel, K. A. 2004. *Environmental Regulations and the Housing Market: A Review of the Literature.* Paper for U.S. Department of Housing and Urban Development conference on regulatory barriers and housing markets, Washington, DC, April.
11. Lewis, P., and Max Neiman. 2002. *Cities under Pressure: Local Growth Controls and Residential Development Policy.* San Francisco: Public Policy Institute of California.
12. Minnesota Office of Legislative Auditor. 2001. *Affordable Housing Report 01-03*. Available at http://www.auditor.leg.state.mn.us/PED/2001/pe0103.htm.
13. National Association of Home Builders. 2000. *The Truth about Regulatory Barriers to Housing Affordability.* Washington, DC: Author.
14. Washington Research Council. 2001. Impact of Government Regulations and Fees on Housing Costs. e-Policy Brief, May 24. http://www.researchcouncil.org/publications_container/growth9.pdf.
15. Russell, R. 2002. Equity in Eden: Can Environmental Protection and Affordable Housing Comfortably Cohabit in Suburbia? *Boston College Environment Law Review* 30 (3). Available at http://www.bc.edu/schools/law/lawreviews/meta-elements/journals/bcealr/30_3/02_TXT.htm.
16. Salins, P. 2002. *New York City's Housing Gap Revisited.* New York: Manhattan Institute.
17. Schill, Michael H. 2002. Regulatory Barriers to Housing Development in the United States. In *Land Law in Comparative Perspective,* ed. Maria Elena Sanchez Jordan and Antonio Gambaro. The Hague: Kluwer Law International.
18. Schill, Michael H. 2002. The Cost of Good Intentions. *Civic Bulletin* No. 28. Available at http://www.manhattan-institute.org/html/cb_28.htm.
19. Schill, Michael H. *Regulations and Housing Development: What We Know and What We Need to Know.* Prepared for U.S. Department of Housing and Urban Development Conference on Regulatory Barriers to Affordable Housing, Washington, DC, April. Available at http://www.huduser.org/rbc/pdf/Regulations_Housing_Development.pdf.

20. U.S. Department of Housing and Urban Development. 2001. *Barriers to Rehabilitation of Affordable Housing. Volume 2: Case Studies.* Washington, DC: Author.
21. U.S. Department of Housing and Urban Development. 1998. *Effects of Environmental Hazards and Regulation on Urban Development.* Washington, DC: Author. Available at http://www.huduser.org/publications/econdev/bfield.html.
22. U.S. Department of Housing and Urban Development. 1978. *Final Report of the Task Force on Housing Costs.* Washington, DC: Author.
23. Washington Research Council. 2001. *Impact of Government Regulations and Fees on Housing Costs.* e-Policy Brief 01-18. Available at http://www.researchcouncil.org/publications_container/growth9.pdf.

Efforts at Regulatory Reform

24. Engel, David. 2004. Regulatory Barriers: Secret (and Not so Secret) Weapons Against Affordable Housing. *Bright Ideas* (Spring).
25. Urban Land Institute. 1979. *Thirteen Perspectives on Regulatory Simplification.* Washington, DC: Author.

State (all from HUD Regulatory Barriers Clearinghouse, http://www.huduser.org/rbc/)

26. Department of Community Affairs Division of Housing and Community Resources. 1996. *1996 Fair Housing Plan.* Trenton, NJ: New Jersey State Department of Community Affairs Division of Housing and Community Resources.
27. The Affordable Housing Subcommittee of Maine's Community Preservation Advisory Committee. 2003. *Affordable Housing: Barriers and Solutions for Maine.* 2003. Available at http://www.state.me.us/spo/landuse/docs/cpachousingrecs.pdf.
28. Association of New Jersey Environmental Commissions. 2003. *Affordable Housing: Meeting a Town's Affordable Housing Obligation While Protecting Natural Resources.* Available at http://www.anjec.org/pdfs/SG_AH.pdf.
29. California Housing Law Project. 2003. *Anti-NIMBY Tools.* Available at http://www.hcd.ca.gov/hpd/nimby.htm.

30. Colorado Department of Local Affairs. 1998. *Reducing Housing Costs through Regulatory Reform: A Handbook for Colorado Communities.*
31. Colorado Department of Local Affairs. 2000. *State of Colorado: Affordable Housing Regulatory Barriers Impact Report.*
32. Massachusetts, Commonwealth, Executive Office for Administration and Finance. 2000. *Bringing Down the Barriers: Changing Housing Supply Dynamics in Massachusetts.* Boston: Author. Available at http://www.dola.state.co.us/Doh/Documents/ReducingCosts.htm.
33. State of Arizona. 2002. *State of Housing in Arizona 2000.* Available at http://azcms.housingaz.com/uploads/PUBLICATIONS/State%20of%20Housing/2000%20State%20of%20Housing.pdf.
34. State of California. 2000. *State of California Consolidated Plan 2000–2005.* Sacramento: California State Department of Housing and Community Development.
35. State of Colorado. 2000. *State of Colorado Consolidated Plan.* Denver: Author. Available at http://www.dola.state.co.us/doh/Documents/RegBarriers00.pdf.
36. State of Maryland. 2000. *Maryland Consolidated Plan for 2000–2004.* Annapolis: Author.
37. State of Massachusetts. 2002. *Report of the Governor's Special Commission on Barriers to Housing Development.* Boston: Governors Special Commission on Barriers to Housing.
38. State of Texas. 2000. *2001–2003 State of Texas Consolidated Plan.* 2000. Austin, TX: Texas Department of Housing and Community Affairs.
39. U.S. Department of Housing and Urban Development. 2008. Connecticut Enacts Legislation to Increase Housing Affordability. *Breakthroughs* 7 (4). Available at http://www.huduser.org/rbc/newsletter/vol7iss4more.html.

Local (all from HUD Regulatory Barriers Clearinghouse, http://www.huduser.org/rbc/)

40. Department of Community Affairs. 2000. *Certification of Affordable Single- and Multifamily Developments Policy.* Tallahassee: Florida State Department of Community Affairs.

41. City of Los Angeles. 2002. *City of Los Angeles General Plan Chapter 4 Housing*. Available at http://www.ci.la.ca.us/PLN/Cwd/GnlPln/HsgElt/HE/Ch4ResDv.htm.
42. Community Action Network. 1999. *Through the Roof: A Report on Affordable Housing in Austin*. Austin, TX: Author.
43. Rappaport Institute for Greater Boston, John F. Kennedy School of Government, Harvard University. 2003. *Getting Home: Overcoming Barriers to Housing in Greater Boston*. Available at http://www.ksg.harvard.edu/rappaport/downloads/gettinghome.pdf.
44. Salama, Jerry J., Michael H. Schill, Jonathan D. Springer. 2005. *Reducing the Cost of New Housing Construction in New York City: 2005 Update*. New York: Furman Center for Real Estate and Urban Policy, The New York University School of Law, and Robert F. Wagner Graduate School of Public Service. Available at http://furmancenter.nyu.edu/CREUP_Papers/cost_study_2005/NYCHousingCost2005.pdf
45. San Francisco Chamber of Commerce. 2003. *Building Workforce Housing: Meeting San Francisco's Challenge*. Available at http://www.sfchamber.com/BestPractices.pdf.

Administrative Considerations

46. Beierle, Thomas C. 2000. The Quality of Stakeholder-Based Decisions: Lessons from the Case Study Record. Discussion Paper 00-56. Washington, DC: Resources for the Future.
47. Beierle, Thomas C., and David M. Konisky. 2000. Values, Conflict, and Trust in Participatory Environmental Planning. *Journal of Policy Analysis and Management* 19: 587–602.
48. Burby, Raymond J. 2003. Making Plans That Matter: Citizen Involvement and Government Action. *Journal of the American Planning Association* 69 (1): 33–49.
49. Conroy, Maria Manta, and Jennifer Evans-Cowley. 2004. *E-Government*. Chicago: American Planning Association.
50. May, Peter J. 2003. Performance-Based Regulation and Regulatory Regimes: The Saga of Leaky Buildings. *Law and Policy* 25 (4): 381–401.
51. May, Peter J. Regulatory Implementation: Examining Barriers from Regulatory Processes. *Cityscape* 8 (1): 209–32.

52. National Conference of States on Building Codes and Standards, Inc. 2001. *Enhancing Public Safety and the States' Role in the Global Economy through Uniform Construction Codes and Standards.* A Report to the National Governors Association. Washington, DC: U.S. Department of Commerce.
53. National Institute of Building Sciences. 2003. *Minimum Property Standards for One- and Two-Family Dwellings and Technical Suitability of Product Programs.* Washington, DC: Author.
54. Susskind, Lawrence, Sarah McKearnan, and Jennifer Thomas-Larmer. 1999. *The Consensus Building Handbook.* Cambridge, MA: Massachusetts Institute of Technology.

APPENDIX B
Chesapeake Bay Program

In the metropolitan Washington, DC, area, concerns over the long-term health of the Chesapeake Bay have prompted regional cooperation between federal and state agencies to develop policies for protecting the bay. This appendix outlines the governance, regulatory, and procedural elements of the program.

Established in 1983 as part of the Clean Water Act (CWA) to restore and protect the Chesapeake Bay, the "program brings together members of various state, federal, academic, and local watershed organizations to build and adopt policies that support bay restoration" (Chesapeake Bay Program n.d.). The program collaboratively involves members of organizations affiliated with Maryland, Virginia, Pennsylvania, the District of Columbia, and the U.S. Environmental Protection Agency (EPA). Members participate in three types of committees to drive and implement the program efforts:

- Committees that govern the Bay Program and guide policy changes
- Advisory committees that provide external perspectives on current issues and events
- Internal subcommittees that work to coordinate restoration activities

The Chesapeake Bay protection legislation greatly influences the environmental regulatory systems for both Fairfax and Montgomery counties. Compliance with the regulations and incentives developed by each state to implement the program has played a role in the unique environmental regulations found in each county—such as Resource Protection Areas (RPAs) in Fairfax County and Special Protection Areas (SPAs) in Montgomery County.

The Chesapeake Bay Preservation Act of Virginia, adopted in 1988, requires that state and local governments work to balance economic development and water quality protection. The protection of the Chesapeake Bay and the general welfare of the residents of Virginia require the following (from the Code of Virginia 10.1-2100).

- The counties, cities, and towns of Tidewater Virginia incorporate general water quality protection measures into their comprehensive plans, zoning ordinances, and subdivision ordinances
- The counties, cities, and towns of Tidewater Virginia establish programs, in accordance with criteria established by the commonwealth, that define and protect certain lands, hereinafter called Chesapeake Bay Preservation Areas, which if improperly developed may result in substantial damage to the water quality of the Chesapeake Bay and its tributaries
- The commonwealth makes its resources available to local governing bodies by providing financial and technical assistance, policy guidance, and oversight when requested or otherwise required to carry out and enforce the provisions of this chapter
- All agencies of the commonwealth exercise their delegated authority in a manner consistent with water quality protection provisions of local comprehensive plans, zoning ordinances, and subdivision ordinances when it has been determined that they comply with the provisions of this chapter.

The act gives local governments the role of planning and implementing the provisions of the act. Accordingly, the Commonwealth is to support these local efforts by establishing criteria and providing oversight and the necessary resources to carry out and enforce the act. The act also establishes the Chesapeake Bay Local Assistance Board, which is responsible for coordinating state, regional, and local initiatives for implementing the act. More specifically, the board is to "ensure local government comprehensive plans, zoning ordinances, and subdivision ordinances are in accordance with the provisions of" the act (Code of Virginia 10.1-2103). The board is required to assist local governments with the programs that, in concert with other state water quality programs, encourage and promote:

- Protection of existing high-quality state waters and restoration of all other state waters to a condition or quality that will permit all reasonable public uses and will support the propagation and growth of all aquatic life, including game fish, which might reasonably be expected to inhabit them
- Safeguarding the clean waters of the commonwealth from pollution

- Prevention of any increase in pollution
- Reduction of existing pollution
- Promotion of water resource conservation to provide for the health, safety, and welfare of the present and future citizens of the commonwealth

The act requires the following elements be part of a local Chesapeake Bay preservation program (Virginia Department of Conservation and Recreation n.d.):

1. A map delineating Chesapeake Bay Preservation Areas
2. Performance criteria applying in Chesapeake Bay Preservation Areas that will become mandatory on the local program adoption date. These criteria will:
   - Prevent a net increase in nonpoint (such as vehicular as opposed to home-based) source pollution from new development and development on previously developed land where the runoff was treated by a water quality protection best management practice
   - Achieve a 10-percent reduction in nonpoint source pollution from development on previously developed land where the runoff was not treated by one or more water quality best management practices
   - Achieve a 40 percent reduction in nonpoint source pollution from agricultural and silvicultural uses
3. A comprehensive plan or revision that incorporates the protection of Chesapeake Bay Preservation Areas and of the quality of state waters and ensures consistency between the act and the local comprehensive plan
4. A zoning ordinance or revision that:
   - Incorporates measures to protect the quality of state waters in Chesapeake Bay Preservation Areas, ensuring their consistency with the act
   - Requires compliance with all criteria set forth in number 2
5. A subdivision ordinance or revision that:
   - Incorporates measures to protect the quality of state waters in Chesapeake Bay Preservation Areas, ensuring their consistency with the act
   - Requires compliance with all criteria set forth in number 2
6. An erosion and sediment control ordinance or revision that requires compliance with the criteria in number 2

7. A plan of development process prior to the issuance of a building permit to ensure that use and development of land in Chesapeake Bay Preservation Areas is accomplished in a manner that protects the quality of state waters

Virginia Chesapeake Bay Preservation Act— Area Designation and Management Regulations

The Virginia Chesapeake Bay Preservation Area Designation and Management Regulations establish the criteria by which local governments must model ordinances.[1] The regulations outline the criteria for designating RPAs, Resource Management Areas (RMAs), Intensely Developed Areas (IDAs), and the performance measures that development requirements are to achieve.

Designation Criteria for Chesapeake Bay Preservation Areas

- Resource Protection Areas (RPA) (sensitive areas with intrinsic water quality value)
  - Tidal wetlands
  - Nontidal wetlands connected to tidal wetlands
  - Tidal shores
  - Other lands with intrinsic water quality value
  - Buffer areas at least 100 feet landward of above areas and on both sides of perennial streams
- RMAs (areas outside of RPA with potential water quality impacts)
  - Floodplains
  - Highly erodible soils
  - Steep slopes
  - Highly permeable soils
  - Nontidal wetlands not included in RPA
  - Other lands necessary to protect water quality
- IDAs (developed areas as an overlay to CBPA available for redevelopment where little natural environment remains)
  - Existing development has more than 50 percent impervious cover
  - Public water and sewer or constructed stormwater drainage system currently serves the area
  - Housing density greater than or equal to four dwelling units per acre

Performance Criteria for Chesapeake Bay Preservation Areas

- Generalized Performance Criteria
    - Minimize
        - Land disturbance
        - Indigenous vegetation removal
        - Impervious cover
    - Maximize rainwater infiltration
    - Ensure long-term performance of BMPs
    - Land disturbance exceeding 2,500 square feet requires plan of development review and erosion and sediment control compliance
    - New septic systems to have reserve system equal to primary system
    - Postdevelopment nonpoint source runoff load shall not exceed predevelopment; redevelopment requires additional 10 percent reduction if no existing BMPs
    - Evidence of wetlands permits, if required
- Additional requirements for RPAs
    - Only water-dependent development in RPA or redevelopment of existing development allowed
    - Buffer requirements
        - 100 feet of vegetation effective in retarding runoff, preventing erosion, filtering nonpoint source pollution
        - If none are present, reestablish to provide woody vegetation that assures the buffer functions
    - Buffer maintenance required
    - If buffer preclude prior buildable lot, buffer may be reduced if reduction minimized (but no more than 50 feet) and additional buffer provided elsewhere on lot
    - Redevelopment within IDA may be exempt from additional buffer requirement but consideration should be given to establishing buffer over time.
    - Water quality assessment required demonstrating compliance with the program's established goals and requirements

Traditionally more lax in its regulatory role, Fairfax County has been increasing environmental regulations to emulate similar requirements in Montgomery County. This has been done in compliance with the Chesapeake Bay Preservation Act, which requires the local comprehensive plan, zoning ordi-

196   Appendix B

nance, and subdivision ordinance implement the Chesapeake Bay program agreements.

Fairfax County Chesapeake Bay Ordinance

The Fairfax County Chesapeake Bay Ordinance, adopted in 1993, designates RPAs, RMAs, and the requirements developers must follow when completing a project in the county.[2]

Designation Criteria for Chesapeake Bay Preservation Areas

- Resource Protection Areas (RPA) (sensitive areas with intrinsic water quality value)
  - Tidal wetlands
  - Tidal shores
  - Water body with perennial flow
  - Nontidal wetlands connected to tidal wetlands or to a water body with perennial flow
  - Buffer areas
    - At least 100 feet landward of above areas
    - Any land within major floodplain
- RMAs (areas outside of RPA with potential water quality impacts)
  - Any area not designated as an RPA
    - Floodplains
    - Highly erodible soils
    - Steep slopes
    - Highly permeable soils
    - Other lands necessary to protect water quality
- IDAs (developed areas as an overlay to CBPA available for redevelopment where little natural environment remains)
- Performance Criteria for Chesapeake Bay Preservation Areas
- Generalized Performance Criteria
  - Prevent a net increase of nonpoint source pollution
  - Achieve a 10-percent reduction in nonpoint source pollution from redevelopment
  - Minimize
    - Land disturbance

- Indigenous vegetation removal
- Impervious cover
- Maximize rainwater infiltration
- Ensure long-term performance of BMPs
- Development and redevelopment projects shall employ BMPs to control stormwater runoff to reduce projected phosphorous loading by 40 percent (development) or 10 percent (redevelopment)
- BMPs of adjacent projects may be combined to satisfy water quality protection requirements
- Land disturbance exceeding 2,500 square feet requires plan of development review and erosion and sediment control compliance
- New septic systems to have reserve system equal to primary system
- Postdevelopment nonpoint source runoff load shall not exceed predevelopment; redevelopment requires additional 10 percent reduction if no existing BMPs
- Wetlands permits, if required, shall be procured prior to commencement of land disturbing activities
- Additional requirements for RPAs
  - Water quality assessment required demonstrating compliance with the program's established goals and requirements
  - Only water-dependent development in RPA or redevelopment of existing development allowed
  - Buffer requirements
    - Vegetation effective in retarding runoff, preventing erosion, and filtering nonpoint source pollution
    - Indigenous vegetation may be removed (subject to approval) to provide for reasonable sight lines, access paths, general woodlot management, and habitat management
    - If are none present, reestablish with mixture of overstory trees, understory trees, shrubs, and groundcovers to provide woody vegetation that assures the buffer functions
  - Buffer maintenance required
  - If buffer preclude prior buildable lot, buffer may be reduced if reduction minimized (but no more than 50 feet) and additional buffer provided elsewhere on lot
  - Redevelopment within IDA may be exempt from additional buffer requirement but consideration should be given to establishing buffer over time.

Maryland Critical Area Program of 1984 (Expanded in 2002)

The Critical Area Program[3] establishes a Resource Protection Program as the state recognizes:

- The significance of the Chesapeake and Atlantic Coastal Bays and their tributaries to the state and nation
- Human activity can have an immediate and adverse impact on water quality and natural habitats
- The capacity of the shoreline and adjacent lands to withstand continuing demands without further degradation to water quality and natural habitats is limited
- It is necessary wherever possible to maintain a minimum 100-foot buffer landward from the mean high-water line
- The restoration of the Chesapeake Bay and Atlantic Coastal Bays and their tributaries is dependent, in part, on minimizing further adverse impacts to the water quality and natural habitats of the shoreline and adjacent lands, particularly in the buffer
- The cumulative impact of current development and of each new development activity in the buffer is inimical to these purposes
- There is a critical and substantial state interest for the benefit of current and future generations in fostering a more sensitive development activity in a consistent and uniform manner to minimize damage to water quality and natural habitats

The Chesapeake Bay Critical Area and Atlantic Coastal Bays Critical Area

- All waters of and lands under the bays and their tributaries to the head of tide and all state and private wetlands
- All land and water areas within 1,000 feet beyond the landward boundaries of state or private wetlands and heads of tides
- A local jurisdiction may exclude:
  - Developed, urban areas (or portions thereof) where the imposition of a program would not substantially improve protection of tidal water quality, wildlife, or their habitats
  - Areas located 1,000 feet from open water and separated by an area of wetlands that is found will serve to protect tidal water quality, wildlife, or their habitats

- A portion of urban land to be excluded must be at least 50 percent developed and not less than 2,640,000 square feet
- Local jurisdictions shall have primary responsibility for developing and implementing a program, subject to review and approval by the commission. A program shall consist of those elements necessary or appropriate to:
  - Minimize adverse impacts on water quality discharged from structures or conveyances or runoff from surrounding lands
  - Conserve fish, wildlife, and plant habitat
  - For development in the critical areas, establish land use policies that accommodate growth and address the fact that, even if pollution is controlled, the number, movement, and activities of persons in that area can create adverse environmental impacts
- A local program includes:
  - A map designating critical areas
  - Comprehensive zoning map for the critical areas
  - New or amended:
    - Subdivision regulations
    - Comprehensive or master plan
    - Zoning ordinances or regulations
    - Enforcement provisions
    - Grandfathering provisions
  - Provisions to limit impervious coverage and to require or encourage cluster development
  - Establish buffer areas for agricultural activities and minimum setbacks for development
- Conditions for development within the critical areas
  - Growth allocation for a locality shall be calculated based on 5 percent of the total resource conservation are in a local jurisdiction
  - When locating new development:
    - New intensively designed development should be located in limited development areas or adjacent to existing intensely developed areas
    - New limited development areas should be located adjacent to existing limited development areas or intensely developed areas
    - No more than 50 percent of the expansion may be located in resource conservation areas

- New intensely or limited development areas located in the resource conservation area shall conform with all criteria and shall be designated on the comprehensive zoning map
- Resource conservation area private wetlands may be included in land area of a one-in-twenty-acre density if:
  - The upland density does not exceed a one-in-eight-acre density
- One additional dwelling unit may be considered per lot or parcel as part of a primary unit for the purpose of the density calculation if:
  - The unit is located within the primary unit or its entire perimeter is within 100 feet of the primary unit
  - It does not exceed 900 square feet
  - Is served by the same sewage disposal system as the primary unit
  - Its construction does not increase the impervious surface area attributed to the primary unit
- Intrafamily transfers of property may take place on properties between seven and sixty acres and are subject to the following conditions:
  - Parcels seven to twelve acres may be subdivided into two lots
  - Parcels twelve to sixty acres may be subdivided into three lots
  - Cannot be subdivided for commercial sale
- Impervious surface limitations in limited development areas and resource conservation areas:
  - Manmade impervious surfaces are limited to 15 percent of a parcel or lot
  - Lots or parcels up to one-half acre are limited to 25 percent impervious surface
  - Lots or parcels between one-half and one acre are limited to 15 percent impervious surface
  - Individual lots one acre or less that are part of a subdivision may not exceed 25 percent imperviousness, but the entire subdivision may not exceed 15 percent imperviousness
- Impervious surface limitations may be exceeded if the following conditions exist:
  - New impervious surfaces have been properly minimized
  - Lots or parcels up to one-half acre are limited to 25 percent or 500 square feet, whichever is greater
  - Lots or parcels between one-half and one acre are limited to 15 percent or 5,445 square feet, whichever is greater

- Water quality impacts can be and have been minimized through site design or BMPs
- Onsite mitigation is implemented or fees are paid
- Development sites in intensely developed areas are to provide a forest or developed woodland cover of at least 15 percent after development or a fee-in-lieu payment adequate to ensure the restoration or establishment of an equivalent forest area
- Localities may develop:
  - A provision encouraging the use of bioretention for stormwater management associated with redevelopment in intensely developed areas
- The approving authority of any subdivision plat approval or approval of a zoning amendment, variance, special exception, conditional use permit, or use of a floating zone affecting any land or water area located within the critical area shall render its decision based on the specific findings that:
  - The proposed development will minimize adverse impacts on water quality
  - The development has been designed to minimize adverse impacts on any identified fish, wildlife, or plant habitat whose loss would substantially diminish the continued ability of those populations to sustain themselves
- Undeveloped lots in existence prior to the adoption of this program are entitled to construct a single-family dwelling unit in accordance with the local critical area program to the extent possible

Maryland Economic Growth, Resource Protection, and Planning Act of 1992

Development regulations must be consistent with comprehensive plan.[4]

- Statement of goals and objectives, principles, policies, and standards that serve as a guide for development and economic and social growth.
- A land-use plan element that shows proposals for the most appropriate and desirable patterns for the general location, character, extent, and interrelationships of the manner in which the community should use its public and private land.
- A transportation element that shows proposals for the most appropriate and desirable patterns for the general location, character, and extent of the channels, routes, and terminals for transportation facilities, and for

the circulation of persons and goods. The transportation element shall also provide for bicycle and pedestrian access and travel ways.
- A community facilities plan element that shows proposals for the most appropriate and desirable patterns for the general location, character, and extent of public and semipublic buildings, land, and facilities.
- A mineral resources element
- An element that contains recommendations that:
  - Encourage streamlined review of development applications within areas designated for growth
  - Encourage the use of flexible development regulations to promote innovative and cost-saving site design while protecting the environment
  - Use innovative techniques to foster economic development in areas designated for growth.

(Please refer to Models and Guidelines # 94-02: Regulatory Streamlining, and #95-06, Achieving Environmentally Sensitive Design through Flexible and Innovative Regulations, for more information.)

The predominant effect of these activities in Fairfax and Montgomery counties has been in the areas of nutrient and sediment pollution. Increased review processes, land-use and development performance criteria, and erosion and sediment control requirements are employed in an effort to restore the health of the Chesapeake Bay.

APPENDIX C

Outline of Environmental Regulations and Review Processes in Fairfax County, Virginia, and Montgomery County, Maryland

This appendix provides an outline of the environmental regulations and review processes used in the two largest—and most dominant—jurisdictions in the metropolitan Washington, DC, housing market: Fairfax and Montgomery counties.

Fairfax County's Environmental Regulatory Ordinances and Guidelines

Beyond the environmental consultant's inventory of relevant environmental regulations, Fairfax County has several special environmental ordinances and guidelines that have a significant effect on housing developments:

- The Chesapeake Bay Ordinance
  - Resource Protection Areas (RPAs)
  - Resource Management Areas (RMAs)
- Environmental Quality Corridors (EQCs)
- Open Space Preservation
- Vegetation Preservation and Planting
- Outfall Analysis

The county's compliance with the Chesapeake Bay Ordinance through the creation of RPAs and RMAs affects development planning in significant ways by requiring more detailed data analysis and mitigation efforts. Amendments to the Chesapeake Bay Ordinance affect stormwater management expectations and require more detailed information in the graphic and narrative portions of special permits, special exceptions, rezoning, and development plan applications. Other amendments expanded the area of RPAs by 11,300 acres through changing the definition of what constituted a perennial stream in the county.

RPAs are buffered areas around perennial streams where development must be very limited to protect water quality from degradation associated with pollutants and other adverse impacts associated with human activities. No expansions or additions to current property may be allowed and no new development is permitted within a RPA.

RMAs are designated adjacent to RPAs to provide a buffer from certain types of development in an effort to preserve RPA functional integrity for protecting water resources from contaminants. Chapter 118 of the Fairfax County Code establishes requirements for development in and adjacent to RPAs and RMAs (Fairfax County Code: Chapter 118 n.d.).

Fairfax County's Chesapeake Bay Ordinance, which establishes RPAs, RMAs, and provides authority to designate Intensely Developed Areas (IDAs), sets forth the following requirements:

- It is on the burden of the applicant to show appropriate RPA and RMA boundaries
- If a conflict arises, the greater requirement or higher standard shall govern

EQCs are a more broad application of the RPA system. EQCs are designed to protect and restore the ecological quality of streams, which provide habitat, replenish water supplies, and provide recreation and aesthetic amenities. As stream corridors represent the central feature of the EQC system as well as a significant portion of the county's parkland, objectives and policies to minimize the adverse impacts of land use and development in relation to these corridors are established in the environment section of the Fairfax County Comprehensive Plan (n.d.).

Open Space Preservation is required by Fairfax County through the Zoning Ordinance when completing a development (Fairfax County Code: Article 2 n.d.). This requirement may be enforced through by-right development regulations or through proffered conditions of approval when working through the rezoning process. Another method of conserving open space encouraged within the county is through easements.

A Vegetation Preservation and Planting ordinance was passed by the county to regulate the removal of vegetation from public and private property in order to preserve, protect, and enhance forest cover and trees. The ordinance reads such that it establishes standards for limiting the removal and ensuring the replacement of vegetation sufficient to safeguard the ecological and aesthetic environment (Fairfax County Public Facilities Manual 12-0100 n.d.).

Outfall analysis monitoring and mitigation is required to minimize the impacts of concentrated flow increases on existing streambeds by demonstrating that no adverse impacts will result in existing stream corridors postdevelopment. In areas where impact is considered unacceptable by county regulators, mitigation measures may be required. This process is currently atypical but, as less-challenging developable sites become scarce, it is likely to increase in prominence as the county recently adopted amendments to the Public Facilities Manual, Zoning Ordinance, and Subdivision Ordinances establishing review and notification requirements.[1]

- **Mitigation and Permit Modifications.** A few of the projects required mitigation measures and changes to the original project design because of stream erosion and subsequent CWA permit violations. These may take place onsite or offsite and can be in the form of fines.
- **Routine Stream Monitoring and Reporting.** Stream monitoring costs were also involved in one project to determine the outfall impact of development on existing watercourses.

Montgomery County's Environmental Regulatory Ordinances and Guidelines

Important tools in the county's land-use regulatory toolbox are its environmental guidelines, which it can use in guiding developers to achieve environmental protection goals during the development process. Some, such as Special Protection Areas, are directly linked to the comprehensive plan while others, such as conservation easements, rely on the voluntary actions of developers and residents. Environmental regulations specific to Montgomery County include:

- Chesapeake Bay Protection: Special Protection Areas (SPAs)
- Forest Conservation

SPAs are areas within a watershed where natural features, especially those related to water, are of a high quality. Unlike many environmental regulations in Fairfax County, which are directives of the state, the SPA program is derived from the county's comprehensive plan goal of watershed and stream protection. The SPA program was established by the Montgomery County Code Chapter 19, Article V, in 1994 (Montgomery County Department of Environmental Protection 2002). Since that time, four SPAs have been designated in the county: Upper Paint Branch, Piney Branch, Clarksburg, and Upper Rock Creek. Existing single-family homes within SPAs may expand as long as they are consistent with zoning laws. However, the development process is different for projects proposed within a SPA. The local government must work closely with environmental agencies to minimize impacts; a one-year, presubmission stream monitoring program is required; and a multi-agency review process is involved. There is a conservation plan for each SPA and an annual report on stream data and development activities. The developer's design requirements include a higher level of erosion and sediment control, stormwater management, environmental buffers around streams, and provision of long-term protection of these areas through easements or park dedications (Montgomery County Department of Parks 2000).

The preliminary plan approval time does not include the one-year water monitoring period required for development projects in a SPA. This monitoring is used to establish a water quality baseline to measure effects of the new development on the high-quality water resources. The new development is monitored for five years after construction to evaluate the effectiveness of the installed mitigation facilities. In addition, a $500-per-acre environmental impact fee is assessed by the Department of Environment on developments in a SPA to be used for additional studies. The preliminary plan required the completion of a natural resources inventory, conceptual stormwater management plan, and preliminary grading plan. With a significant level of detail involved in the preparation of these components, the developer invests heavily in meeting environmental regulations at the front end of the project.

Planning for forest conservation was given priority in the county following Maryland's 1991 Forest Conservation Act, after which the County Council passed the Montgomery County Forest Conservation Law. The purpose of the law is to preserve and protect existing trees and forest cover in the county because of their numerous environmental benefits. It established procedures, standards, and requirements for afforestation and reforestation of land subject to an application for development approval or a sediment control permit. In addition, regulations exist to minimize tree loss as a result of development and to protect trees and forests during and after land development activities (Montomery County n.d.).

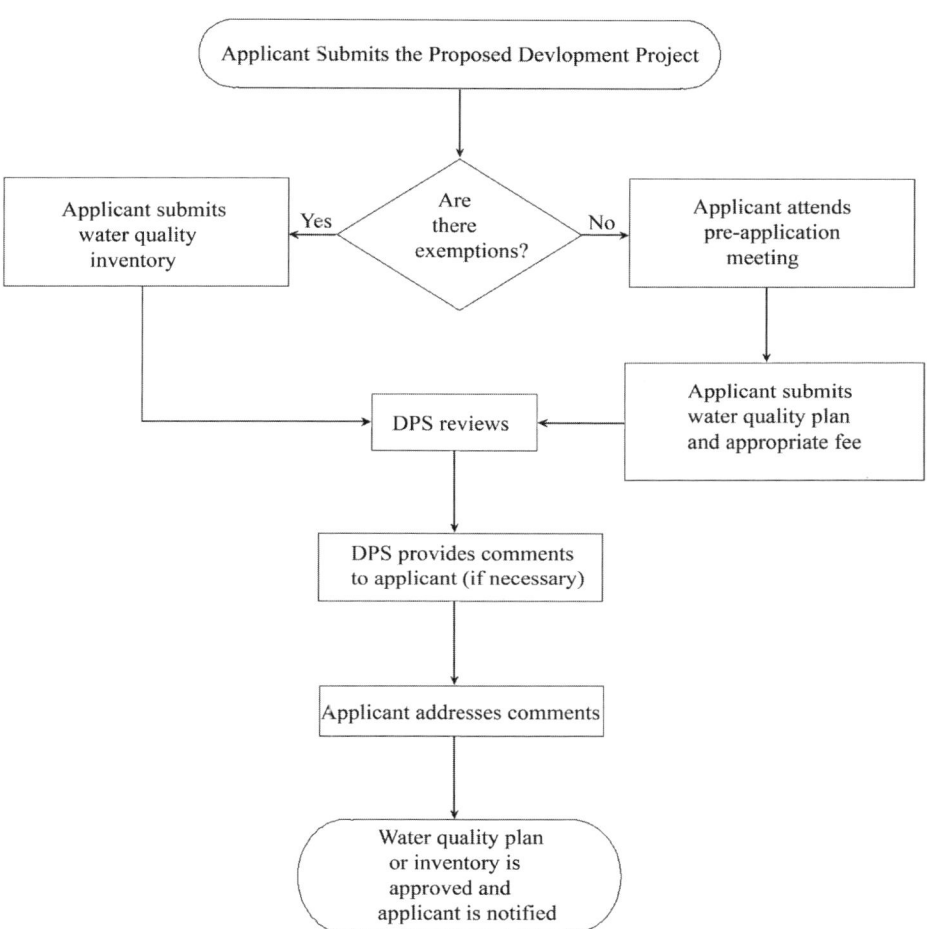

Figure C.1 Special Protection Review Process, Montgomery County, Maryland.
Source: Figure provided by Montgomery County Planning Board.

APPENDIX D
Special References for Cost Reduction and Best Development Practices

Time-Saver Standards

DeChaira, Joseph. 1984. *Time-Saver Standards for Residential Development*. New York: McGraw-Hill.

DeChaira, Joseph, and John Callender. 1990. *Time-Saver Standards for Building Types*. 3rd ed. New York: McGraw-Hill.

DeChaira, Joseph, and Lee E. Koppelman. 1984. *Time-Saver Standards for Site Planning*. New York: McGraw-Hill.

DeChaira, Joseph, Julius Panero, and Martin Zelnick. 1985. *Time-Saver Standards for Housing and Residential Development*. 2nd ed. New York: McGraw-Hill.

Dines, Nicholas T., and Kyle D. Brown. 1998. *Time-Saver Standards Concise Site Construction Details Manual*. New York: McGraw-Hill.

Watson, Donald. 2000. *Time-Saver Standards for Building Materials and Systems*. New York: McGraw-Hill.

Watson, Donald, Alan Plattus, and Robert Shibley. 2003. *Time-Saver Standards for Urban Design*. New York: McGraw-Hill.

Best Development Practices

Ben-Joseph, Eran, and Terry S. Szold. 2004. *Regulating Place: Standards and the Shaping of Urban America*. New York: Routledge.

Corbett, Michael, Judy Corbett, and Robert L. Thayer. 1999. *Designing Sustainable Communities: Learning From Village Homes*. Washington, DC: Island Press.

Ewing, Reid H. 1998. *Best Development Practices: A Primer for Smart Growth.* Washington, DC: International City-County Management Association.

Ewing, Reid H., Christine C. Heflin, MaryBeth DeAnna, and Douglas R. Porter. 1996. *Best Development Practices: Doing the Right Thing and Making Money at the Same Time.* Chicago: American Planning Association.

Porter, Douglas R. 2002. *Making Smart Growth Work.* Washington, DC: Urban Land Institute.

NOTES

Introduction

1. The term "housing affordability" is used to prevent confusion with the specific definition provided by the U.S. Department of Housing and Urban Development (HUD) on what constitutes "affordable housing" technically. We focus on the relationship between environmental regulations and housing costs, but we occasionally use the term "housing affordability" to suggest the possibility that housing costs associated with environmental regulations may rise to a point where substantially fewer households could afford to buy a home.

Chapter One

1. Much of this section is adapted from HUD's Administrative Service Center 1, Solicitation Number R-2004-R-00126, "Study of Impact of Environmental Regulatory Processes on Affordable Housing."
2. Much of the discussion in this section is based on Peter J. May, "Regulatory Implementation: Examining Barriers from Regulatory Processes," *Cityscape* vol. 8, no. 1, pp. 209–32.
3. Much of the historical discussion is adapted from Robert H. Freilich and Michael M. Schultz, *Model Subdivision Regulations*, 2nd Edition, American Planning Association (Chicago: 1995).
4. This attitude prevailed into the 1990s in some communities.

Chapter Two

This chapter follows an alternative reference style. All references are numbered and contained in brackets. Please refer to Appendix A for full citations.

1. [10, 19].
2. [10, 11, 15, 17, 19, 25].
3. See, for example, the 1991 Kemp Commission. [9, 20, 21, 22].
4. [26, 27, 28, 29, 30, 31, 32, 33, 34, 35, 36, 37, 38, 39].
5. [40, 41, 42, 43, 44, 45].
6. [2, 6].
7. [2, 3, 6].
8. [1, 5, 6, 7, 8].
9. [2, 6].
10. [13, 14].
11. [11].
12. [9, 27, 34, 38, 43].
13. [42].
14. [18].
15. [9, 16, 34, 43].
16. [16, 27, 29].
17. [14].
18. [9, 14, 16, 34, 43].
19. [13].
20. [10, 19].
21. [32].
22. [10].
23. [1, 11, 38, 42].
24. Including national permitting and state requirements. [10, 12, 19].
25. [42].
26. [1, 7, 8].
27. [24].
28. [18, 25, 26, 34, 45].
29. [25, 27, 28].
30. [27].
31. [9, 29, 40, 41, 44].
32. [26, 33, 37].
33. [15, 36].
34. [45].
35. [11, 12, 13, 14, 17, 19].
36. [17, 25, 31].
37. [51].
38. [51].
39. [53].
40. [52].
41. [47].

42. [50].
43. [50].
44. [50].
45. [50].
46. [48, page 38].
47. [46, 47, 48].
48. [50].
49. [54].

Chapter Four

1. Data from "Economic Indicators" is available at http://www.fairfax county.gov/economic/indicat/2006/02.pdf.

2. Data from "Economic Indicators" is available at http://www.fairfax county.gov/economic/indicat/1998/02.pdf.

3. For more information, see "Affordable Housing Partnership Program," available at http://www.fairfaxcounty.gov/rha/ahpp.htm.

4. Data from Maryland-National Capital Park and Planning Commission, Montgomery Planning Board, "Montgomery County at a Glance—Current Estimates: Population, Housing, Employment," available at http://www.mc-mncppc.org/research/data_library/montgomery_county_glance/ata glance.pdf.

5. Data from Maryland-National Capital Park and Planning Commission, Montgomery Planning Board, "Montgomery County at a Glance—Current Estimates: Population, Housing, Employment," available at http://www.mc-mncppc.org/research/data_library/montgomery_county_glance/ata glance.pdf.

6. Data from Montgomery County Maryland, Department of Housing and Community Affairs, "Federal Programs Section," available at http://www.montgomerycountymd.gov/dhctmpl.asp?url=/content/dhca/community/conplan99exsum.asp.

7. Data from Montgomery County Maryland, Department of Housing and Community Affairs, "Consolidated Plan for Montgomery County, Maryland," available at http://www.montgomerycountymd.gov/content/dhca/community/conplan07_exec_summary.doc.

8. Data from Montgomery County Maryland, Department of Housing and Community Affairs, "Consolidated Plan for Montgomery County, Maryland," available at http://www.montgomerycountymd.gov/content/dhca/community/conplan07_exec_summary.doc.

9. Data from Montgomery County Maryland, Department of Housing and Community Affairs, "Consolidated Plan for Montgomery County, Maryland," available at http://www.montgomerycountymd.gov/content/dhca/community/conplan07_exec_summary.doc.

10. Data from MNCPPC Research and Technology Center (RTC), the Department of Housing and Community Affairs, the Housing Opportunities Commission, and the City of Rockville, County MPDU, available at http://www.mc-mncppc.org/research/data_library/real_estate_development/housing/pdfs/countympdu.pdf.

11. For more details, visit Fairfax County Department of Planning and Zoning, "Zoning Application Process," available at http://www.fairfaxcounty.gov/dpz/zoning/applaccept.htm.

12. For more details, see the "Fairfax County Rezoning Application Package," available at http://www.fairfaxcounty.gov/dpz/zoning/applications/nofind/2005/rzconvpkg.pdf.

13. For more information, see also Fairfax County Zoning Applications, "Rezoning Process," available at http://www.fairfaxcounty.gov/dpz/zoning/rzprocess.htm.

14. For additional information, see Fairfax County Department of Planning and Zoning, "Zoning Application Process," available at www.fairfaxcounty.gov/dpz/zoning/applaccept.htm.

15. For more information, see "Fairfax County Rezoning Application Package," available at http://www.fairfaxcounty.gov/dpz/zoning/applications/nofind/2005/rzconvpkg.pdf.

16. For more information, see also "Fairfax County Rezoning Application Package," available at http://www.fairfaxcounty.gov/dpz/zoning/applications/nofind/2005/rzconvpkg.pdf.

17. For more information, visit MNCPPC, "Community Based Planning Master Plans Master List," available at http://www.mc-mncppc.org/community/plan_areas/master_plans.shtm.

18. For more details, visit DPS/General Information, "Permitting Process," available at http://permittingservices.montgomerycountymd.gov/dpstmpl.asp?url=/permitting/gi/nfatm.asp.

19. For more information, see "How to Participate Effectively in the Subdivision Process in Montgomery County, Maryland," available at http://www.mc-mncppc.org/development/about/subdivision.pdf.

20. For more information, see Montgomery County Department of Permitting Services, "About DPS," available at http://permittingservices.montgomerycountymd.gov/dpstmpl.asp?url=/aboutdps.asp.

21. For more information, see Montgomery County Department of Permitting Services, "About DPS," available at http://permittingservices.montgomerycountymd.gov/dpstmpl.asp?url=/aboutdps.asp.

22. For more information, see FY05PRELIM document, available at http://www.mcparkandplanning.org/development/forms/prelimplan_aug04/FY05PRELIM.pdf.

23. For more information, see FY05SITE document, available at http://www.mcparkandplanning.org/development/forms/siteplan_aug04/FY05SITE.pdf.

24. For more information, see FY05PLAT document, available at http://www.mcparkandplanning.org/development/forms/plat_Oct_04/FY05PLAT.pdf.

25. For more information, see "Comprehensive Plan Glossary," available at http://www.fairfaxcounty.gov/dpz/comprehensiveplan/glossary/.

26. For more information, see *Fairfax County Zoning Ordinance—Article 2: General Regulations*, available at http://www.fairfaxcounty.gov/dpz/zoningordinance/articles/art02.pdf.

27. For more information, see *In Brief: The MPDU Process for Builders and Developers*, available at http://www.montgomerycountymd.gov/dhctmpl.asp?url=/content/dhca/housing/housing_P/mpdu/MPDU_Process_Developers.asp.

28. Afforestation is the creation of a biological community dominated by trees and other woody plants at a density of at least 100 trees per acre. For more information, see "Appendix A" of the document available at http://www.mcparkandplanning.org/Environment/forest/trees/append_trees.pdf.

29. One could speculate that perhaps the difference is not significant in light of the robust regional housing market from 1997 to 2006. Maybe the additional environmental costs affected the home builders' rate of return for Montgomery County, but had little financial impact given the multiple projects in multiple counties; thus, the costs are spread across the companies' portfolio of projects.

Chapter Five

1. Fairfax County also does not have broad authority to impose impact fees compared with local governments in Maryland.

2. This development/acquisition strategy makes sense for smaller home builders/developers because they tend to acquire properties with such preliminary approvals; while many larger, regional, or national home builders have

business models that now focus on the acquisition and development of raw land.

3. In addition to natural features, archeological and cultural resources are frequently required for inventory during the early planning approval phases of the project.

4. According to yearlong study by University of Pennsylvania researchers Susan Wachter and Kevin Gillen (2006), investment in "green infrastructure" (natural open space) strategies not only enhanced the overall vitality of Philadelphia neighborhoods but also increased the values of adjacent and nearby properties (based on 2004 median home price of $82,700):

- Adjacent to stabilized and greened lot: 17 percent increase in value, or $14,059
- Near a new tree planting: 9 percent increase in value, or $7,443
- Near a excellent commercial corridor: 23 percent increase in value, or $19,021
- Near streetscape improvements: 28 percent increase in value, or $23,156
- Located within Business Improvement Districts: 30 percent increase in value, or $24,397

Appendix B

1. For additional information, see www.cblad.virginia.gov/docs/Regs 3-01-02.pdf.

2. For additional information, see www.fairfaxcounty.gov/dpwes/environmental/cbay/ch118final.pdf.

3. For additional information, see www.dsd.state.md.us/comar/Annot_Code_Idx/NaturalResIndex.htm, Title 8, Subtitle 18.

4. For additional information, refer to www.mdp.state.md.us/general/planact.htm.

Appendix C

1. For more information on these amendments, see "Fairfax County Public Facilities Manual, 6-0000 Storm Drainage Amendment 1," available at http://www.fairfaxcounty.gov/dpwes/publications/pfm/ao/amendment1.pdf, and "6-0000 Storm Drainage Amendment 2," available at http://www.fairfaxcounty.gov/dpwes/publications/pfm/ao/amendment2.pdf.

REFERENCES AND SELECTED BIBLIOGRAPHY

Abbott, William W., Peter M. Detwiler, M. Thomas Jacobson, Margaret Sohagi, and Harriet A. Steiner. 2001. *Exactions and Impact Fees in California*. Point Arena, CA: Solano Press.

Adams, Gerard F., Grace Milgram, Edward W. Green, and Christine Mansfield. 1968. Undeveloped Land Prices during Urbanization: A Micro-Empirical Study over Time. *Review of Economics and Statistics* 50 (2):248–58.

Advisory Commission on Intergovernmental Relations. 1966. *Building Codes: A Program for Intergovernmental Reform*. Report A-26. Washington, DC: Superintendent of Documents, U.S. Government Printing Office.

Advisory Commission on Regulatory Barriers to Affordable Housing. 1991. *"Not in My Back Yard": Removing Barriers to Affordable Housing*. Final report. Washington, DC: U.S. Department of Housing and Urban Development.

Ahlbrandt, Roger S. Jr. 1976. *Flexible Code Enforcement: A Key Ingredient in Neighborhood Preservation Planning*. Washington, DC: National Association of Housing and Redevelopment Officials.

Alterman, Rachelle. 2001. *National-Level Planning in Democratic Countries: An International Comparison of City and Regional Policy-Making*. Town Planning Review Book Series. Liverpool: Liverpool University Press.

Altshuler, Alan A., and Jose A. Gómez-Ibáñez. 1993. *Regulation for Revenue*. Cambridge, MA: Lincoln Institute of Land Policy.

American Bar Association. 1976. *Model Land Development Code*. Chicago: Author.

American Farmland Trust. 2001. *Purchase of Development Rights and Transfer of Development Rights Case Studies*. Prepared for Boone County Planning Commission. Available at www.ctahr.hawaii.edu/awg/downloads/rp_AFT_TDRstudies_Boone.doc.

American Institute of Planners (AIP). 1976. *Survey of State Land Use Planning Activity.* Report to the U.S. Department of Housing and Urban Development. Washington, DC.

American Planning Association. 2002. *Planning for Smart Growth: State of the States.* Chicago: Author.

Anthony, Jerry. 2003. The Effects of Florida's Growth Management Act on Housing Affordability. *Journal of the American Planning Association* 69 (3):282–95.

Apgar, William, Allegra Calder, Michael Collins, and Mark Duda. 2003. *An Examination of Manufactured Housing as a Community- and Asset-Building Strategy.* Cambridge, MA: Neighborhood Reinvestment Corp. and the Joint Center for Housing Studies, Harvard University.

Asabeare, Paul K., and Peter F. Colwell. 1984. Zoning and the Value of Urban Land. *Real Estate Issues* 8 (1):22–27.

Ayres, Ian, and John Braithwaite. 1992. *Responsive Regulation: Transcending the Deregulation Debate.* New York: Oxford University Press.

Babcock, Richard F. 1966. *The Zoning Game: Municipal Practices and Policies.* Madison: University of Wisconsin Press.

Babcock, Richard F., and Fred P. Bosselman. 1973. *Exclusionary Zoning.* New York: Praeger.

Baden, Brett M., and Don L. Coursey. 1999. An Examination of the Effects of Impact Fees on Chicago's Suburbs. Working Paper 99: 20. Harris School of Public Policy Studies, University of Chicago.

Bailey, Martin J. 1959. A Note on the Economics of Residential Zoning and Urban Renewal. *Land Economics* 35 (2):288–92.

Bailey, Martin J., Richard Muth, and Hugh O. Nourse. 1963. A Regression Model for Real Estate Price Index Construction. *Journal of the American Statistical Association* 58 (304):933–42.

Baldassare, Mark, and Georjeanna Wilson. 1996. Changing Sources of Suburban Support for Local Growth Controls. *Urban Studies* 33:459–71.

Bardach, Eugene, and Robert Kagan. 1982. *Going by the Book: The Problem of Regulatory Unreasonableness.* Philadelphia: Temple University Press.

Bauman, Gus, and William H. Ethier. 1987. Development Exactions and Impact Fees: A Survey of American Practice. *Law & Contemporary Problems* 50:51–68.

Beaton, W. Patrick. 1991. The Impact of Regional Land-Use Controls on Property Values: The Case of the New Jersey Pinelands. *Land Economics* 67 (2):172–94.

Beaton, W. Patrick, and Marcus Pollock. 1992. Economic Impact of Growth Management Policies Surrounding the Chesapeake Bay. *Land Economics* 68 (4):434–53.

Been, Vicki. 1991. "Exit" as a Constraint on Land Use Exactions: Rethinking the Unconstitutional Conditions Doctrine. *Columbia Law Review* 91 (3): 473–506.

———. Impact Fees and Housing Affordability. *Cityscape* 8 (1):139–86.

Beierle, Thomas C. 1998. Public Participation in Environmental Decisions: An Evaluation Framework Using Social Goals. Discussion Paper 99-06. Washington, DC: Resources for the Future.

———. 2000. The Quality of Stakeholder-Based Decisions: Lessons from the Case Study Record. Discussion Paper 00-56. Washington, DC: Resources for the Future.

Beierle, Thomas C., and Jerry Cayford. 2001. Evaluating Dispute Resolution as an Approach to Public Participation. Discussion Paper 01-40. Washington, DC: Resources for the Future.

Beierle, Thomas C., and David M. Konisky. 2000. Values, Conflict, and Trust in Participatory Environmental Planning. *Journal of Policy Analysis and Management* 19:587–602.

Ben-Joseph, Eran. 2003. Subdivision Regulations: Practices and Attitudes. Working Paper WP03EB1. Cambridge, MA: Lincoln Institute of Land Policy. Available at http://www.lincolninst.edu/pubs/pub-detail.asp?id=846.

Bernstein, Harvey, and Andrew Lemer. 1996. *Solving the Innovation Puzzle: Challenges Facing the U.S. Design and Construction Industry.* New York: American Society of Civil Engineers.

Black, J. Thomas, and James Hoben. 1985. Land Price Inflation and Affordable Housing: Causes and Impacts. *Urban Geography* 6 (1):27–47.

Blaesser, Brian, and Christene M. Kentopp. 1990. Impact Fees: The Second Generation. *Washington University Journal of Urban and Contemporary Law* 38 (1):55–100.

Blewett, Robert A., and Arthur C. Nelson. 1988. A Public Choice and Efficiency Argument for Development Impact Fees. In *Development Impact Fees: Policy Rationale, Practice, Theory, and Issues*, ed. Arthur C. Nelson, 281–89. Chicago: Planners Press, American Planning Association.

Blomquist, Glenn C., Mark C. Berger, and John P. Hoehn. 1988. New Estimates of Quality of Life in Urban Areas. *American Economic Review* 78 (1):89–107.

Bogart, William T. 1993. "What Big Teeth You Have!" Identifying the Motivations for Exclusionary Zoning. *Urban Studies* 30 (10):1669–81.

Bogdon, Amy S. 2001. Monitoring Housing Affordability. In *Land Market Monitoring for Smart Urban Growth*, ed. Gerrit J. Knaap, 307–22. Cambridge, MA: Lincoln Institute of Land Policy.

Boyle, Melissa A., and Katherine A. Kiel. 2001. A Survey of House Price Hedonic Studies of the Impact of Environmental Externalities. *Journal of Real Estate Literature* 9 (2):117–44.

Braconi, Frank P. 1996. Environmental Regulation and Housing Affordability. *Cityscape* 2 (3):81–106.

Branfman, Eric J., Benjamin I. Cohen, and David M. Trubek. 1973. Measuring the Invisible Wall: Land Use Controls and the Residential Patterns of the Poor. *Yale Law Journal* 82:483–508.

Braun, Mark Edward. 2003. Suburban Sprawl in Southeastern Wisconsin: Planning, Politics, and the Lack of Affordable Housing. In *Suburban Sprawl: Culture, Theory, and Politics*, ed. Matthew J. Lindstrom and Hugh Bartling, 257–72. Lanham, MD: Rowman & Littlefield.

Briffault, Richard. 1990. Our Localism: Part I—The Structure of Local Government Law. *Columbia Law Review* 90 (1):1–115.

Bright Future Business Consultants. 2006. *Housing Market Letter*. Tucson, AZ: Author.

Bringardner, Bruce W. 2000. Exactions, Impact Fees, and Dedications: National and Texas Law after *Dolan* and *Del Monte Dunes*. *Urban Lawyer* 32:561–85.

Brueckner, Jan K. 1990. Growth Controls and Land Values in an Open City. *Land Economics* 66 (3):237–48.

———. 1995. Strategic Control of Growth in a System of Cities. *Journal of Public Economics* 57 (3):393–416.

———. 1997. Infrastructure Financing and Urban Development: The Economics of Impact Fees. *Journal of Public Economics* 66 (3):383–407.

———. 1998. Testing for Strategic Interaction among Local Governments: The Case of Growth Controls. *Journal of Urban Economics* 44 (3):438–67.

———. 2001. "Urban Sprawl: Lessons from Urban Economics." In *Brookings-Wharton Papers on Urban Affairs: 2001*, ed. William G. Gale and Janet Rothenberg Pack. Washington, DC: Brookings Institution.

Brueckner, Jan K., and Fu-Chuan Lai. 1996. Urban Growth Controls with Resident Homeowners. *Regional Science and Urban Economics* 26:125–43.

Building Technology Inc. 1981. *Building Regulations and Existing Buildings: Improved Techniques for Regulation of Existing Buildings*. Report prepared for the U.S. Department of Housing and Urban Development. Silver Spring, MD: Author.

———. 1982. *Building Regulations and Existing Buildings: Final Report*. Report prepared for the U.S. Department of Housing and Urban Development. Silver Spring, MD: Author.

———. 1987. *Rehabilitation Technology: A State of the Art Overview*. Report prepared for the U.S. Department of Housing and Urban Development. Silver Spring, MD: Author.

Building Technology Inc., Melvyn Green and Associates, Inc., and John G. Degenkolb. 1979. *Final Report: Evaluation and Analysis of Current Effective Building and Fire Prevention Code Administration and Enforcement Programs*. Silver Spring, MD: Building Technology Inc.

Buist, H. 1991. The Wharton Urban Decentralization Database. Unpublished paper. University of Pennsylvania.

Bullard, Robert, J. Eugene Grigsby III, and Charles Lee, ed. 1994. *Residential Apartheid*. Los Angeles: CAAS Publications.

Burby, Raymond J. 2003. Making Plans That Matter: Citizen Involvement and Government Action. *Journal of the American Planning Association* 69 (1): 33–49.

Burby, Raymond J., and Peter J. May. 1998. Intergovernmental Environmental Planning: Addressing the Commitment Conundrum. *Journal of Environmental Planning and Management* 41 (1):95–110.

———. 1999. Making Building Codes an Effective Tool for Earthquake Hazard Mitigation. *Environmental Hazards: Human and Policy Dimensions* 1 (1):27–37.

Burby, Raymond J., Peter J. May, Emil Malizia, and Joyce Levine. 2000. Building Code Enforcement Burdens and Central City Decline. *Journal of the American Planning Association* 66 (2):143–61.

Burby, Raymond J., Peter J. May, and Robert C. Paterson. 1998. Improving Compliance with Regulations Choices and Outcomes [for] Local Government. *Journal of the American Planning Association* 64 (3):324–34.

Burby, Raymond J., Arthur C. Nelson, Dennis Parker, and John Handmer. 2001. Urban Containment Policy and Exposure to Natural Hazards: Is There a Connection? *Journal of Environmental Planning and Management* 44 (4):475–90.

Burby, Raymond J., David Salvesen, and Mike Creed. 2003. Beating the Building Code Burden with Smart Codes. Unpublished PowerPoint presentation, available at http://www.huduser.org/Publications/pdf/BarriersVol1_part3.pdf.

Burchell, Robert W., and David Listokin. 1995. *Land, Infrastructure, Housing Costs, and Fiscal Impacts Associated with Growth: The Literature on the Impacts of Sprawl versus Managed Growth*. Cambridge, MA: Lincoln Institute of Land Policy.

Burchell, Robert W., David Listokin, and William R. Dolphin. 1994. *Development Impact Assessment Handbook*. Washington, DC: The Urban Land Institute.

Burchell, Robert W., Naveed A. Shad, David Listokin, Hilary Phillips, Anthony Downs, Samuel Seskin, Judy S. Davis, Terry Moore, David Helton, and Michelle Gall. 1998. *The Costs of Sprawl—Revisited*. Washington, DC: Transportation Cooperative Research Program.

Butler, Richard. 1982. The Specification of Hedonic Indexes for Urban Housing. *Land Economics* 58 (1):96–110.

Callan, Scott J., and Janet M. Thomas. 2004. *Environmental Economics and Management: Theory, Policy and Applications*, 3rd ed. Mason, OH: Thomson/South-Western.

Capozza, Dennis R. 1994. The Risk Structure of Land Markets. *Journal of Urban Economics* 35 (3):297–331.

Chambers, Daniel N., and Douglas B. Diamond Jr. 1988. Regulation and Land Prices. Paper presented at meeting of American Real Estate and Urban Economics Association (AREUEA), June.

Changing Seasons, Changing Markets. *Washington Post*, March 26, 2006.

Chesapeake Bay Program. n.d. *Bay Program Overview*. Available at www.chesapeakebay.net/overview.htm.

Cheshire, Paul, and Stephen Sheppard. 1989. British Planning Policy and Access to Housing: Some Empirical Estimates. *Urban Studies* 26 (5): 469–85.

———. 2002. The Welfare Economics of Land Use Planning. *Journal of Urban Economics* 52 (2):242–69.

Chicoine, David L. 1981. Farmland Values at the Urban Fringe. *Land Economics* 57 (3):353–62.

Cho, Man. 1990. The Exclusionary and Spillover Effect of Land Use Regulations: A Model and Empirical Evidence. Unpublished paper. University of Pennsylvania.

Chressanthis, George A. 1986. The Impact of Zoning Changes on Housing Prices: A Time Series Analysis. *Growth and Change* 17 (1):49–70.

City of Knoxville. 2000. *Five-Year Consolidated Plan for Housing and Community Development: Program Years 2000–2004*. Knoxville, TN: Author.

City of San Antonio. 2000. *City of San Antonio Consolidated Plan: Fiscal Year 2000–2004*. San Antonio, TX: Author.

City of Tampa. 1998. *City of Tampa Comprehensive Plan*. Tampa, FL: Author.
Clarke, Wes, and Jennifer Evans. 1999. Development Impact Fees and the Acquisition of Infrastructure. *Journal of Urban Affairs* 21 (3):281–88.
Clingermayer, James. 1996. Quasi-Judicial Decision Making and Exclusionary Zoning. *Urban Affairs Review* 31 (4):544–53.
Code of Virginia 10.1-2100. n.d. Available at http://leg1.state.va.us/cgi-bin/legp504.exe?000+cod+10.1-2100.
Code of Virginia 10.1-2103. n.d. Available at http://leg1.state.va.us/cgi-bin/legp504.exe?000+cod+10.1-2103.
Coglianese, Cary, and David Lazer. 2003. Management-Based Regulation: Prescribing Private Management to Achieve Public Goals. *Law & Society Review* 37 (4):691–730.
Cohn, Jeffrey P., and Jeffrey A. Lerner. 2003. *Integrating Land Use Planning and Biodiversity*. Washington, DC: The Biodiversity Partnership, Defenders of Wildlife, Northwest Office. Available at www.biodiversitypartners.org/pubs/landuse/01.shtml.
Coleman, Margaret D. 1989. *Building Codes and Historic Preservation*. Washington, DC: National Trust for Historic Preservation.
Colorado Department of Local Affairs. 1998. *Reducing Housing Costs through Regulatory Reform: A Handbook for Colorado Communities*. Denver: Colorado Division of Housing.
Colwell, Peter F., and James B. Kau. 1982. The Economics of Building Codes and Standards. In *Resolving the Housing Crisis: Government Policy, Decontrol, and the Public Interest*, ed. M. Bruce Johnson. San Francisco: Pacific Institute for Public Policy Research.
Colwell, Peter F., and C. F. Sirmans. 1993. A Comment on Zoning, Returns to Scale, and the Value of Undeveloped Land. *Review of Economics and Statistics* 75 (4):783–86.
Commonwealth of Massachusetts. 2000. *Bringing Down the Barriers: Changing Housing Supply Dynamics in Massachusetts*. Boston: Executive Office for Administration and Finance.
———. 2002. *Massachusetts Consolidated Plan 2000–2004*. Boston: Author.
Conroy, Maria Manta, and Jennifer Evans-Cowley. 2004. *E-Government*. Chicago: American Planning Association.
Consensus Building Institute. 1999. Study on the Mediation of Land Use Disputes. Prepared for the Lincoln Institute of Land Policy. Available at www.communitytools.net/cbi/.
Cooke, Patrick. 1977. *Research and Innovation in the Building Regulatory Process: Proceedings of the First NBS/NCSBCS Joint Conference*. Washington, DC: U.S. Department of Commerce.

Cooley, Thomas F., and C. J. LaCivita. 1972. A Theory of Growth Controls. *Journal of Urban Economics* 12 (2):129–45.

Courant, Paul N. 1976. On the Effect of Fiscal Zoning on Land and Housing Values. *Journal of Urban Economics* 3 (1):88–94.

Crecine, John P., Otto A. Davis, and John E. Jackson. 1967. Urban Property Markets: Some Empirical Results and Their Implications for Municipal Zoning. *Journal of Law and Economics* 10 (2):79–100.

Crellin, Glenn E. n.d. Assessment of Endangered Species Act Enforcement on Real Property Values: A Case Study of Three Washington Counties. Available at www.realtor.org/Research.nsf/files/Crellinfinal2.pdf/$FILE/Crellinfinal2.pdf.

Daniels, T. 2003. *The Environmental Planning Handbook*. Chicago: Planners Press.

Danielson, Michael N. 1976. *The Politics of Exclusion*. New York: Columbia University Press.

Dawkins, Casey J., and Arthur C. Nelson. 2002. Urban Containment Policies and Housing Prices: An International Comparison with Implications for Future Research. *Land Use Policy* 19 (1):1–12.

Deakin, Elizabeth. 1989. Growth Control: A Summary and Review of Empirical Research. In *Understanding Growth Management: Critical Issues and a Research Agenda*, ed. David Brower, David R. Godschalk, and Douglas R. Porter, 3–21. Washington, DC: The Urban Land Institute.

Delaney, Charles J., and Marc T. Smith. 1989a. Impact Fees and the Price of New Housing: An Empirical Study. *AREUEA Journal* 17 (1):41–54.

———. 1989b. Pricing Implications of Development Exactions on Existing Housing Stock. *Growth and Change* 20 (4):1–12.

Denver Economic Development Corporation. 2006. *Monthly Economic Summary*. Denver, CO: Author.

Department of Housing and Urban Development. 1991. *"Not In My Backyard": Removing Barriers to Affordable Housing*. Washington, DC: Department of Housing and Urban Development.

Department of Housing and Urban Development. 1991. *"Why Not in Our Community": An Update to the Report of the Advisory Commission on Regulatory Barriers to Affordable Housing*. Washington, DC: Department of Housing and Urban Development.

DiMento, Joseph, Michael D. Dozier, Steven L. Emmons, Donald G, Hagman, Christopher Kim, Karen Greenfield-Sanders, Paul F. Waldau, and Jay A. Woollacott. 1980. Land Development and Environmental Control in the California Supreme Court: The Deferential, the Preservationist, and Preservationist-Erratic Eras. *UCLA Law Review* 27 (4):859–1066.

Dowall, David E. 1984. *The Suburban Squeeze: Land Conversion and Regulation in the San Francisco Bay Area.* Berkeley: University of California Press.

Dowall, David E., and John D. Landis. 1982. Land Use Controls and Housing Costs: An Examination of San Francisco Bay Area Communities. *AREUEA Journal* 10 (1):67–93.

Downing, Paul B. 1970. Estimating Residential Land Value by Multivariate Analysis. In *The Assessment of Land Value*, ed. Daniel M. Holland, 101–24. Madison: University of Wisconsin Press.

———. 1973a. Factors Affecting Commercial Land Values: An Empirical Study of Milwaukee, Wisconsin. *Land Economics* 49 (1):44–56.

———. 1973b. User Charges and the Development of Urban Land. *National Tax Journal* 26 (4):631.

Downing, Paul, and Thomas S. McCaleb. 1987. The Economics of Development Exactions. In *Development Exactions*, ed. J. Frank and R. Rhodes, 42–69. Chicago: Planners Press, American Planning Association.

Downs, Anthony. 1991. The Advisory Commission on Regulatory Barriers to Affordable Housing: Its Behavior and Accomplishments. *Housing Policy Debate* 2 (4):1095–1137.

———. 2002. Have Housing Prices Risen Faster in Portland than Elsewhere? *Housing Policy Debate* 13 (1):7–31.

Dresch, Marla, and Steven M. Sheffrin. 1997. *Who Pays for Development Fees and Exactions?* San Francisco: Public Policy Institute of California.

Ducker, Richard. 1988. Land Subdivision Regulation. In *The Practice of Local Government Planning*, ed. Frank S. So and Judith Getzels, 198–250. Washington, DC: International City-County Association.

Dukes, E. Franklin. 2004. What We Know about Environmental Conflict Resolution: An Analysis Based on Research. *Conflict Resolution Quarterly* 22 (1-2):191–220.

Dwyer, John P., and Peter S. Menell. 1998. *Property Law and Policy: A Comparative Institutional Perspective.* Westbury, NY: Foundation Press.

Ellickson, Robert C. 1973. Alternatives to Zoning: Covenants, Nuisance Rules, and Fines as Land Use Controls. *University of Chicago Law Review* 40 (4): 681–781.

———. 1977. Suburban Growth Controls: An Economic and Legal Analysis. *Yale Law Journal* 86 (3):385–511.

———. 1981. The Irony of "Inclusionary" Zoning. *Southern California Law Review* 54 (September):1167–1216.

———. 1982. The Irony of "Inclusionary Zoning." In *Resolving the Housing Crisis: Government Policy, Decontrol, and the Public Interest*, ed. M. Bruce

Johnson, 197–216. San Francisco: Pacific Institute for Public Policy Research.

Ellickson, Robert C., and Vicki L. Been, eds. 2005. *Land Use Controls*. New York: Aspen Law and Business.

Elliott, Michael. 1981. The Impact of Growth Control Regulations on Housing Prices in California. *AREUEA Journal* 9 (2):115–33.

Engel, David. 2004. Regulatory Barriers: Secret (and Not so Secret) Weapons against Affordable Housing. *Bright Ideas* Spring.

Epple, Dennis, and Glenn Platt. 1998. Equilibrium and Local Redistribution in an Urban Economy When Households Differ in Both Preferences and Incomes. *Journal of Urban Economics* 43 (1):23–51.

Euchner, Charles C., and Elizabeth G. Frieze. 2003. *Getting Home: Overcoming Barriers to Housing in Greater Boston*. Cambridge, MA: Pioneer Institute for Public Policy Research and the Rappaport Institute for Greater Boston, Kennedy School of Government. Available at www.pioneerinstitute.org/pdf/wp21.pdf.

Evans, Alan W. 1988. *No Room! No Room! The Costs of the British Town and Country Planning System*. London: Institute of Economic Affairs.

Evans, Brock. 1996. An Environmentalist's Response to Environmental Regulation and Housing Affordability. *Cityscape* 2 (3):107–14.

Evans-Cowley, Jennifer S., and Larry L. Lawhon. 2003. The Effects of Impact Fees on the Price of Housing and Land: A Literature Review. *Journal of Planning Literature* 17 (3):351–59.

Fairfax County Code: Article 2. n.d. Available at http://www.fairfaxcounty.gov/dpz/zoningordinance/articles/art02.pdf.

Fairfax County Code: Chapter 118—Chesapeake Bay Preservation Ordinance. n.d. Available at http://www.fairfaxcounty.gov/dpwes/environmental/cbay/ch118final.pdf.

Fairfax County Comprehensive Plan: Environment. n.d. Available at http://www.fairfaxcounty.gov/dpz/comprehensiveplan/policyplan/environment.pdf.

Fairfax County Public Facilities Manual 12-0100. n.d. Available at http://www.fairfaxcounty.gov/dpwes/publications/pfm/12-0100.htm.

Falk, David. 1976. Building Codes and Manufactured Housing. *National Housing Policy Review* 2:793–815.

Fenster, Mark. 2004. Takings Formalism and Regulatory Formulas: Exactions and the Consequences of Clarity. *California Law Review* 92:609–82.

Ferrera, Salvatore. 1988. *Chicago's Building Code: An Impediment to Affordable Housing Development*. Chicago: Metropolitan Housing Development Corporation.

Ferro, Maximilian L. 1993. Building Codes and Older Structures: The Massachusetts Experience. In *Preservation and Affordable Housing: Accomplishments, Constraints, and Opportunities*, ed. David Listokin and Barbara Listokin, 100–108. New Brunswick: Center for Urban Policy Research, Rutgers, The State University of New Jersey.

Field, Charles G. 1997. Building Consensus for Affordable Housing. *Housing Policy Debate* 8 (4):801–32.

Field, Charles G., and Steven R. Rivkin. 1975. *The Building Code Burden*. Lexington, MA: Lexington Books.

Field, Charles G., and Francis T. Ventre. 1971. Local Regulation of Building: Agencies, Codes, and Politics. In *The Municipal Year Book*, 139–65. Washington, DC: International City Management Association.

Fischel, William A. 1980. Zoning and the Exercise of Monopoly Power: A Reevaluation. *Journal of Urban Economics* 8 (3):283–93.

———. 1981. Is Local Government Structure in Large Urbanized Areas Monopolistic or Competitive? *National Tax Journal* 34 (1):95–104.

———. 1985. *The Economics of Zoning Laws: A Property Rights Approach to American Land Use Controls*. Baltimore: Johns Hopkins University Press.

———. 1987. The Economics of Land Use Exactions: A Property Rights Analysis. *Law and Contemporary Problems* 50 (1):101–13.

———. 1989. What Do Economists Know about Growth Controls? In *Understanding Growth Management*, ed. David J. Brower, David R. Godschalk, and Douglas R. Porter, 59–86. Washington, DC: The Urban Land Institute.

———. 1990. *Do Growth Controls Matter? A Review of Empirical Evidence on the Effectiveness and Efficiency of Local Government Land Use Regulation*. Cambridge, MA: Lincoln Institute of Land Policy.

———. 1992. Property Taxation and the Tiebout Model: Evidence for the Benefit View from Zoning and Voting. *Journal of Economic Literature* 30 (1):171–77.

———. 1995. *Regulatory Takings: Law, Economics, and Politics*. Cambridge, MA: Harvard University Press.

———. 1999. Does the American Way of Zoning Cause the Suburbs of U.S. Metropolitan Areas to Be Too Spread Out? In *Governance and Opportunity in Metropolitan Areas*, ed. Alan Altshuler, William Morrill, Harold Wolman, and Faith Mitchell, 151–91. Washington, DC: National Academy Press.

———. 2001. *The Homevoter Hypothesis*. Cambridge, MA: Harvard University Press.

Fisher, Richard. 2001. Rehabilitation Subcode Success. *Public Management* (March):12–17.

Florida Advisory Council on Intergovernmental Relations. 1991. *1991 Florida Impact Fee Report*. Available at www.floridalcir.gov/UserContent/docs/File/reports/impactfee91.pdf.

Ford, Richard Thompson. 1994. The Boundaries of Race: Political Geography in Legal Analysis. *Harvard Law Review* 107 (8):1841–44.

Forest, Ben. 1999. New Jersey Revs Up Its Rehabs. *Planning* 65 (8):10–12.

Frank, James E. 1989. *The Costs of Alternative Development Patterns: A Review of the Literature*. Washington, DC: The Urban Land Institute.

Frech, H.E. III, and Ronald N. Lafferty. 1984. The Effect of the California Coastal Commission on Housing Prices. *Journal of Urban Economics* 16 (4):105–23.

Freeman, A. Myrick III. 1992. *The Measurement of Environmental and Resource Values: Theory and Methods*. Washington, DC: Resources for the Future.

Freilich, Robert H. 1973. *Model Subdivision Regulations: Text and Commentary*. Washington, DC: American Society of Planning Officials.

Freilich, Robert H., and David W. Bushek, eds. 1995. *Exactions, Impact Fees and Dedications: Shaping Land-Use Development and Funding Infrastructure in the Dolan Era*. Chicago: State and Local Government Law Section, American Bar Association.

Frey, William H. 2001. *Melting Pot Suburbs: A Census 2000 Study of Suburban Diversity*. Census 2000 Series. Washington, DC: Brookings Institution.

Frug, Gerald. 1980. The City as a Legal Concept. *Harvard Law Review* 93 (6): 1057–154.

———. 1996. The Geography of Community. *Stanford Law Review* 48: 1047–108.

Fu, Yuming, and C. Tsuriel Somerville. 2001. Site Density Restrictions: Measurements and Empirical Analysis. *Journal of Urban Economics* 49 (2): 404–23.

Gabriel, Stuart A., and Jennifer R. Wolch. 1980. Local Land Use Regulation and Urban Housing Values. Center for Real Estate and Urban Economics Working Paper No. 80–18. Berkeley, CA: Center for Real Estate and Urban Economics.

Galster, George C. 2003. Review of the Literature on Impacts of Affordable and Multi-Family Housing on Market Values of Nearby Single-Family Homes. Paper presented at the Brookings Symposium on the Relationships between Affordable Housing and Growth Management, Brookings Institution, May 29.

Gatzlaff, Dean H., and Marc T. Smith. 1993. Uncertainty, Growth Controls, and the Efficiency of Development Patterns. *Journal of Real Estate Finance and Economics* 6 (2):147–55.

Genesis Group. 2008. *Denver Metropolitan Area Historical Price Trends*. Available at http://www.thegenesisgroup.net/documents/Metro0AveragePrice Trends.pdf.

Gilliland, C. E., L. D. Krebs, and T. J. Vanderberg. 1992. *Texas Development Impact Fees*. Real Estate Center Technical Report. College Station, TX: Texas A&M University.

Glaeser, Edward L., and Joseph Gyourko. 2002. *The Impact of Zoning on Housing Affordability*. Discussion Paper 1948. Cambridge, MA: Harvard Institute of Economic Research.

———. 2003a. Why Is Manhattan So Expensive? *Civic Report* 39. New York: Manhattan Institute.

———. 2003b. The Impact of Building Restrictions on Housing Affordability. *Federal Reserve Bank of New York Economic Policy Review* 9 (2):21–39.

Glaeser, Edward L., Joseph Gyourko, and Raven Saks. 2003. Why Is Manhattan So Expensive? Regulation and the Rise in House Prices. Cambridge, MA: National Bureau of Economic Research Working Paper No. 10124.

Gleeson, Michael E. 1979. Effects of an Urban Growth Management System on Land Values. *Land Economics* 55 (3):350–65.

Glickfeld, Madelyn, and Ned Levine. 1992. *Regional Growth . . . Local Reaction: The Enactment and Effects of Local Growth Control and Management Measures in California*. Cambridge, MA: Lincoln Institute of Land Policy.

Godshalk, D., T. Beatley, P. Berke, D. Brower, and E. Kaiser. 1999. *Natural Hazard Mitigation: Recasting Disaster Policy and Planning*. Washington, DC: Island Press.

Goering, John, and Judith D. Feins. 2003. *Choosing a Better Life? Evaluating the Moving to Opportunity Social Experiment*. Washington, DC: The Urban Institute.

Goldberg, M., and P. Horwood. 1980. *Zoning: Its Costs and Relevance for the 1980s*. Vancouver, BC: The Fraser Institute.

Goldman, Arthur S. 1976. The Influence of Model Codes and Their Associations on Acceptance of Innovative Technology at the Local Level. *National Housing Policy Review* 2:816–31.

Gómez-Ibáñez, Jose A. 1996. The Debate over Impact Fees. *Illinois Real Estate Letter* Winter/Spring:1–3. Available at www.business.uiuc.edu/orer/V10-1-1.pdf.

Gordon, Peter, and Harry W. Richardson. 1997. Are Compact Cities a Desirable Planning Goal? *Journal of the American Planning Association* 63 (1): 95–106.

Gordon, Tracy. 2004. *Planned Developments in California: Private Communities and Public Life.* San Francisco: Public Policy Institute of California.

Green, Richard K. 1999. Land Use Regulation and the Price of Housing in a Suburban Wisconsin County. *Journal of Housing Economics* 8 (2): 144–59.

Green, Richard K., and Stephen Malpezzi. 2003. *A Primer on U.S. Housing Markets and Housing Policy.* Washington, DC: The Urban Institute.

Greulich, Erica, John M. Quigley, and Steven Raphael. 2004. The Anatomy of Rent Burdens: Immigration, Growth and Rental Housing. *Brookings-Wharton Papers on Urban Affairs* 4 (1):149–206.

Guidry, Krisandra, James D. Shilling, and C. F. Sirmans. 1991. An Econometric Analysis of Variation in Urban Residential Land Prices and the Adoption of Land-Use Controls. Working paper. Center for Urban Land Economics Research, University of Wisconsin–Madison.

Guttery, Randall S., Stephen L. Poe, and C. F. Sirmans. 2000. Federal Wetlands Regulation: Restrictions on the Nationwide Permit Program and the Implications for Residential Property Owners. *American Business Law Journal* 37 (2):299–341.

Gyourko, Joseph. 1991. Impact Fees, Exclusionary Zoning, and the Density of New Development. *Journal of Urban Economics* 30 (2):242–56.

Haar, Charles M. 1996. *Suburbs under Siege: Race, Space, and Audacious Judges.* Princeton, NJ: Princeton University Press.

Hamilton, Bruce. 1976. Capitalization of Intrajurisdictional Differences in Local Tax Prices. *American Economic Review* 66 (5):743–53.

———. 1978. Zoning and the Exercise of Monopoly Power. *Journal of Urban Economics* 5 (1):116–30.

Hammit, James K., Eric S. Belsky, Jonathan I. Levy, and John D. Graham. 1999. *Residential Building Codes, Affordability, and Health Protection: A Risk-Tradeoff Approach.* Cambridge, MA: Joint Center for Housing Studies, Harvard University.

Harper, R. Eugene, and Hydie Hopkins. 1988. *To Save Our Past for Our Future. . . . A Report.* West Virginia: Task Force for Historic Preservation Legislation.

Hartman, Chester. 1991. Comment on Anthony Downs's "The Advisory Commission on Regulatory Barriers to Affordable Housing: Its Behavior and Accomplishments." *Housing Policy Debate* 2 (4):1161–68.

Hassell, Scott, Anny Wong, Ari Houser, Debra Knopman, and Mark Bernstein. 2003. *Building Better Homes: Government Strategies for Promoting Innovation in Housing.* Washington, DC: U.S. Department of Housing and Urban Development.

Hattis, David B., and Howard M. Markman. 1982. *A Study into the Economic Impact of Retroactive Implementation of Building Safety and Fire Safety Code Provisions.* Final report, executive summary. New York: Office of Fire Prevention and Control, Department of State, State of New York.

Hendershott, Patrick H., and Thomas G. Thibodeau. 1990. The Relationship between Median and Constant Quality Housing Prices: Implications for Setting FHA Loan Limits. *AREUEA Journal* 18 (3):323–34.

Henry, John R. 2001. *Providing Safer Buildings through Modern Building Codes.* Washington, DC: Building Standards Publication, National Conference of State Legislatures, International Conference of Building Officials.

Ho, Alfred Tat-Kei. 2002. Reinventing Local Government and the E-Government Initiative. *Public Administration Review* 62 (4):434–44.

Hodge, Ian, and Gordon Cameron. 1989. Raising Infrastructure Charges on Land Development: Incidence and Adjustments. *Land Development Studies* 6 (3):171–82.

Holcombe, Randall G. 2001. Growth Management in Action: The Case of Florida. In *Smarter Growth*, ed. Randall G. Holcombe and Samuel R. Staley, 203–19. Westport, CT: Greenwood Publishing Group.

Holmes, Nicholas H. Jr. 1977. Contemporary Codes and Old Building Recycling. *Construction Specifier* October:34–39.

Housing Research and Development Building Research Council, University of Illinois. 1998. *National Survey of Rehabilitation Enforcement Practices.* Report prepared for U.S. Department of Housing and Urban Development, Office of Policy Development and Research. Urbana, IL: School of Architecture, University of Illinois at Urbana–Champaign.

Huffman, Forrest E., Arthur C. Nelson, M.T. Smith, and Michael A. Stegman. 1988. Who Bears the Burden of Development Impact Fees? *Journal of the American Planning Association* 54 Winter:49–55.

Hushak, Leroy J. 1975. The Urban Demand for Urban-Rural Fringe Land. *Land Economics* 51 (2):112–23.

Ihlanfeldt, Keith R., and Timothy M. Shaughnessy. 2004. An Empirical Investigation of the Effects of Impact Fees on Housing and Land Markets. *Regional Science and Urban Economics* 34 (6):639–61.

Inman, Robert, and Daniel Rubinfeld. 1979. The Judicial Pursuit of Local Fiscal Equity. *Harvard Law Review* 92 (8):1662–89.

International Code Council, Inc. 2001. *ICC Performance Code for Buildings and Facilities*. Whittier, CA: International Conference of Building Officials.

International Code Council. *International Code Adoptions*. Available at www.iccsafe.org/government/adoption.html.

James, Franklin J., and Thomas Muller. 1977. Environmental Impact Evaluation, Land Use Planning, and the Housing Consumer. *American Real Estate and Urban Economics Association Journal* 5 (3):279–301.

Jones, Bryan D. 1985. *Governing Buildings and Building Government: A New Perspective on the Old Party*. Tuscaloosa: University of Alabama Press.

Juergensmeyer, Julian C., and Thomas Roberts. 2007. *Handbook on Land Use Planning and Development Regulation Law*. 2nd ed. St. Paul, MN: Thomson West.

Kagan, Robert A. 1991. Adversarial Legalism and American Government. *Journal of Policy Analysis and Management* 10 (3):369–407.

———. 1994. Regulatory Enforcement. In *Handbook of Regulation and Administrative Law*, ed. David H. Rosenbloom and Richard D. Schwartz, 383–422. New York: Marcel Decker.

———. 2001. *Adversarial Legalism: The American Way of Law*. Cambridge, MA: Harvard University Press.

Kaplan, Marilyn E. 1988. Working with the Code Official. *Preservation Forum* (Spring).

Kaplow, Louis. 1986. An Economic Analysis of Legal Transitions. *Harvard Law Review* 99 (3):509–617.

Kapsch, Robert J. 1979. *Building Codes: Preservation and Rehabilitation*. Washington, DC: Department of Commerce, National Bureau of Standards.

Kasowski, Kevin. 1993. The Costs of Sprawl, Revisited. Planners Advisory Service Memo. February 1993. Chicago: American Planning Association.

Katz, Bruce, Karen Destorel Brown, Margery Austin Turner, Mary Cunningham, and Noah Sawyer. 2003. *Rethinking Local Affordable Housing Strategies: Lessons from 70 Years of Policy and Practice*. Washington, DC: The Brookings Institution and The Urban Institute.

Katz, Lawrence, and Kenneth T. Rosen. 1987. The Interjurisdictional Effects of Growth Controls on Housing Prices. *Journal of Law and Economics* 30 (1):149–60.

Kenyon, Daphne A. 1991. *The Economics of NIMBYs*. Working Paper Series. Cambridge, MA: Lincoln Institute of Land Policy.

Kiel, Katherine A. 1995. Measuring the Impact of the Discovery and Cleaning of Identified Hazardous Waste Sites on House Values. *Land Economics* 74 (4):428–35.

———. 2004. *Environmental Regulations and the Housing Market: A Review of the Literature.* Paper for U.S. Department of Housing and Urban Development conference on regulatory barriers and housing markets. Washington, DC, April.

———. 2005. Environmental Regulations and the Housing Market: A Review of the Literature. *Cityscape* 8 (1):187–208.

Kirp, David L., John P. Dwyer, and Larry A. Rosenthal. 1995. *Our Town: Race, Housing, and the Soul of Suburbia.* New Brunswick, NJ: Rutgers University Press.

Knaap, Gerrit. 1985. The Price Effects of Urban Growth Boundaries in Metropolitan Portland, Oregon. *Land Economics* 61 (1):26–35.

———. 1991. Comment: Measuring the Effects of Growth Controls. *Journal of Policy Analysis and Management* 10 (3):469–73.

———, ed. 2001. *Land Market Monitoring for Smart Urban Growth.* Cambridge, MA: Lincoln Institute of Land Policy.

———. 2004. *Monitoring Land and Housing Markets: An Essential Tool for Smart Growth. National Center for Housing and the Environment.* College Park, MD: National Center for Smart Growth.

Koebel, C. Theodore, Maria Papadakis, Ed Hudson, and Marilyn Cavell. 2004. *The Diffusion of Innovation in the Residential Building Industry.* Washington, DC: U.S. Department of Housing and Urban Development. Available at www.toolbase.org/PDF/CaseStudies/Diffusion_Reporta.pdf.

Landis, John D. 1992. Do Growth Controls Work? A New Assessment. *Journal of the American Planning Association* 58 (4):489–508.

———. 2001. Characterizing Urban Land Capacity: Alternative Approaches and Methodologies. In *Land Market Monitoring for Smart Urban Growth,* ed. Gerrit J. Knaap, 3–50. Cambridge, MA: Lincoln Institute of Land Policy.

Landis, John, Michael Larice, Deva Dawson, and Lan Deng. 2001. *Pay to Play: Residential Development Fees in California Cities and Counties 1999.* Sacramento: State of California Department of Housing and Community Development.

Leithe, Joni L., with Matthew Montavon. 1990. *Impact Fee Programs: A Survey of Design and Administrative Issues.* Washington, DC: Government Finance Research Center.

Levine, Jonathan C. 1994. Equity in Infrastructure Finance: When Are Impact Fees Justified? *Land Economics* 70 (2):210–22.

Levine, Ned. 1999. The Effects of Local Growth Controls on Regional Housing Production and Population Redistribution in California. *Urban Studies* 36 (12):2047–68.

Levmore, Saul. 1999. Changes, Anticipations, and Reparations. *Columbia Law Review* 99 (7):1657–1700.

Lewis, Paul G., and Max Neiman. 2000. *Residential Development and Growth Control Policies: Survey Results from Cities in Three California Regions.* San Francisco: Public Policy Institute of California.

———. 2002. *Cities under Pressure: Local Growth Controls and Residential Development Policy.* San Francisco: Public Policy Institute of California.

Lillydahl, Jane H., and Larry D. Singell. 1987. The Effects of Growth Management on the Housing Market: A Review of Theoretical and Empirical Evidence. *Journal of Urban Affairs* 9 (1):63–77.

Linneman, Peter, and Anita A. Summers. 1993. Patterns and Processes of Employment and Population Decentralization in the United States, 1970–87. In *Urban Change in the United States and Western Europe: Comparative Analysis and Policy*, ed. Anita A. Summers, Paul C. Cheshire, and Lanfranco Senn, 87–144. Washington, DC: Urban Institute Press.

Linneman, Peter, A. Summers, N. Brooks, and H. Buist. 1990. The State of Local Growth Management. Real Estate Working Paper no. 81. The Wharton School, University of Pennsylvania.

Listokin, David. 1995. *Building Codes and Housing Rehabilitation.* Study prepared for the New Jersey Department of Community Affairs. New Brunswick: Center for Urban Policy Research, Rutgers, The State University of New Jersey.

Listokin, David, and David B. Hattis. 2005. Building Codes and Housing. *Cityscape* 8 (1):21–68.

Listokin, David, and Barbara Listokin, eds. 1993. *Preservation and Affordable Housing: Accomplishments, Constraints, and Opportunities.* New Brunswick: Center for Urban Policy Research, Rutgers, The State University of New Jersey.

———. 2001. *Barriers to the Rehabilitation of Affordable Housing.* Vol. 1, *Findings and Analysis.* Washington, DC: U.S. Department of Housing and Urban Development, Office of Policy Development and Research.

Lubove, Roy. 1962. *The Progressives and the Slums: Tenement House Reform in New York City, 1890–1917.* Westport, CT: Greenwood Press.

Luger, Michael I., and Kenneth Temkin. 2000. *Red Tape and Housing Costs.* New Brunswick: Center for Urban Policy Research, Rutgers, The State University of New Jersey.

Maisel, Sherman J. 1953. *Housebuilding in Transition.* Berkeley: University of California Press.

Malizia, Emil, Richard Norton, and Craig Richardson. 1997. Reading, Writing, and Impact Fees. *Planning* 63 (9):17–19.

Malpezzi, Stephen. 1996. Housing Prices, Externalities, and Regulation in U.S. Metropolitan Areas. *Journal of Housing Research* 7 (2):209–42.

Malpezzi, Stephen, Gregory H. Chun, and Richard K. Green. 1998. New Place-to-Place Housing Price Indexes for U.S. Metropolitan Areas, and Their Determinants: An Application of Urban Indicators. *Real Estate Economics* 26 (2):235–74.

Malpezzi, Stephen, and Stephen K. Mayo. 1997. Getting Housing Incentives Right: A Case Study of the Effects of Regulation, Taxes and Subsidies on Housing Supply in Malaysia. *Land Economics* 73 (3):372–91.

Mann, Dean E., ed. 1982. *Environmental Policy Implementation: Planning and Management Options and Their Consequences.* Lexington, MA: Lexington Books.

Manufactured Housing Research Alliance. 2003. *Technology Roadmapping for Manufactured Housing.* Report prepared for the U.S. Department of Housing and Urban Development, Affordable Housing Research and Technology Division. New York: Author.

Mark, Jonathan H., and Mark A. Goldberg. 1986. A Study of the Impacts of Zoning on Housing Values over Time. *Journal of Urban Economics* 20 (4): 254–73.

Martín, Carlos. 1999. Riveting: Building Codes, Steel Technology, and the Production of Modern Place. PhD dissertation, Department of Civil and Environmental Engineering, Stanford University.

Maryland-National Capital Park and Planning. 2001. *Inventory of Affordable Housing 2000, Montgomery County, Maryland.* Introduction available at www.mcparkandplanning.org/research/analysis/housing/affordable/intro.pdf.

Maryland-National Capital Park and Planning Commission. n.d. Chapter 22A: Forest Conservation—Trees. Available at www.mc-mncppc.org/environment/forest/law.pdf.

———. n.d. Special Protection Areas. Available at www.mc-mncppc.org/environment/spa/index.shtm.

Masnick, George S. 2001. *Home Ownership Trends and Racial Inequality in the United States in the 20th Century.* Working Paper W01-4. Cambridge, MA: Joint Center for Housing Studies, Harvard University.

Massey, Douglas S., and Nancy A. Denton. 1993. *American Apartheid: Segregation and the Making of the Underclass.* Cambridge, MA: Harvard University Press.

May, Peter J. 1997. State Regulatory Roles: Choices in the Regulation of Building Safety. *State and Local Government Review* 29 (Spring):70–80.

———. Social Regulation. In *Tools of Government: A Guide to the New Governance*, ed. Lester M. Salamon, 156–216. Oxford: Oxford University Press.

———. 2003. Performance-Based Regulation and Regulatory Regimes: The Saga of Leaky Buildings. *Law and Policy* 25 (4):381–401.

———. 2004. Compliance Motivations: Affirmative and Negative Bases. *Law and Society Review* 38 (1):41–67.

———. 2005. Regulatory Implementation: Examining Barriers from Regulatory Processes. *Cityscape* 8 (1):209–32.

May, Peter J., and Thomas A. Birkland. 1994. Earthquake Risk Reduction: An Examination of Local Regulatory Efforts. *Environmental Management* 18 (6):923–937.

May, Peter J., and Raymond J. Burby. 1998. Making Sense out of Regulatory Enforcement. *Law and Policy* 20 (2):157–82.

May, Peter J., and T. Jens Feeley. 2000. Regulatory Backwaters: Earthquake Risk Reduction in the Western United States. *State and Local Governmental Review* 32 (1):20–33.

May, Peter J., and Robert S. Wood. 2003. At the Regulatory Frontlines: Inspectors' Enforcement Styles and Regulatory Compliance. *Journal of Public Administration Research and Theory* 13 (2):117–39.

Mayer, Christopher J., and C. Tsuriel Somerville. 2000. Land Use Regulation and New Construction. *Regional Science and Urban Economics* 30 (6): 639–62.

Mayo, Stephen, and Stephen Sheppard. 1996. Housing Supply under Rapid Economic Growth and Varying Regulatory Stringency: An International Comparison. *Journal of Housing Economics* 5 (3):274–89.

McConnaughey, John S. Jr. 1978. *An Economic Analysis of Building Code Impacts: A Suggested Approach*. Washington, DC: U.S. Department of Commerce, National Bureau of Standards.

McElfish, James M. Jr. 2004. *Nature-Friendly Ordinances*. Washington, DC: Environmental Law Institute.

———. 2005. Response to Environmental Regulations and the Housing Market: A Review of the Literature. *Cityscape* 8 (1):273–76.

McElfish, James M. Jr., and C. Casey-Lefkowitz. 2001. *Smart Growth and the Clean Water Act*. Washington, DC: Northeast-Midwest Institute.

McFarlane, Alastair. 1999. Taxes, Fees, and Urban Development. *Journal of Urban Economics* 46 (3):416–36.

McKenna, William F. 1982. *The Report of the President's Commission on Housing*. Washington, DC: U.S. Government Printing Office.

McKenzie, Evan. 1994. *Privatopia: Homeowner Associations and the Rise of Residential Private Government*. New Haven, CT: Yale University Press.

Metropolitan Washington Council of Governments. 2006a. *Economic Trends in Metropolitan Washington 2000–2004*. Available at www.mwcog.org/uploads/pub-documents/y1tXVw20050914134641.pdf.

———. 2006b. *Metropolitan Washington Annual Regional Housing Report*. Available at www.mwcog.org/uploads/pub-documents/9VlcXg20060717084410.pdf.

———. 2006c. *2003 Housing Data Survey*. Available at www.mwcog.org/uploads/pub-documents/8V1WXA20041029084116.pdf.

———. 2007. *Growth Trends to 2030: Cooperative Forecasting in the Washington Region*. Washington, DC: Author. Available at www.mwcog.org/uploads/pub-documents/z1dfVw20080117203640.pdf.

Metz, F. Eugene. 1977. *Housing Conservation Technology*. Washington, DC: Center for Building Technology.

Metz, F. Eugene, H. W. Berger, and T. H. Boone. 1978. Housing Conservation Technology Assessment Shows Need for Progress in Accomplishments, Attitudes. *Journal of Housing* 35 (1):21–22.

Mid-Atlantic RESAC. 2006. *Measuring Sprawl in the Washington Metropolitan Region*. Available at www.geog.umd.edu/resac/sprawl.htm.

Millennial Housing Commission. 2002. Meeting our Nation's Housing Challenges. Report of the Bipartisan Millennial Housing Commission Appointed by the Congress of the United States. Washington, DC: Superintendent of Documents, U.S. Government Printing Office.

Mills, Edwin S. 1979. Economic Analysis of Land-Use Controls. In *Current Issues in Urban Economics*, ed. Peter Mieszkowski and Mahlon Straszheim, 511–41. Baltimore: Johns Hopkins University Press.

———. 2002. *Why Do We Have Urban Density Controls?* Paper presented at Analysis of Land Markets and the Impact of Land Market Regulation conference, July 10–12.

Monk, Sarah, and Christine M. E. Whitehead. 1999. Evaluating the Economic Impact of Planning Controls in the United Kingdom: Some Implications for Housing. *Land Economics* 75 (1):74–93.

Montgomery County Department of Environmental Protection. 2002. *SPA Annual Report for 2001*. Available at www.montgomerycountymd.gov/content/dep/SPA/2001annualreport/summary.pdf.

Montgomery County Department of Park and Planning. 2004. *Census Update Survey 2003*. Available at www.mc-mncppc.org/research/data_library/CUS2003/summary/CUS03Summary.pdf.

Montgomery County Department of Parks. 2000. *Environmental Guidelines Guidelines for Environmental Management of Development in Montgomery County*. Silver Spring, MD: Maryland National Capital Park and Planning Commission.

Montgomery County, MD. n.d. Montgomery County Code 22-A. Gaithersburg, MD: Montgomery County Commission.

Moon, M. Jae. 2002. The Evolution of E-Government among Municipalities: Rhetoric or Reality? *Public Administration Review* 62 (4):424–33.

Morgan, Terry D. 1984. Exclusionary Zoning: Remedies under Oregon's Land Use Planning Program. *Environmental Law* 14 (2):779–830.

Mullen, Clancy. 2005. 2005 National Impact Fee Survey. Unpublished paper. Duncan Associates, available at www.impactfees.com/surveys.htm.

Muth, Richard F., and Elliot Wetzler. 1976. The Effect of Constraints on House Costs. *Journal of Urban Economics* 3 (1):57–67.

Muto, Sheila. 1999. Cattlemen Act to Save Ranch Land. *Wall Street Journal*, January 6.

NAHB Research Center Inc. 1999. *Innovative Rehabilitation Provisions: A Demonstration of the National Applicable Recommended Rehabilitation Provisions*. Washington, DC: U.S. Department of Housing and Urban Development.

———. 2007. *Study of Subdivision Requirements as a Regulatory Barrier*. Washington, DC: Office of Policy Development and Research, U.S. Department of Housing and Urban Development.

National Association of Home Builders. 1976a. *Cost Effective Site Planning: Single Family Development*. Washington, DC: Author.

———. 1976b. *Impact of Government Regulations on Housing Costs: A Selected Annotated Bibliography*. Washington, DC: National Association of Home Builders.

———. 1982a. *Density Development Cost Effective and Affordable*. Washington, DC: Author.

———. 1982b. *The Affordable Housing Demonstration Case Study—Lincoln, Nebraska*. Washington, DC: U.S. Government Printing Office.

———. 1998. *The Truth about Regulatory Barriers to Housing Affordability*. Washington, DC: Author.

———. 2004. *Annual New Home Sales (1963–2003)*. Washington, DC: National Association of Home Builders.

National Bureau of Standards. 1979. *Impact of Building Regulations on Rehabilitation—Status and Technical Needs*. Washington, DC: U.S. Department of Commerce, National Bureau of Standards.

National Commission on Urban Problems. 1968. *Building the American City.* Washington, DC: Superintendent of Documents, U.S. Government Printing Office.

National Conference of States on Building Codes and Standards, Inc. 1998. *Annual Progress Report for Streamlining the Nation's Building Regulatory Process Project.* Washington, DC: U.S. Department of Commerce.

———. 1999. *Annual Progress Report for Streamlining the Nation's Building Regulatory Process Project.* Washington, DC: U.S. Department of Commerce.

———. 2000a. *Introduction to Building Codes: A Guide to Understanding the Codes and How They Work.* Herndon, VA: NCSBCS Publications.

———. 2000b. *Streamlining the Nation's Building Regulatory Process: 2000 Business Plan.* Washington, DC: U.S. Department of Commerce.

———. 2001. *Enhancing Public Safety and the States' Role in the Global Economy through Uniform Construction Codes and Standards.* A Report to the National Governors Association. Washington, DC: U.S. Department of Commerce.

———. 2003. *The National Alliance on Building Regulatory Reform in the Digital Age: The Need for the Alliance and Sample Streamlining Benefits.* Available at www.ncsbcs.org/newsite/New%20Releases/3rdNatlForum_NR_102803.htm.

———. 2004. *Introduction to Building Codes.* Herndon, VA: NCSBCS Publications.

National Fire Protection Association. 2002. *NFPA 5000, Building Construction and Safety Code.* Quincy, MA: Author.

National Institute of Building Sciences. 1981. *Rehabilitation Guidelines 1980: Egress Guidelines for Residential Rehabilitation.* Report prepared for the U.S. Department of Housing and Urban Development, Office of Policy Development and Research. Washington, DC: U.S. Government Printing Office.

———. 2002. *Electronic Permitting Systems and How to Implement Them.* Prepared for U.S. Department of Housing and Urban Development, Office of Policy Development and Research. Washington, DC: U.S. Department of Housing and Urban Development.

———. 2003. *Minimum Property Standards for One- and Two-Family Dwellings and Technical Suitability of Product Programs.* Washington, DC: Author.

National Multi Housing Council. 1982. *Rent Control Activities through May 31, 1982.* Washington, DC: Author.

Navarro, Peter, and Richard Carson. 1991. Growth Controls: Policy Analysis for the Second Generation. *Policy Sciences* 24 (2):127–52.

Nelson, Arthur C. 1988. An Empirical Note on How Regional Urban Containment Policy Influences an Interaction between Greenbelt and Exurban Land Markets. *American Planning Association Journal* 54 (2):178–84.

———. 2000a. Effects of Urban Containment on Housing Prices and Landowner Behavior. *Land Lines* 12 (3):1–3.

———. 2000b. *Housing Price Effects and Landowner Behavior: Implications of Urban Containment*. Cambridge, MA: Lincoln Institute of Land Policy.

———. 2006. Leadership in a New Era. *Journal of the American Planning Association* 72 (4):393–406.

Nelson, Arthur C., Casey J. Dawkins, and Thomas W. Sanchez. 2003. *Urban Containment and Residential Segregation: A Preliminary Investigation*. Discussion paper. Metropolitan Institute, Virginia Polytechnic Institute and State University.

Nelson, Arthur C., and James B. Duncan. 1995. *Growth Management Principles and Practices*. Chicago: Planners Press, American Planning Association.

Nelson, Arthur C., James E. Frank, and James C. Nicholas. 1992. Positive Influence of Impact Fee in Urban Planning and Development. *Journal of Urban Planning and Development* 118 (1):59–64.

Nelson, Arthur C., Jane H. Lillydahl, James E. Frank, and James C. Nicholas. 1992. Price Effects of Road and Other Impact Fees on Urban Land. *Transportation Research Record* 1305:36–41.

Nelson, Arthur C., Rolf Pendall, Casey J. Dawkins, and Gerrit J. Knaap. 2002. *The Link between Growth Management and Housing Affordability: The Academic Evidence*. Discussion Paper. Washington, DC: Brookings Institution Center for Urban and Metropolitan Policy.

Netzer, Dick. 1988. Exactions in the Public Finance Context. In *Private Supply of Public*, ed. Rachelle Alterman, 35–50. New York: New York University Press.

Netzer, Dick, Michael Schill, and Scott Susin. 2001. Changing Water and Sewer Finance: Distributional Impacts and Effects on the Viability of Affordable Housing. *Journal of the American Planning Association* 67 (4): 420–36.

New York City Department of Housing Preservation and Development. 2002. *The New Housing Marketplace*. New York: Author.

Nicholas, James C. 1992. On the Progression of Impact Fees. *Journal of the American Planning Association* 58 (4):517–25.

Noam, Eli M. 1983. The Interaction of Building Codes and Housing Prices. *Journal of American Real Estate and Urban Economics Association* 10 (4): 394–403.

Nolon, John R. 2003. *New Ground: The Advent of Local Environmental Law.* Washington, DC: Environmental Law Institute.

Office of Building Standards and Codes Services. 1975. *Status of Statewide Building Code Regulatory Programs.* Washington, DC: Author.

Ohls, J. C., R. C. Weisberg, and Michelle J. White. 1974. The Welfare Effects of Zoning on Land Value. *Journal of Urban Economics* 1 (3):428–44.

Oster, Sharon M., and John M. Quigley. 1977. Regulatory Barriers to the Diffusion of Innovation: Some Evidence from Building Codes. *Bell Journal of Economics* 8(2):360–76.

Ozanne, Larry, and Thomas Thibodeau. 1983. Explaining Metropolitan Housing Price Differences. *Journal of Urban Economics* 13 (1):51–66.

Parsons, George R., and Yangru Wu. 1991. The Opportunity Cost of Coastal Land-Use Controls: An Empirical Analysis. *Land Economics* 67 (3): 308–16.

Peiser, Richard B. 1981. Land Development Regulation: A Case Study of Dallas and Houston, Texas. *American Real Estate and Urban Economics Association Journal* 9 (4):397–417.

Pendall, Rolf. 1995. *Growth Controls and Affordable Housing in the United States: Results from a Recent Survey.* Working Paper 636. Berkeley: University of California Press.

———. 2000. Local Land Use Regulation and the Chain of Exclusion. *Journal of the American Planning Association* 66 (2):125–42.

Peterson, George E. 1974. *The Influence of Zoning Regulations on Land and Housing Prices.* Working Paper no. 1207-24. Washington, DC: The Urban Institute.

Phillips, Justin, and Eban Goodstein. 2000. Growth Management and Housing Prices: The Case of Portland, Oregon. *Contemporary Economic Policy* 18 (3):334–44.

Pima County, Arizona. 2005. *Regional Plan Policy: Conservation Lands System.* Tucson, AZ: Pima County, Development Services, Tucson. Available at www.pimaxpress.com/Planning/ComprehensivePlan/PDF/CLS/CLS_Adopted_Policy.pdf.

Pollakowski, Henry O., and Susan M. Wachter. 1990. The Effects of Land-Use Constraints on Housing Prices. *Land Economics* 66 (3):315–24.

Potoski, Matthew, and Aseem Prakash. 2002. Protecting the Environment: Voluntary Regulations in Environmental Governance. *Policy Currents* 11 (4):9–14.

President's Committee on Urban Housing. 1968. *Report of the President's Committee on Urban Housing: A Decent Home.* Washington, DC: Author.

Pressman, Jeffrey, and Aaron Wildavsky. 1972. *Implementation*. Berkeley: University of California Press.

Purdum, Elizabeth D., and James E. Frank. 1987. Community Use of Exactions: Results of a National Survey. In *Development Exactions*, ed. J. Frank and R. Rhodes, 123–52. Chicago: Planners Press, American Planning Association.

QuantEcon. 2002. *Smart Growth and Its Effects on Housing Markets: The New Segregation*. Washington, DC: National Center for Public Policy Research.

Quigley, John M., and Stephen Raphael. 2004. Is Housing Unaffordable? Why Isn't It More Affordable? *Journal of Economic Perspectives* 18 (1):191–214.

Quigley, John M., Stephen Raphael, and Larry A. Rosenthal. 2004. Local Land Use Controls and Demographic Outcomes in a Booming Economy. *Urban Studies* 41 (2):389–421.

Quigley, John M., and Larry A. Rosenthal. 2005. The Effects of Land Use Regulation on the Price of Housing: What Do We Know? What Can We Learn? *Cityscape* 8 (1):69–138.

Rabinowitz, Alan. 1988. *Land Investment and the Redevelopment Process*. New York: Quorum Books.

Randolph, John. 2004. *Environmental Land Use Planning and Management*. Washington, DC: Island Press.

Real Estate Research Corporation. 1973. *Costs of Sprawl*. Washington, DC: U.S. Department of Housing and Urban Development.

Redfearn, Christian L., and Larry A. Rosenthal. 2001. The Case for Monitoring Real Estate Prices. In *Land Supply Monitoring for Smart Growth*, ed. Gerrit J. Knaap, 307–32. Cambridge, MA: Lincoln Institute of Land Policy.

Riddel, Mary. 2001. A Dynamic Approach to Estimating Hedonic Prices for Environmental Goods: An Application to Open Space Purchase. *Land Economics* 77 (4):494–512.

Rolleston, Barbara Sherman. 1987. Determinants of Restrictive Suburban Zoning: An Empirical Analysis. *Journal of Urban Economics* 21 (1):1–21.

Rose, Louis A. 1989. Urban Land Supply: Natural and Contrived Restrictions. *Journal of Urban Economics* 25 (3):325–45.

Rosen, S. 1974. Hedonic Prices and Implicit Markets: Product Differentiation in Pure Competition. *Journal of Political Economy* 82 (1):34–55.

Rosenbaum, Lee. 2004. Destroying the Museum to Save It. *The New York Times*, January 10.

Rosenberg, Nick. 2003. Development Impact Fees: Is Limited Cost Internalization Actually Smart Growth? *Boston College Environmental Affairs Law Review* 30:641–88.

Rosenthal, Larry A. 2000. Long Division: California's Land Use Reform Policy and the Pursuit of Residential Integration. Unpublished paper. University of California, Berkeley.

Ross, H. Laurence. 1995. Housing Code Enforcement as Law in Action. *Law and Policy* 17:133–60.

Ross, Stephen, and John Yinger, 1999. Sorting and Voting: A Review of the Literature on Urban Public Finance. In *Handbook of Regional and Urban Economics: Applied Urban Economics*, ed. Paul Cheshire and Edwin S. Mills, 2003–42. New York: Elsevier Science.

Rueter, Frederick J. 1973. Externalities in Urban Property Markets: An Empirical Test of the Zoning Ordinance of Pittsburgh. *Journal of Law and Economics* 16 (2):313–50.

Russell, R. 2002. Equity in Eden: Can Environmental Protection and Affordable Housing Comfortably Cohabit in Suburbia. *Boston College Environment Law Review* 30 (3). Available at www.bc.edu/schools/law/lawreviews/meta-elements/journals/bcealr/30_3/02_TXT.htm.

Salama, Jerry J., Michael H. Schill, and Martha E. Stark. 1999. *Reducing the Cost of New Housing Construction in New York City*. A Report to The New York City Partnership and Chamber of Commerce, The New York City Housing Partnership and The New York City Department of Housing Preservation and Development. New York: New York University School of Law, Center for Real Estate and Urban Policy. Available at www.law.nyu.edu/realestatecenter/CREUP_Papers/Cost_Study_1999/NYCHousing-Cost.pdf.

Salins, P. 2002. *New York City's Housing Gap Revisited*. New York: Manhattan Institute.

Schill, Michael H. 1992. The Federal Role in Reducing Regulatory Barriers to Affordable Housing in the Suburbs. *Journal of Law and Politics* 8 (6): 703–30.

———. 2002a. Regulatory Barriers to Housing Development in the United States. In *Land Law in Comparative Perspective*, ed. Maria Elena Sanchez Jordan and Antonio Gambaro, 101–20. The Hague: Kluwer Law International.

———. 2002b. The Cost of Good Intentions. *Civic Bulletin* No. 28. Available at www.manhattan-institute.org/html/cb_28.htm.

———. 2003. *Comments on Smart Growth and Affordable Housing*. Paper presented at the Brookings Symposium on the Relationships between Affordable Housing and Growth Management. Brookings Institution, May 29.

———. 2004. Regulations and Housing Development: What We Know and What We Need to Know. Prepared for U.S. Department of Housing and Urban Development Conference on Regulatory Barriers to Affordable Housing, Washington, DC, April. Available at www.huduser.org/rbc/pdf/ Regulations_Housing_Development.pdf.

———. 2005. Regulations and Housing Development: What We Need To Know. *Cityscape* 8 (1):243–50.

Schwartz, Seymour I. 1982. Equity Implications of Local Growth Management. In *Environmental Policy Implementation: Planning and Management Options and Their Consequences*, ed. Dean E. Mann. Lexington, MA: Lexington Books.

Schwartz, Seymour I., David E. Hansen, and Richard Green. 1981. Suburban Growth Controls and the Price of New Housing. *Journal of Environmental Economics and Management* 8 (4):303–20.

Schwartz, Seymour I., David E. Hansen, and Richard Green. 1984. The Effect of Growth Management on the Production of Moderate Priced Housing. *Land Economics* 60 (1):110–14.

Schwartz, Seymour I., and Peter M. Zorn. 1988. A Critique of Quasiexperimental and Statistical Controls for Measuring Program Effects: Application to Urban Growth Control. *Journal of Policy Analysis and Management* 7 (3):491–505.

Segal, David, and Philip Srinivasan. 1985. The Impact of Suburban Growth Restrictions on U.S. Housing Price Inflation, 1975–78. *Urban Geography* 6 (1):14–26.

Segal, Lewis M., and Daniel G. Sullivan. 1998. Trends in Homeownership: Race, Demographics, and Income. *Federal Reserve Bank of Chicago Economic Perspectives* 22:53–72. Available at www.chicagofed.org/publications/ economicperspectives/1998/ep2Q98_4.pdf.

Seidel, Stephen R. 1978. *Housing Costs and Government Regulations: Confronting the Regulatory Maze*. New Brunswick: Center for Urban Policy Research, Rutgers, The State University of New Jersey.

Shaviro, Daniel. 2000. *When Rules Change: An Economic and Political Analysis of Transition Relief and Retroactivity*. Chicago: University of Chicago Press.

Shilling, James D., C. F. Sirmans, and Krisandra A. Guidry. 1991. The Impact of State Land-Use Controls on Residential Land Values. *Journal of Regional Science* 31 (1):83–92.

Shoshkes, Ellen. 1991. *Balanced Housing Evaluation: Promise, Process, and Product Rehabilitation*. Newark: New Jersey Institute of Technology/Architecture and Building Science.

Siegan, Bernard H. 1972. *Land Use without Zoning*. Lexington, MA: DC Heath.
Simmie, James, Simon Olsberg, and Christopher Tunnell. 1992. Urban Containment and Land Use Planning. *Land Use Policy* 9 (1):36–46.
Simmons, Patrick A. 2001. *Changes in Minority Homeownership during the 1990s*. Census Note 07. Washington, DC: Fannie Mae Foundation.
Singell, Larry D., and Jane H. Lillydahl. 1990. Housing Impact Fees. *Land Economics* 66 (1):82–92.
Skaburskis, Andrejs, and Mohammad Qadeer. 1992. An Empirical Estimation of the Price Effects of Development Impact Fees. *Urban Studies* 29 (5): 653–67.
Skidmore, Mark, and Michael Peddle. 1998. Do Development Impact Fees Reduce the Rate of Residential Development? *Growth and Change* 29: 383–400.
Slack, Enid. 1990. *An Economic Analysis of Development Charges in British Columbia and Ontario*. Waterloo, ON: Laurier Institute.
Slack, Enid, and Richard Bird. 1991. Financing Urban Growth through Development Charges. *Canadian Tax Journal* 39 (5):1288–1304.
Smith, Jennifer Esway, and Margot W. Garcia. 2002. From Superfund Site to Developable Property: The Case of Rentokil. *Journal of Environmental Planning and Management* 45 (2):157–79.
Snyder, Thomas P., and Michael A. Stegman. 1986. *Paying for Growth: Using Impact Fees to Finance Infrastructure*. Washington, DC: The Urban Land Institute.
Somerville, C. Tsuriel, and Christopher J. Mayer. 2002. Government Regulation and Changes in the Affordable Housing Stock, Centre for Urban Economics and Real Estate. Working paper 02-02. University of British Columbia.
Sparrow, Malcolm K. 2000. *The Regulatory Craft: Controlling Risks, Solving Problems, and Managing Compliance*. Washington, DC: Brookings Institution.
Speir, Cameron, and Kurt Stephenson. 2002. Does Sprawl Cost Us All? Isolating the Effects of Housing Patterns on Public Water and Sewer Costs. *Journal of the American Planning Association* 68 (1):56–70.
Spreyer, Janet Furman. 1989. The Effect of Land Use Restrictions on the Market Value of Single Family Homes in Houston. *Journal of Real Estate Finance and Economics* 2 (2):117–30.
Staley, Samuel R., and Gerard Mildner. 1999. *Urban Growth Boundaries and Housing Affordability*. Los Angeles: Reason Public Policy Institute.
State of Colorado. 2000. *State of Colorado Consolidated Plan*. Denver, CO: Author.

State of Connecticut. 2000. *Connecticut Consolidated Plan 2000*. Hartford, CT: Author.
State of Maryland. 2000. *Maryland Consolidated Plan for 2000–2004*. Annapolis, MD: Author.
State of Minnesota, Office of the Legislative Auditor. 2001. *Affordable Housing; Program Evaluation Report*. St. Paul, MN: Author.
State of Montana, Department of Commerce, Housing Division. 2000. *Montana Five-Year Consolidated Plan*. Helena, MT: Author.
State of New Jersey. 2000. *State of New Jersey-Summary Draft of the Consolidated Plan*. Trenton, NJ: Author.
State of North Carolina. 2000. *2001–2005 North Carolina Consolidated Plan*. Raleigh, NC: Author.
Stein, Seth, and Joseph Tomasello. 2004. When Safety Costs Too Much. *The New York Times*, January 10.
Steiner, Frederick. 2001. Identifying Environmental Constraints to and Opportunities for Development. In *Land Market Monitoring for Smart Urban Growth*, ed. Gerrit J. Knaap, 107–37. Cambridge, MA: Lincoln Institute of Land Policy.
Stoker, Gerry. 1995. Regime Theory and Urban Politics. In *Theories of Urban Politics*, ed. David Judge, Gerry Stoker, and Harold Wolman, 54–71. London: Sage Publications.
Sunding, David. 2004a. *Economic Impacts of Critical Habitat Designation for the Coastal California Gnatcatcher*. Sacramento: California Resource Management Institute.
———. 2004b. Housing and Habitat: A Review of the Literature. Prepared for the National Center for Housing and the Environment Urban University Symposium, Alexandria, Virginia, November 5–6.
———. 2005. Response to Environmental Regulations and the Housing Market: A Review of the Literature. *Cityscape* 8 (1):277–82.
Sunding, David, and Aaron Swoboda. 2004. Does Regulation Ration Housing? Paper presented at Annual Meeting of the American Agricultural Economics Association, Denver, August 2004.
Sunding, David, Aaron Swoboda, and David Zilberman. 2004. The Welfare Economics of Environmental Regulation of Land Use Changes. Working paper. University of California, Berkeley.
Sunding, David, and David Zilberman. 2002. The Economics of Environmental Regulation by Licensing: An Assessment of Recent Changes to the Wetland Permitting Process. *Natural Resources Journal* 42: 59–90.

Syal, Matt, Chris Shay, and Faron Supanich-Goldner. 2001. Streamlining Building Rehabilitation Codes to Encourage Revitalization. *Housing Facts & Findings* 3 (2):3–5.

Tatum, C. B. 1987. Process of Innovation in Construction Firm. *Journal of Construction Engineering and Management* 113 (4):648–63.

Thorson, James A. 1996. An Examination of the Monopoly Zoning Hypothesis. *Land Economics* 72 (1):43–55.

Tietenberg, Tom. 2001. *Environmental Economics and Policy*, 3rd ed. Boston, MA: Addison Wesley Longman.

Time Again to Redo the Building Code. 1999. *Chicago Tribune*, January 3.

Turque, Bill. 2006. Developers' Neglect Is Costly for Fairfax. *Washington Post*, June 25.

Turnbull, Geoffrey K. 2003. Urban Growth Controls: The Transitional Dynamics of Development Fees and Growth Boundaries. Working Paper No. 03-05, Urban and Regional Analysis Group. Atlanta: Andrew Young School of Policy Studies, Georgia State University.

Turner, Margery A., and Veronica M. Reed. 1990. *Housing America: Learning from the Past, Planning for the Future*. Washington, DC: The Urban Institute Press.

Urban Land Institute. 1979. *Thirteen Perspectives on Regulatory Simplification*. Washington, DC: Author.

———. 1990. *Residential Development Handbook*, 2nd ed. Community Builders Handbook Series. Washington, DC: Author.

———. 1999. Regulatory Burden on New Home Buyers Averages 10 Percent. *Builder* January.

U.S. Bureau of the Census. 2006. 2004 Data Profiles—American Community Survey. Available at www.census.gov/acs/www/Products/index.htm.

———. 2008a. Housing Units Authorized by Building Permits. Washington, DC: Author. Available at www.census.gov/const/www/C40/table3.html.

———. 2008b. STF 4. United States Census 2000. Available at www.census.gov/main/www/cen2000.html.

U.S. Department of Agriculture. 2005. Economic Research Service. Available at www.ers.usda.gov/Data/Unemployment/RDList2.asp?ST=AZ.

U.S. Department of Commerce, U.S. Bureau of the Census. 2004. Annual Estimates of the Population of Metropolitan and Micropolitan Statistical Areas: April 1, 2000 to July 1, 2007. Available at www.census.gov/population/www/estimates/CBSA-est2007-annual.html.

U.S. Department of Commerce, U.S. Department of Housing and Urban Development. 1991. *American Housing Survey for the United States in 1989*.

Washington, DC: U.S. Department of Commerce. Available at www2.census.gov/prod2/ahsscan/h150-89.pdf.

———. 2002. *American Housing Survey for the United States: 2001.* Washington, DC: U.S. Department of Commerce. Available at www.census.gov/prod/2002pubs/h150-01.pdf.

U.S. Department of Housing and Urban Development. n.d. Regulatory Barriers Clearinghouse. Available at www.huduser.org/rbc.

———. 1978. *Final Report of the Task Force on Housing Costs.* Washington, DC: Author.

———. 1982. *Building Affordable Homes: A Cost Savings Guide for Builder/Developers.* Washington, DC: Author.

———. 1990a. Unedited Transcript of the First Hearing of the Advisory Commission on Regulatory Barriers to Affordable Housing. Washington, DC: Ann Riley & Associates, Transcript Service.

———. 1990b. Unedited transcript of the Second Hearing of the Advisory Commission on Regulatory Barriers to Affordable Housing. Washington, DC: Ann Riley & Associates, Transcript Service.

———. 1991. *Not in My Backyard.* Washington, DC: U.S. Government Printing Office.

———. 1998a. *Factory and Site-Built Housing Analysis.* Report prepared for the U.S. Department of Housing and Urban Development, Office of Policy Development and Research. Upper Marlboro, MD: NAHB Research Center, Inc.

———. 1998b. *Effects of Environmental Hazards and Regulation on Urban Development.* Washington, DC: Author. Available at www.huduser.org/publications/econdev/bfield.html.

———. 2001. *Barriers to Rehabilitation of Affordable Housing. Volume 2: Case Studies.* Washington, DC: Author.

———. 2004. America's Affordable Communities Initiative. HUD's Initiative on Removal of Regulatory Barriers: Announcement of Incentives Criteria on Barrier Removal in HUD's FY 2004 Competitive Funding Allocations. *Federal Register* 69 (55):13449–454.

———. 2005. *Why Not in Our Community.* Washington, DC: U.S. Government Printing Office.

U.S. Department of Transportation, Federal Highway Administration. n.d. State Environmental Streamlining Practices Database. Available at environment.fhwa.dot.gov/strmlng/es6stateprac.asp.

———. 2002. *Environmental Commitment Implementation: Innovative and Successful Approaches.* Washington, DC: Author.

U.S. Environmental Protection Agency. n.d. *Brownfields Cleanup and Redevelopment: About Brownfields.* Available at www.epa.gov/swerosps/bf/about.htm.

———. n.d. *Endangered Species.* Available at www.epa.gov/ebtpages/ecosspecieendangeredspecies.html.

———. 2000. Wetlands, in 2000 *National Water Quality Inventory.* Available at www.epa.gov/305b/2000report/chp5.pdf.

———. 2001a. Critical Pollutants—National Trends (Part 1 of 3). In *National Air Quality and Emissions Trends Report 1999.* Available at www.epa.gov/air/airtrends/aqtrnd99/pdfs/Chapter2a.pdf.

———. 2001b. Critical Pollutants—National Trends (Part 3 of 3). In *National Air Quality and Emissions Trends Report 1999.* Available at www.epa.gov/air/airtrends/aqtrnd99/pdfs/Chapter2c.pdf.

U.S. General Accounting Office. 2000. *Local Growth Issues—Federal Opportunities and Challenges.* Washington, DC: U.S. Government Printing Office. Available at www.gao.gov/archive/2000/rc00178.pdf.

U.S. House of Representatives, Committee on Small Business. 2000. Regulatory Reform Initiatives and Their Impact on Small Business. Hearing before the Committee, Serial No. 106–60. Washington DC: U.S. Government Printing Office.

U.S. National Commission on Urban Problems. 1969. *Building the American City.* Washington, DC: U.S. Government Printing Office.

University of Illinois at Urbana–Champaign. 1998. *A National Survey of Rehabilitation Enforcement Practices.* Washington, DC: U.S. Department of Housing and Urban Development, Office of Policy Development and Research.

Vaillancourt, François, and Luc Monty. 1985. The Effect of Agricultural Zoning on Land Prices, Quebec, 1975–81. *Land Economics* 61 (1):36–42.

Virginia Department of Conservation and Recreation. n.d. Regs3-01-02, Available at www.cblad.virginia.gov/docs/Regs3-01-02.pdf.

Wachter, Susan M. 2002. Comments on "An Empirical Investigation of the Effects of Impact Fees on Housing and Land Markets" by Keith R. Ihlandfeldt and Timothy M. Shaughnessy. Paper presented at Lincoln Institute of Land Policy Conference, July 10–12. Philadelphia: Wharton School of Business, University of Pennsylvania.

Wachter, Susan M., and Man Cho. 1991. Interjurisdictional Price Effects of Land Use Controls. *Journal of Urban and Contemporary Law* 40 (1):49–63.

Wachter, Susan M., and Kevin C. Gillen. 2006. Public Investment Strategies: How They Matter for Neighborhoods in Philadelphia. Working Paper, The Wharton School, University of Pennsylvania.

Wachter, Susan M., and I. Megbolugbe. 1992. Racial and Ethnic Disparities in Homeownership. *Housing Policy Debate* 3 (2):333–70.

Warner, Kee, and Harvey Molotch. 1992. *Growth Control: Inner Workings and External Effects*. Berkeley: California Policy Seminar.

———. 1995. Power to Build: How Development Persists Despite Local Limits. *Urban Affairs Review* 30 (3):378–406.

Washington Research Council. 2001. *Impact of Government Regulations and Fees on Housing Costs*. Available at www.researchcouncil.org/publications _container/growth9.pdf.

Watkins, Andrew R. 1999. Impacts of Land Development Charges. *Land Economics* 75 (3):415–24.

Weinstein, Alan C. 1997. *Anderson's American Law of Zoning*. 4th ed., Vol. 5. Deerfield, IL: Clark Boardman Callaghan.

———. 1982. *Affordable Housing: How Local Regulatory Improvements Can Help*. Washington, DC: U.S. Department of Housing and Urban Development, Office of Policy Development and Research.

Weitz, Stevenson. 1985. Who Pays Infrastructure Benefit Charges—The Builder or the Home Buyer? In *The Changing Structure of Infrastructure Finance*, ed. James C. Nicholas. Cambridge, MA: Lincoln Institute of Land Policy.

Wermiel, Sara E. 2000. *The Fireproof Building: Technology and Public Safety in the Nineteenth-Century American City*. Baltimore: Johns Hopkins University Press.

White, James. 1988. Large Lot Zoning and Subdivision Costs: A Test. *Journal of Urban Economics* 23 (3):370–84.

White, Michelle J. 1975. Fiscal Zoning in Fragmented Metropolitan Areas. In *Fiscal Zoning and Land Use Controls*, ed. Edwin S. Mills and Wallace E. Oates, 79–98. Lexington, MA: DC Heath.

White, S. Mark. *Affordable Housing: Proactive and Reactive Planning Strategies*. PAS Report No. 441. Chicago: American Planning Association.

Wible, Robert, and Mari Cote. 1997. *Annual Progress Report for Streamlining the Nation's Building Regulatory Process Project*. Washington, DC: U.S. Department of Commerce.

Williams, Norman Jr., and Thomas Norman. 1971. Exclusionary Land Use Controls: The Case of North-Eastern New Jersey. *Syracuse Law Review* 22 (2):475–507.

Windsor, Duane. 1979. *Fiscal Zoning in Suburban Communities*. Lexington, MA: Lexington Books.

Winter, Soeren C., and Peter J. May. 2001. Motivation for Compliance with Environmental Regulations. *Journal of Policy Analysis and Management* 20 (4):675–98.

Witte, Ann D., Howard J. Sumka, and Homer Erekson. 1979. An Estimate of a Structural Hedonic Price Model of the Housing Market: An Application of Rosen's Theory of Implicit Markets. *Econometrica* 47 (5):1151–73.

Wolch, Jennifer, and Stuart A. Gabriel. 1981. Local Land Development Policies and Urban Housing Values. *Environment and Planning* 13 (10):1253–76.

Wood, Robert S. 2003. At the Regulatory Front Lines: Building Inspectors and the New Public Management. PhD Dissertation, Department of Political Science. Seattle, WA: University of Washington.

Woods and Poole Economics. 2005. *Complete Economics and Demographic Data Source*. Washington, DC: Author.

———. 2007. *Complete Economics and Demographic Data Source*. Washington, DC: Author.

Yinger, John. 1986. Measuring Racial Discrimination with Fair Housing Audits: Caught in the Act. *American Economic Review* 76 (5):881–93.

———. 1995. *Closed Doors, Opportunities Lost: The Continuing Costs of Housing Discrimination*. New York: Russell Sage Foundation.

———. 1998. The Incidence of Development Fees and Special Assessments. *National Tax Journal* 51 (1):23–42.

Yinger, John, H. S. Bloom, A. Boersch-Supan, and H. F. Ladd. 1988. *Property Taxes and House Values: The Theory and Estimation of Intrajurisdictional Property Tax Capitalization*. New York: Academic Press.

Zabel, Jeffrey E., and Katherine A. Kiel. 2000. Estimating the Demand for Air Quality in Four U.S. Cities. *Land Economics* 76 (2):174–94.

Zorn, Peter M., David E. Hansen, and Seymour I. Schwartz. 1986. Mitigating the Price Effects of Growth Control: A Case Study of Davis, California. *Land Economics* 62 (1):46–57.

INDEX

Page numbers in italics indicate figures, tables, and boxes, respectively.

Administrative process
  benefits of, 167–169
  duplication in, 3–4
  Fairfax/Montgomery study and, *49*
  recommendations for improvement of, 29–32, 169–170, 173–177
  regulatory cost inventories and, 179
Affordability, 58, 77–79, *78*, 109–110, 137–138, 180–181
Affordable dwelling units, 78–79, 85, 99–100
Affordable Housing Trust Fund, 94
Aggregated models, 42–43
Agricultural land, 24, 58–59
Air quality, 2. *See also* Clean Air Act
Amenity benefits, 14, 166
American Planning Association, 33, 37
Archaeological surveys, 62, 67, 72, 91, 95, 113
Area master plans, 74–76
Arizona. *See* Pima County (Tucson), AZ study
Army Corps of Engineers, 126, 134, 155
Atlantic Coastal Bays Critical Area, 198–201
Audits, 177–180

Backward capitalization, 16–17
Barriers
  inconsistency as, 116–117, 126, 155, 169–170, 176
  overview of, 2–3, 27
  research recommendations and, 181
  state and local governments and, 27
  survey of research on, 3–6
Baselines
  costs and, *37*, 37–38
  excessive regulations and, 41–44, *43*
  limitations, caveats and, 41
  overview of, 36–37, 44
  processes and, 38–41, *39*, *40*
  special protection areas and, 206
Benefits of regulations, 122–124, 165–170, 181
Best development practices, 208–209
Best management practices, 89, 175, 177–180, 195, 197
Bioretention, 201
Brownfields, 27, 118–119, 177
Buffers, 195, 197. *See also* Resource Management Areas; Resource Protection Areas
Building codes, 23, 24

253

254 Index

By-right development projects, 69–70, 90–93, *91*, *92*, *93*, 113, 129, 141

Capitalization,
  Backwards, 16–17, 109
  Forward-shifting, 17
Captured costs, 123–124
Center for Municipal Dispute Resolution (CMDR), 33–34
Chesapeake Bay, 54, 57, 198–202
Chesapeake Bay Critical Area, 198–201
Chesapeake Bay Local Assistance Board, 192
Chesapeake Bay Ordinance, 57, 203–205
Chesapeake Bay Preservation Act, 57, 63–64, 191–193
Chesapeake Bay Program, 60, 116, 191–194
Children, design and, 182–183
Clarksburg SPA, 206
Clean Air Act, 8, 21–22
Clean Water Act, 8, 21, 22, 59, 63, 65–67, 191
CLS. *See* Conservation Lands System
CMDR. *See* Center for Municipal Dispute Resolution
Coastal Zone Management Act (CZMA), 22, 23–24
Coastal zone protection, 2
COGCC. *See* Colorado Oil and Gas Conservation Commission
Collaborative review, 176–177
Colorado. *See* Denver, CO study
Colorado Oil and Gas Conservation Commission (COGCC), 135–136

Complexity, compliance costs and, 117–118
Compliance costs
  by activity, 109–113, *112*
  affordability and, 109–110
  benefits vs., 167–169
  enforcement and, 163–164
  environmental benefits vs., 122–124
  Fairfax/Montgomery study and, *49*, 105–106, 107–110
  political factors affecting, 119–120
  reduction of, 120–122
  regulatory and market factors influencing, 114–119
  table of significant, *160*
Comprehensive plans, 175–176, 193, 201–202
Concept phase, 129–130
Conflict reduction, 32–34, 173–174
Conflicting regulations, 116–117, 126, 155, 169–170, 176
Consensus building, 32–34, 173–174
Conservation Lands System (CLS), 156–157
Consultants, 120–122, 134, 167–168
Cost Effective Site Planning (NAHB), 36, 37
Costs of Sprawl (Real Estate Research Corporation), 36
Critical areas, 198–202
Cultural resources, 62, *64*, *65*, *67*
CZMA. *See* Coastal Zone Management Act

Dallas, TX, 138–139
Dallas-Fort Worth-Plano market study
  developer input and, 144–149
  developers participating in, 143–144

development process in, 140–141, 149
overview of, 138–149
Plano approval process and, 141–143
results of, 159–164, 160
Decision making, 3–4, 27
Deferral of payment, 16–17f
Delays
  baseline value and, 38–41, 39, 40
  FEMA and, 127, 143, 146, 155–156, 158, 162, 168
  financing and, 109
  free look agreements and, 15
  overview of cost impacts of, 18–20
  predictability of, 119
  regulatory barriers and, 3–4, 27, 172
  subdivision process and, 8–10, 9
  Washington, D.C. area case study and, 113–114
Demonstration programs, 175
Density, 14, 43, 43, 177
Denver, CO study
  developer input and, 132–138
  developers participating in, 132
  development process in, 129–131, 138
  overview of, 127–128
  results of, 159–164, 160
  rezoning process in, 131–132
Development Review Committee (DRC), 77
Dillon's Rule, 55–56, 114–115. *See also* Proffers
Disaggregated models, 42–43
Dispute resolution, 32–34, 173–174
District of Columbia. *See* Washington, D.C. area case study

Drilling, natural gas, 127, 147, 162–163
Due diligence, 7, 15–17, 109, 116, 135

Economic Development Corporation (EDC), 128
Efficiency benefits, 166
Electronic permitting, 30
Endangered species
  Pima County development and, 154–155
  Prince William County project and, 96–97
  regulations for, 24, 62, 63–64, 65, 67
Endangered Species Act (ESA)
  Clean Air Act and, 8
  Dallas-Fort Worth-Plano development and, 143, 146
  Denver, CO development and, 132, 136
  habitat conservation plans and, 21
  land availability and, 168
  overview of, 63
  program-related costs and, 27
  typical compliance costs and, 112
Enforcement, 30–31, 163–164, 173
Engineering design costs, 117–118
Environmental impact statements (EIS), 2, 21, 26
Environmental Protection Agency (EPA), 7, 21–22, 36, 126, 131–132, 191
Environmental Quality Corridors (EQC), 61, 69, 204
EPA. *See* Environmental Protection Agency
Erosion control, 23, 25, 63–64, 110–111, 193

ESA. *See* Endangered Species Act
Externalities, internalization of, 10, 13–14

Fairfax County Chesapeake Bay Ordinance, 196–197
Fairfax County, VA. *See also* Washington, D.C. area case study
  Chesapeake Bay Program and, 191, 196–197
  compliance costs and, 108–109
  development process of, 68–74, 73
  environmental regulatory ordinances of, 203–205
  housing affordability in, 77–79, 78
  overview of project study in, 101–102, 114–115
  planning process in, 114–116
  profile of, 48, 49, 54–56
  residential subdivision projects of, 81–88, 83, 84, 85, 86, 87
  review process in, 49, 177
Federal Emergency Management Agency (FEMA)
  compliance costs and, 162, 163
  Dallas-Fort Worth-Plano development and, 146, 148–149
  delays and, 127, 143, 146, 152, 155–156, 158, 162, 168
  floodplain zoning and, 22
  Pima County development and, 155–156
Federal government
  Dallas-Fort Worth-Plano development and, 143
  Denver, CO development and, 131
  environmental regulations and, 21–23, 63, 161–162
  Pima County development and, 152
  regulatory cost inventories and, 179–180
  suggestions for improvements in, 175
Federal Water Pollution Control Act. *See* Clean Water Act
FEMA. *See* Federal Emergency Management Agency
Financing, 17, 109
Fish and Wildlife Service (FWS), 8, 21, 126, 133–134, 154–155
Flood insurance, 22
Floodplain management. *See also* Federal Emergency Management Agency
  benefits of, 166
  Dallas-Fort Worth-Plano development and, 142, 146, 148
  Denver, CO development and, 132, 136
  local regulations and, 24
  Pima County development and, 152, 155–156
  regulations for, 63–64
  state regulations and, 23, 61
Forest conservation plans, 88–90, 94–95, 206
Forest preservation, 62
Forests and trees, 63–64, 65, 112
Formal phase, 130
Fort Worth, TX. *See* Dallas-Fort Worth-Plano market study
Fragmentation. *See* Inconsistencies
Free look agreements, 15
FWS. *See* Fish and Wildlife Service

Golding, Susan, 31
Grayfields, 118–119

Green Tape Process, 79
Groundwater, 24

Habitat preservation, 21, 61–62, 154–155
Hazard mitigation, 23, 24
Hillside Development Overlay Zones, 156
Historical preservation, 62
Home Rule Charters, 74
Housing and Urban Development (HUD), 19, 175
Housing Barriers Clearinghouse, 175
Housing Preservation and Development Fund, 95
HUD. See Housing and Urban Development

IDAs. See Intensely Developed Areas
Impact fees, 25, 206
Impacts, regulation of implementation and, 27
Impervious surface limitations, 200–201
Implementation
  Chesapeake Bay Preservation Act and, 192
  framework for improvement of, 172–173
  inventories, best practices, incentives and, 177–180
  policy improvements and, 173–176
  regulation of, 27
  regulatory cost inventories and, 179
  research recommendations and, 180–182
  simplification of, 173–174
Incentives, 179–180

Inconsistencies, 116–117, 126, 155, 169–170, 176
Individual permits, 66
Infill urban development, 82, 118–119, 177
Insurance, flood, 22
Intensely Developed Areas (IDAs), 194, 195, 196, 204
Interest rates, 17
Inventories, 177–180, 206

Joint permit applications, 66

Kemp Commission report, 2–3

Land availability, 13, 14, 18–20, 158, 168
Land costs, development costs vs., 81
Land purchase price, 16
Landscaping, local regulations and, 25
Leadership in Energy and Environmental Design (LEED), 180
Liability, paper trail and, 145
Local governments
  case study lessons and, 104–105
  Dallas-Fort Worth-Plano development and, 140–141
  Denver, CO and, 129–131
  development costs and, 127
  Dillon's Rule and, 55–56
  environmental regulations and, 24–25
  impacts of regulations of, 162–163
  Maryland Critical Area Program and, 199
  Pima County development and, 150–152
  regulatory acts of (DC area case study), 63–64

Local governments (cont.)
  regulatory cost inventories and, 179–180
  state governments vs., 55–56
  suggestions for improvements in, 174, 176–177
Lot releases, 16–17
Loudon County, VA, 90–95, *91*, *92*, *93*, *94*, *101–102*. See also Washington, D.C. area case study

Mapping, 178, 193, 199
Market factors, 114–119
Maryland Critical Area Program, 198–202
Maryland Economic Growth, Resource Protection, and Planning Act, 201–202
Maryland-National Capital Park and Planning Commission (MNCPPC), 75–76
Master plans, 74–76
Metropolitan statistical area. See Dallas-Fort Worth-Plano market study
Mineral exploration cleanup, 135–136
Mineral resources, 202
Mitigation costs
  Fairfax County, VA and, *84*, *87*, 205
  Loudon County, VA and, *92*
  overview of, 107, 111, 124
  Prince William County, VA and, *98*
MNCPPC. See Maryland-National Capital Park and Planning Commission
Model Land Development Code (American Bar Association), 36
Model Subdivision Regulations (American Society of Planning Officials), 36

Moderately Priced Dwelling Units (MPDU) Ordinance, 78–79, 88
Monetary benefits, 123–124
Monitoring, 205, 206
Montgomery County Forest Conservation Law, 206
Montgomery County, MD. *See also* Washington, D.C. area case study
  Chesapeake Bay Program and, 191
  compliance costs and, 108–109
  development process of, 74–77
  environmental regulatory ordinances of, 205–206, 207
  housing affordability in, 77–79, *78*
  overview of project study in, *101–102*
  planning process in, 114–116
  profile of, *48*, *49*, 54–56, 57–59
  residential subdivision projects of, 88–90, *89*
MPDU Ordinance. See Moderately Priced Dwelling Units Ordinance

National Association of Home Builders (NAHB), 3, 36, 37, 41–44, *43*
National Charrette Institute, 33
National Environmental Policy Act (NEPA), 7, 21
National Flood Insurance Program (NFIP), 22
National Marine Fisheries Service (NMFS), 8, 21
National Oceanic and Atmospheric Administration (NOAA), 8, 22
National Pollutant Discharge Elimination System (NPDES), 22, 131–132
Nationwide permit #39, 66

Nationwide permit #43, 66
Native plants, 155
Natural gas drilling, 127, 147, 162–163
NEPA. *See* National Environmental Policy Act
NFIP. *See* National Flood Insurance Program
NIMBY, 26, 173–174
NMFS. *See* National Marine Fisheries Service
NOAA. *See* National Oceanic and Atmospheric Administration
Noise abatement, 64, 113, 135
Nonrecourse loans, 17
Not In My Back Yard (NIMBY). *See* NIMBY
"Not in My Backyard": Removing Barriers for Affordable Housing (Kemp Commission), 2–3
NPDES. *See* National Pollutant Discharge Elimination System

Ombudsmen, 32
One-stop permitting, 30
Open space preservation, 25, 62, 112, 204
Outfall analysis monitoring, 205

Patchwork regulatory process. *See* Inconsistencies
Performance criteria, 193, 195–196
Permit expeditors, 121
Permit modifications, 67, 205
Permitting, electronic and one-stop, 30
Phased development projects, 82–85, *83, 84, 85,* 93–95
Pima County (Tucson), AZ study
 developer input and, 153–157
 developers participating in, 153
 development process in, 150–152, 158–159
 overview of, 149–150
 perceptions of regulations and, 157–158
 results of, 159–164, *160*
Piney Branch SPA, 206
Planning process, regulatory reviews and, 114–115
Plano, TX, 139–140, 141–143, 145. *See also* Dallas-Fort Worth-Plano market study
Plat review process, flow chart of, *11, 12*
PMSA. *See* Primary metropolitan statistical area
Political process, 119–120
Preconstruction notification, 67, 87
Primary metropolitan statistical area (PMSA), 54
Prince William County, VA, 95–98, *96, 97, 98, 100, 101–102. See also* Washington, D.C. area case study
Priority funding areas, 175
Proffers, 68, 82–83, 85–86, 96–97, 113, 114, 177
Property transfers, 200
Purchase price, 16

Ratings systems, 180
Real Estate Research Corporation, 37
Recordation phase, 130
Recourse loans, 17
Regional Flood Control Districts, 151, 152, 156
Regulatory barriers. *See* Barriers
Regulatory cost inventories, 177–180
Reilly, William K., 183

260 Index

Remediation, infill development and, 82
Research, recommendations for, 170, 180–182
Residential Development Handbook (Urban Land Institute), 38
Residuals, 16
Resource Management Areas (RMAs), 57, 194, 196, 203–204
Resource Protection Areas (RPAs), 57, 191, 194, 195, 196–197, 203–204
Resource Protection Program, 198–202
Review procedures, 49, 176–177, 179
Rezoning. *See also* Proffers; Zoning
  Dallas-Fort Worth-Plano and, 141
  Denver, CO and, 131–132
  Fairfax County and, 70–72
  Pima County and, 151–152, 156–158, 161
Riparian protection areas (RPA), 61, 154, 156–157
Risk reduction, 166
Risks, backward capitalization and, 16
RMAs. *See* Resource Management Areas
Roads, subdivisions and, 6–7
RPAs. *See* Resource Protection Areas

Safe Drinking Water Act (SDWA), 8, 22–23
Safety, research and, 181–182
Saguaro Cactus, 127, 155, 157, 162
SDWA. *See* Safe Drinking Water Act
Security, loans and, 17
Sediment control, 23, 25, 63–64, 110–111
Seismic zoning, 24
Septic systems, 7, 147

Single-phase development project, 85–88, *86*, *87*
Site preparation, 14, 108–109, 111
Smart growth programs, 27, 55, 175
Sonoran Desert Conservation Plan, 152, 154, 156–157
SPA. *See* Special Protection Areas
SPEA. *See* Standard Planning Enabling Act
Special Protection Areas (SPA), 58, 61, 191, 205–206, 207
Standard Planning Enabling Act (SPEA), 6
Standards, 174, 180
State governments
  Dallas-Fort Worth-Plano development and, 142–143
  Denver, CO development and, 130
  environmental regulations and, 23–24
  local governments vs., 55–56
  Pima County development and, 152
  primacy of, 25
  regulatory acts of (DC area case study), *63*
  regulatory cost inventories and, 179–180
  suggestions for improvements in, 174–176
  water resource management and, 60–61
State primacy, 25
Stormwater management
  Clean Water Act and, 67
  Dallas-Fort Worth-Plano development and, 142–143, 144–145
  Denver, CO development and, 132, 136–137
  federal regulations and, 22, 162

impacts of on costs, 160
local regulations and, 24–25
Maryland Critical Area Program and, 201
Montgomery County project and, 89
phased development project and, 82, 84
Pima County development and, 151, 153–154, 157
regulations for, 63–64
as significant cost, 126
special protection areas and, 206
state regulations and, 23, 61
subdivisions and, 7
typical costs from, 110–111
Stormwater pollution prevention plan (SWPP), 142, 144
Stream monitoring and reporting, 205
Subdivisions
baseline costs for, 37, 37–38
environmental costs, land capitalization and, 14–17
environmental regulations, housing costs and, 10–14, *11*, *12*
overview of process for residential, 5–10, *9*, *11*, *12*
processing time for approval of, 3
SWPP. *See* Stormwater pollution prevention plan

TCEQ. *See* Texas Commission of Environmental Quality
TDR. *See* Transfer of Development Rights program
Technical assistance grants, 176
Technical response specifications, 178–179

Texas. *See* Dallas-Fort Worth-Plano market study
Texas Commission of Environmental Quality (TCEQ), 144–147
Threatened species, 62, 64, 65, 67, 134
Time-saver standards, 180, 208
Tracking, cost reduction and, 121, 167
Transfer of Development Rights (TDR) program, 58–59
Transparency, 174
Transportation, 201–202
Tree planting, 135, 136
Tree preservation regulations, 25, 72–74, 83, 85–95, 137, 145. *See also* Forest conservation plans
Tucson, AZ. *See* Pima County (Tucson), AZ study

Upper Paint Branch SPA, 206
Upper Rock Creek SPA, 206
Urban forestry programs, 25
Urban Land Institute, 38
Utilities, subdivisions and, 6–7

Vegetation Preservation and Planting ordinance, 204–205
View preservation ordinances, 135
Virginia Chesapeake Bay Preservation Act, 194–196. *See also* Chesapeake Bay Preservation Act
Voter initiatives, affordability and, 137–138

Washington, D.C. area case study
compliance costs and, 105–106, 107–110
costs in, 103–105
development review processes and, 67–77, *73*

Washington, D.C. area case study (*cont.*)
  environmental regulations, programs relevant to, 59–67, 63
  housing affordability and, 77–79, 78
  methodology of, 48–50, 49
  metropolitan Washington, DC overview and, 50–54, 52, 53, 54
  overall regulatory environment of, 160
  overview of, 45–48, 47
  residential subdivision projects of, 79–98, 83, 84, 85, 86, 87, 89, 91, 92, 93, 94, 96, 97, 98
  summary of, 99–103, 101–102, 103
Water resources
  case study lessons and, 103
  Chesapeake Bay Preservation Act and, 192–193
  Fairfax County Chesapeake Bay Ordinance and, 196–197
  Maryland Critical Area Program and, 198–202
  regulations for, 63–64, 65
  state protection of, 60–61
  subdivisions and, 2, 7
  typical compliance costs and, 110–111
  Virginia Chesapeake Bay Preservation Act and, 194–196
Watersheds, 24, 205–206
Wellheads, 24

Wetlands
  Dallas-Fort Worth-Plano development and, 145–146, 148
  delineation of, 65
  Denver, CO development and, 133, 136
  Maryland Critical Area Program and, 200
  permitting of, 21
  Pima County development and, 155
  program-related costs and, 27
  regulations for, 63–64
  state regulations and, 2, 23, 61
  typical compliance costs and, 111–112, 112
Why Not in Our Community report, 2

Zoning. *See also* Proffers
  applications for, 39
  approval time and, 3, 40
  by-right development and, 69–70
  Chesapeake Bay Preservation Act and, 193
  Denver, CO development and, 138
  Fairfax County, VA and, 113, 204
  Maryland Critical Area Program and, 199
  phased development project and, 82–83, 113
  single-phase development project and, 85–86, 113
  Virginia and, 113

Island Press | Board of Directors

ALEXIS G. SANT *(Chair)*
Summit Foundation

DANE NICHOLS *(Vice-Chair)*

HENRY REATH *(Treasurer)*
Nesbit-Reath Consulting

CAROLYN PEACHEY *(Secretary)*
President
Campbell, Peachey & Associates

STEPHEN BADGER
Board Member
Mars, Inc.

KATIE DOLAN
Eastern New York
  Chapter Director
The Nature Conservancy

MERLOYD LUDINGTON LAWRENCE
Merloyd Lawrence, Inc.
  and Perseus Books

WILLIAM H. MEADOWS
President
The Wilderness Society

DRUMMOND PIKE
President
The Tides Foundation

CHARLES C. SAVITT
President
Island Press

SUSAN E. SECHLER

VICTOR M. SHER, ESQ.
Principal
Sher Leff LLP

PETER R. STEIN
General Partner
LTC Conservation Advisory
  Services
The Lyme Timber Company

DIANA WALL, PH.D.
Professor of Biology
  and Senior Research Scientist
Natural Resource Ecology
  Laboratory
Colorado State University

WREN WIRTH
President
Winslow Foundation